Faith Development in the Adult Life Cycle

Project Editor: James T. Morgan
Editor: Jane Dickler Lebow
Design Director: Gail Schneider

Acknowledgements:
Excerpts from *The Modern Practice of Adult Education* by Malcolm Knowles. Copyright © 1980 by Malcolm Knowles. Used by permission of Follett Publishing Company.

Excerpts from *The Seasons of a Man's Life* by Daniel J. Levinson. Copyright © 1978 by Daniel J. Levinson. Reprinted by permission of Alfred A. Knopf, Inc.

Excerpts from pages 172-173, 182-183, 197-198, and portion of Table 5.1 on pages 244-245 in *Stages of Faith: The Psychology of Human Development and the Quest for Meaning* by James W. Fowler. Copyright © 1981 by James W. Fowler. Reprinted by permission of Harper & Row, Publishing, Inc.

Excerpts from *Form of Intellectual and Ethical Development in the College Years* edited by William G. Perry, Jr. Copyright © 1968, 1970 by Holt, Rinehart and Winston, Inc. Reprinted by permission of Holt, Rinehart & Winston, CBS College Publishing.

Library of Congress Catalog Card Number: 81-85337
ISBN: 0-8215-9904-6

Published by William H. Sadlier, Inc.
11 Park Place, New York, New York 10007

Printed and bound in the United States of America
23456789/987654

Faith Development in the Adult Life Cycle

Kenneth Stokes, Editor

W. H. Sadlier

New York   Chicago   Los Angeles

Table of Contents

Appreciation

Literally hundreds of persons contributed to the success of the SYMPOSIUM in addition to those whose work is seen in this book. All cannot be cited individually, but several do need to be noted. Particular appreciation is expressed:

—to Charles Bruning, Research Consultant, and the Research Team—James Berry, Betty Bigelbach, Sr., Isabella Farrell, Tom Myott, Edward Sellner, and Sue Stanek—who spent close to 600 person-hours reading and chronicling the basic material contained in the *Hypotheses Paper;*

—to the Steering Committee of the Project—Neil Parent, Chair; Joanne Chafe, Vasiliki Eckley, Doug Hodgkinson, and Starr Williams—representing the Sponsor Organizations in planning the design of the SYMPOSIUM program;

—to the Project Committee—Gene Scapanski, Chair; Joan Duke, Corrine Geiger, Randy Nelson, Wayne Paulson, and Fr. John Forliti—Twin Cities' area researchers all, who met regularly with Project staff to provide scholarly commentary on the research design;

—to Gene Scapanski and Sr. Mary Paula McCarthy of the Center for Religious Education, College of St. Thomas, and their staff, who represented the College in hosting the SYMPOSIUM and helping 300 people feel very much at home;

—to Loretta Girzaitis, accomplished adult educator, who coordinated and guided the 25 small reflection groups that provided opportunity for involving all SYMPOSIUM participants in dialogue;

—to Connie Davis, the Project's hard-working and gracious Administrative Assistant, who served as Registrar and "communication center" for the SYMPOSIUM;

—to Helen Pye and Corinne Bruning, whose assistance with a myriad of details and responsibilities at the SYMPOSIUM helped the program flow smoothly;

—to Barney Kathan, who, as Executive Secretary of the Religious Education Association of the United States and Canada, provided the support and encouragement that has made the Project possible.

The Faith Development in the Adult Life Cycle Project has been greatly enriched by their contributions, and so many more, who have made and continue to make it all possible. Thank you.

Kenneth Stokes
Editor and Project Director

Foreword

In the late 1950s and 1960s the Religious Education Association carried out an extensive five-stage research project under the leadership of Dr. Herman E. Wornom, its General Secretary, and a committee chaired by Dr. Walter H. Clark. Funded by grants from the Lilly Endowment, the program culminated in the publication in 1971 of the substantial volume, *Research on Religious Development*, edited by Dr. Merton P. Strommen.

At my installation in 1970 as the Association's new executive I asked whether an equally ambitious program could be envisioned and developed in the decade ahead. The project on "Faith Development in the Adult Life Cycle" is a major step toward the meeting of that challenge.

It is not generally known that this current enterprise had its roots in a 1976 conference on adult religious education sponsored by the R.E.A. and in a proposal on "adult moral development" which was submitted to a foundation, unfortunately with negative results. Ken Stokes has taken the initiative in designing this new project, in mustering the support of the R.E.A. and other partner organizations, William H. Sadlier, Inc., the Gallup Organization, and many others in recruiting an able and conscientious steering committee and research team, and in securing much of the funding to implement it.

This volume represents the successful completion of the first phase of the project and includes the *Hypotheses Paper*, the major presentations at the 1981 SYMPOSIUM, and substantial responses by a group of participants. It is a fitting testimony to the creativity and hard work of the Steering Committee, chaired by Neil Parent, and dozens of others who have given generously of their time and talents in the leadership of the project.

> *Boardman W. Kathan*
> *Executive Secretary*
> *The Religious Education Association*

On August 10-14, 1981, nearly 300 men and women gathered on the campus of the College of St. Thomas in St. Paul, Minnesota for a SYMPOSIUM on Faith Development in the Adult Life Cycle. They represented a broad spectrum of religious traditions from Orthodoxy to Humanism; they were teachers, pastors, counselors, educators; there was a good balance of men and women, laity and clergy; one in five was a Canadian. They came for an intensive week together around a common interest—the nature of adult faith development.

This volume is the story of that SYMPOSIUM.

1

The Germ
of an Idea

The six of us stayed at the table long after lunch had been finished. Our mentor was a well known scholar respected for his perceptive research on the developmental patterns of the adult life cycle. As we probed his fertile mind, one of the group asked what his study had found regarding the changes in peoples' understandings of their faith—the spiritual dimension of life—as they moved through adulthood. His answer was simple, honest, and to the point:

> "Oh, we didn't get many religious answers. We'll leave those questions to the preachers!"

He excused himself and left the table, but several of us remained to reflect on his comments.

There is tremendous interest today in the changing patterns of adulthood. *Passages* was a best seller for years because it helped people understand that they are not alone, that countless others have the same struggles dealing with the dynamics of an ever-changing adulthood. Hardly a week passes that a TV show, magazine article or new movie does not deal with some theme related to the physical, psychological, or social dynamics of adult change. Concepts like "generation gap," "mid-life crises," "empty nest," "baby-boom generation," and "senior citizen"—which emphasize the journey of adulthood—are a part of everyday conversation. An understanding of the nature of human adulthood is of increasing interest to all of us.

And yet, that final question and our colleague's brief response continued to intrigue our table group. If everything else about us changes as we grow older, what *might* we expect to happen to our faith? One of us mentioned a close friend—male, age 47, married, occasional churchgoer who puts it succinctly:

> "I'm asking questions now I never even thought of in Confirmation Class."

Another told of a friend in her '40s, a devout Catholic who had just experienced the trauma of divorce. Although a caring priest assured her that the Church's attitude toward divorce has changed, her own feelings and misconception that divorce is a sin forced some difficult soul-searching upon her. Her comment reflects the importance of this new dimension of her faith-life.

> "The social adjustment hasn't been nearly as hard as the faith adjustment. It's going to take me a long time to work this one through."

Traditionally, church leaders have been closely related to the adult life cycle as they participate in the sacraments and ceremonies of life—confirmation and bar/bas mitzvah, marriage, baptism, anniversaries, . . . and that final celebration of life at the grave. We counsel men and women at times of life's crossroad decisions yet, unfortunately, many of us religious professionals are amazingly insensitive to life's ever-changing journey in our preaching, teaching, and program planning in the parish, congregation, and synagogue.

If the young adult really has a sense of powerlessness in society, how does this affect his/her faith attitudes? If there really is a significant mid-life transition in which one's basic values undergo scrutiny and change, what does this suggest for classes and retreats aimed at mid-life adults? If the older adult has to come to grips with the meaning of death and her/his personal preparation for it, does this not suggest some very special opportunities for ministry?

As we talked, the germ of an idea that was to become the Faith Development in the Adult Life Cycle Project was formed. In the months that followed, it was discussed by hundreds of people; it found support in the sponsorship of the Religious Education Association and a source of interested denominations and other organizations. Through several generous gifts and the hard work of many, in 1981 the research began.

In essence, the Project seeks to identify and better understand relationships between the changing dynamics of life through adulthood and an individual's understanding of his/her faith. "Faith" refers not just to a person's church or synagogue relationship and formal belief structures, such as creeds and doctrines. It encompasses and focuses on that dynamic element of the individual's total being which involves issues of ultimate concern, such as the meaning of life and death, the nature of being, the existence and nature of Deity, and the like. "Faith *Development*" reflects the changing nature of one's faith perspective and understandings through the developmental journey of her/his life. It is through faith development that maturing adults function in increasingly complex and adequate responses to life's ultimate questions and meaning.

Theologians have pondered the meaning of "faith" for centuries, but historically it has been seen as something given, constant, unchanging. Only recently have scholars begun to probe the developmental nature of the faith experience. Fowler's concept of "faithing," which suggests a continuing process of growth and development, has appeal for many people.

Psychologists, on the other hand, have been studying human development for about a century, albeit for the most part with a focus on childhood and adolescence. It is only in the last generation that the pattern of *adult* change has become a focus of scholarly interest. But even now, most social science research in adult development deals minimally with that dimension of human life which is fundamental in all of us and of importance to most of us—our faith. Unfortunately, the casual words of our scholarly colleague reflect truth. "Faith" *is* hard to study empirically and "faith development" is a relatively new concept. Therefore, few social scientists have tried to deal with it.

The Faith Development in the Adult Life Cycle Project is a conscious effort to help bridge that gap between the theological and social science disciplines at the point of Faith Development. This research is foundational since it is hoped it will spark other studies which will carry the exploration into countless previously unexplored nooks and crannies of this relationship.

The Project will be more than the collection of data. Its third phase involves the development of practical resources, based on the research findings, for persons in the helping professions—clergy, educators, counselors, etc.—to help them better understand the dynamics between Faith Development and the Adult Life Cycle in their work with people.[1]

The details of structure and research design of the Faith Development in the Adult Life Cycle Project will be found in the Appendix. Later publications will tell the story of the "idea" as it comes to fruition—hopefully to make its contribution in the fullness of time.

This volume, rather, is the story of an event—the SYMPOSIUM

---

[1]See Appendix for details regarding Phase III.

held in Minnesota in August, 1981. It was the first public gathering of persons interested in the topic to discuss, early in the life of the Project, some of the fundamental issues of the research design. The pages that follow recreate, in part, the SYMPOSIUM event through the written reflections of some who were there.

2

The SYMPOSIUM

One week before the SYMPOSIUM began, the U.S. Professional Air Traffic Controllers Organization began a strike which was to disrupt air travel in both the United States and Canada for many months. This confusion notwithstanding, fewer than twenty persons cancelled their SYMPOSIUM registrations, and close to 300 people convened in St. Paul for the five-day event in mid-August, 1981. They had no common identity save their mutual interest in the topic under discussion.

From its first session on Monday to its conclusion on Friday, the concept of *participative research* was emphasized. Built into the Project's research design are several "check-point" experiences in which interested persons could come together to reflect on the research to date. The SYMPOSIUM was the first of these experiences. Not only did the participants *listen* to the presentations of scholars, they were encouraged—through small (10-12 persons) reflection groups with a built-in feed-back mechanism—to contribute their insights and reflection on the data collected and the future directions of the research.

Since early 1981, a Phase I[1] Research Team of six graduate students led by Research Consultant Charles Bruning had been seeking out, reading, and evaluating the major research already available in the fields of Adult Life Cycle and Faith Development. This survey of the literature was collated in the *Hypotheses Paper,* a copy of which was sent to all SYMPOSIUM participants one month before the event as its basic working document.

[1]Phase I of the Project involves background research. See Appendix for details.

Further, the *Hypotheses Paper* proposed 21 hypothesis statements which might become bases for the Phase II[2] research. These hypotheses were discussed not only by the SYMPOSIUM leaders, but also in the reflection groups which met daily. The suggestions for their refinement were incorporated into the Phase II research design. The text of the *Hypotheses Paper* is found in Chapter 3.

The major respondents to the *Hypotheses Paper* at the SYMPOSIUM were the five Subject Matter Consultants who represented important fields related to the study:

—ADULT LEARNING: Malcolm Knowles
—THEOLOGY: James Fowler
—DEVELOPMENTAL PSYCHOLOGY: Winston Gooden
—MORAL DEVELOPMENT: Mary Wilcox
—RELIGIOUS EDUCATION: Gabriel Moran

Each Subject Matter Consultant prepared a written critique of the *Hypotheses Paper.* These comprise Chapters 4-8. The essence of each of these critique papers was presented by its author at the SYMPOSIUM. At the conclusion of each presentation, a public conversation with the other Subject Matter Consultants was held around the major themes of that presentation. Opportunity for questions and comment from SYMPOSIUM participants was also provided.

Seven members of the SYMPOSIUM community, chosen to provide vocational, denominational, and geographic balance, were asked to write Reflection Papers on their SYMPOSIUM experiences. These commentaries comprise Chapters 9-15 of this volume. They approach SYMPOSIUM issues from a wide variety of perspectives and bring a diversity of insights to the significance of the experience.

Many elements of the SYMPOSIUM experience cannot adequately be recorded on paper:

—the intense discussions of 25 Reflection Groups which met daily,
—the interplay of Protestant, Catholic, Jewish, Orthodox, Evangelical, Humanist, and other traditions in dialogue around issues of common concern,

---

[2]Phase II encompasses the primary data collection of the Project. See Appendix for details.

—the culminating SYMPOSIUM Banquet and its choice of two plays, "I Do! I Do!" and "On Golden Pond," both dramatic examples of the human life cycle.

They added a dimension that can only be hinted at in this book. But they were there and they all combined to make the SYMPOSIUM a *total experience.*

On the pages that follow, something of the flavor of the SYMPOSIUM event can be felt through the words of five key leaders who reflect the *Hypotheses Paper* and the research concept, and those of seven participants who reflect on these reflections from their own perspectives. As you read these pages, do so both with a sense of the event itself and also with a larger sense of that event's context in the fuller design of the total Project.

Charles Bruning

is Associate Professor of Adult, Continuing, and Community Education at the University of Minnesota, Minneapolis. As Research Consultant for the Faith Development in the Adult Life Cycle Project in Phase I, he headed the Research Team which gathered the basic data contained in the *Hypotheses Paper*, and developed its bibliographic resource material.

Dr. Bruning was for twelve years a member and eight years chairperson of the Board of the Division of College and University Services of the American Lutheran Church.

Kenneth Stokes, Director of the Project, and Bruning collaborated in the preparation of the *Hypotheses Paper*.

3

The Hypotheses Paper

The *Hypotheses Paper* is the basic document of the SYMPOSIUM. It serves several purposes: provides a review of the literature of the fields of Faith Development and Adult Life Cycle and the interface between them, lifts up some fundamental concepts, and suggests possible hypotheses on which the Phase II research could be based. The *Hypotheses Paper* was sent to, and presumably read by, SYMPOSIUM participants before they arrived. It is the *Hypotheses Paper* to which the Subject Matter Consultants react in their major presentations and papers (Chapters 4-8).

The *Hypotheses Paper* is actually a document-in-process. Its critique by SYMPOSIUM leaders and participants alike suggests much that needs revision. This will be done in time. However, it is published here essentially as it was written and read prior to the SYMPOSIUM as the basis for the papers that follow which spoke to it. In the spirit of the continuing process of refining, suggestions for its improvement will be appreciated.

I. ADULT LIFE CYCLE

Introduction

For many years, considerable research has been done related to childhood and adolescence. Recently, there has been a surge of interest in the adult, both in scholarly research and in the popular media. Sheehy's *Passages* (60) was a best-seller for several months in the late '70's. Erikson has suggested reasons for this interest:

> "Only the century of the child has made us study childhood and indeed youth not only as the casual precursors of adulthood as it was and is, but also as a potential promise for what adulthood may yet become. We still face powerful problems arising from the relativity adhering to the adult's

tasks of defining his position as a person and as an observer in ongoing life." (12)

Adult Life Cycle Research

Adulthood is the latter period of the life span, following adolescence and childhood. Although these are general terms, their usage usually means differences in needs, interests and behavior. This study concentrates on adulthood in terms of "Adult Life Cycle" research in the context of the field of Human Development. According to this literature, there are predictable physical, psychological, and social patterns that affect most, if not all, adults as they move through life. Out of the multitude of stage and age patterns that have been proposed, a selective review is given as background for the tentative operational definition of Adult Life Cycle described at the end of this section.

Before looking at examples of specific research, it may be wise to note a word of caution raised by Kummerow and Hummel (41). They question an over-zealous categorization of individuals into stages or levels, suggesting that such a process tends to become too simplistic and to ignore individual differences. There is value in this counsel, and the reader is urged to keep it in mind in perusing the pages that follow. The writers will try to be mindful of this also in the selective review of the literature which follows.

Erikson identifies eight stages of personality development:

1. Trust vs. Basic Mistrust
2. Autonomy vs. Shame and Doubt
3. Initiative vs. Guilt
4. Industry vs. Inferiority
5. Identity vs. Role Diffusion
6. Intimacy vs. Isolation
7. Generativity vs. Stagnation
8. Ego Integrity vs. Despair (12)

He authored several books in which he expanded upon his basic work. Many succeeding stage theory concepts had their beginning with Erikson's model. Several are noted here to demonstrate the continuing effort to define the ADULT LIFE CYCLE.

Moran (52) attempted to define "adult" and holds that the best operative meaning of adult is the *ideal of maturity*. Thus he subsequently defines adulthood as that "specific form of dependence (or interdependence) in which the illusion of self sufficiency is recognized and one gratefully responds to the pain/pleasure of life." Other meanings of adult are identified: 1) synonymous with pornographic (the counter-image to our dominant ideal of adulthood), 2) a chronological/biological point of development, and 3) an ideal of rational, factual, economically productive individual. The *ideal of maturity* definition, however, is primary because it provides the individual with the ability to integrate life and death, the rational and the non-rational, and is the most complete definition for a total understanding of adulthood.

Bromley suggests seven stages of adulthood from Early Adulthood to a Terminal Stage prior to death (5).

Another structure of life stages is advanced by Boelen (3), who commented that the various stages of human development must *not* be considered as separate biological or psychological phenomena, but as a series of intermittently connected, ultimately fully integrated existential *crises*. Boelen's stages of adulthood include:

16-21 years-Early Adolescence
21-30 years-Late Adolescence
30-40 years-Young Adulthood
40-45 years-Mid Life Crisis—Crises of the Limits (3)

In DeBoy's (7) review of Boelen's work on developmental theory, he concludes that the stages might occur at different ages for males and females:

Early Adolescence (14-20 for women; 16-21 for men)
Late Adolescence (21-25 for women; 22-30 for men)
Young Adulthood (25-30 for women; 30-40 for men)
Crisis of Limits (30-40 for women; 40-45 for men)

Levinson's research on males has probably become the most highly regarded study on the Adult Life Cycle. A significant contribution is his suggestion that the adult life structure (for males at least) evolves through a relatively orderly sequence of alternating stable (structure building) and transitional (structure changing) periods. The stable period is characterized by firm choices, rebuilding one's life structure and enhancing one's life within it. The transitional period is the time

" . . . to question and reappraise the existing structure, explore various possibilities for change in self and world, and to move toward commitment to the crucial choices that form the basis for a new life structure in the ensuing stable period." (42)

Levinson's schema of stages is depicted graphically on the jacket of *The Seasons of a Man's Life* as follows:

DEVELOPMENTAL PERIODS
IN EARLY AND MIDDLE
ADULTHOOD

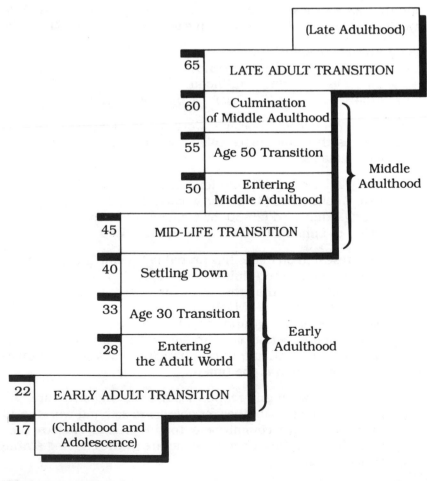

(Late Adulthood)

65	LATE ADULT TRANSITION
60	Culmination of Middle Adulthood
55	Age 50 Transition
50	Entering Middle Adulthood

Middle Adulthood

45	MID-LIFE TRANSITION
40	Settling Down
33	Age 30 Transition
28	Entering the Adult World

Early Adulthood

| 22 | EARLY ADULT TRANSITION |
| 17 | (Childhood and Adolescence) |

Levinson states that these periods overlap, connect, and interpenetrate. While the current period is predominant, the others are present in it, as the life cycle is an organic whole and each period contains all the others. Thus the person works chiefly on the tasks of the current period, but also on the tasks of other periods that are unfinished or anticipated.

Levinson's periods are precise in terms of specific ages of beginning and ending. His position is that although there are individual variations, the great majority of men experience the different "seasons" during the period of years identified.

If one compares Boelen's (3) scheme concerning adulthood with Bromley's (5) and Levinson's (42) Adult Life Cycle stages, age differences can be noted. For example, Boelen would place a 17-year-old in the "Early Adolescence" stage while Levinson would say that he/she would be in the "Early Adult Transition" stage. The 17-year-old is not even included in Bromley's categorization.

In her popular *Passages*, Sheehy develops her own identification for the stages of the life cycle. She uses the decades to delineate the stages, and identifies catch titles for each; viz: the 20-30 period is called the "Trying Twenties." She also provides a colorful description of how transitions occur. She says:

> "We are not unlike a particularly hard crustacean. The lobster grows by developing and shedding a series of hard, protective shells. Each time it expands from within, the confining shell must be sloughed off. It is left exposed and vulnerable until, in time, a new covering grows to replace the old.

> "With each passage from one stage of human growth to the next we, too, must shed a protective structure. We are left exposed and vulnerable—but also yeasty and embryonic again, capable of stretching in ways we hadn't known before." (60)

Warnat (68) reviewed the several types and categories of life cycles. She suggested another systematic set of stages:

1. Foundation—birth to 20 years
2. Anticipation—20 to 30 years
3. Apex—30 to 45 years
4. Plateau—45 to 50 years
5. Reward—55 to 70 years
6. Tranquility—70 onward

The recurring theme in Neugarten's book, *Middle Age and Aging* (54), is that in the first part of life, as well as in the last, centripetal tendencies toward old age were dominant. These centripetal tendencies are caused by factors related to disengagement such as health problems, decreased mobility, and cultural attitudes toward the elderly. Middle age people who have a high degree of fulfillment and maturity have the most positive attitudes. Neugarten comments that in the first half of life our subjective experience is determined by our needs for for the *expansion* of the individual. In the second half, however, one deals more with matters of *conservation* and *integration* of life patterns already established.

Another major categorization that cannot be overlooked, if the Adult Life Cycle is to be viewed holistically, is the pioneering work of Robert Havighurst, who introduces the concept of the Developmental Task.

> "Living in a modern society is a long series of tasks to learn, where learning well brings satisfaction and reward, while learning poorly brings unhappiness and social disapproval. The tasks the individual must learn—*the developmental tasks of life*—are those things that constitute healthy and satisfactory growth in our society." (28)

Havighurst identifies *developmental tasks* for six periods of the life cycle. Those related to adulthood, although somewhat dated, are:

Early Adulthood
1. Selecting a Mate
2. Learning to Live with a Marriage Partner
3. Starting a Family
4. Rearing Children
5. Managing a Home
6. Getting Started in an Occupation
7. Taking on Civic Responsibility
8. Finding a Congenial Social Group

Middle Age
1. Assisting Teen-Age Children to Become Responsible Adults
2. Achieving Adult Social and Civic Responsibility
3. Reaching and Maintaining Satisfactory Performance in One's Occupational Career
4. Developing Adult Leisure-Time Activities
5. Relating Oneself to One's Spouse as a Person

6. To Accept and Adjust to the Physiological Changes of Middle Age
7. Adjusting to Aging Parents

Later Maturity
1. Adjusting to Decreasing Physical Strength and Health
2. Adjustment to Retirement and Reduced Income
3. Adjusting to Death of Spouse
4. Establishing an Explicit Affiliation with One's Age Group
5. Adopting and Adapting Social Roles in a Flexible Way
6. Establishing Satisfactory Physical Living Arrangement

Vivian McCoy (47) has drawn from Havighurst, Levinson, Sheehy, and others to develop a more sophisticated and contemporary set of developmental stages. They are:

Leaving Home (18-22)
Becoming Adult (23-28)
Catch 30 (29-34)
Midlife Reexamination (35-43)
Restabilization (44-55)
Preparation for Retirement (56-64)
Retirement (65 +)

Within each stage are approximately ten developmental tasks similar to those of Havighurst, but more adequately representing contemporary social patterns, some of which appear as appropriate in several of the chronological stages. Several of these appear in several of the chronological stages, in recognition of the recurring nature of developmental tasks throughout the adult life cycle.

Just as it is important to consider the "Developmental Task" construct in relationship to the Adult Life Cycle, it is also important to look at the work done on ego development. In one of her earlier works Loevinger indicated that human development has four main streams or channels; namely, physical, psychosexual, ego and intellectual development (43). She concentrates on ego development and says that her work is a collage from many sources. Her investigation led to the development of a model with the definition of stages and transitions for ego development, together with what she calls "milestones." Loevinger sees "ego development" as a definable and discrete construct:

"... this dimension [in describing characteristics that led to the development of the model] should be called ego development rather than moral development, development of cogni-

tive complexity or development of capacity for interpersonal relations. All of these are involved. Nothing less
than the ego encompasses so wide a scope." (45)

Although Hauser (27) says that Loevinger's "invariant sequence
paradigm" is most akin to Piaget's model of cognitive development and Kohlberg's schema of moral development," he wonders
if the affective and motivational elements can be thought of in the
same way that Piaget and Kohlberg do for their models. To Hauser
there are a number of conceptual as well as empirical issues relative to Loevinger's model that need to be explored. He offers suggestions for the development of a plan of investigation for the
validation and deeper understanding of the model. Although
Hauser and others raise questions about Loevinger's model of
"ego development," her work is advanced enough to be significant for the investigation of the Adult Life Cycle.

Further Considerations in the Literature About the Adult Life Cycle

Jung (29) compared a person's existence to the life cycle of the
sun. He speaks of the inner psychic problems that each person
constantly encounters in life, and about the necessity of entering
these "forms of darkness and uncertainty" so that new life can be
born. When he compares his four stages of life (childhood, young
adulthood, mature adulthood and extreme old age) to the life cycle
of the sun (a day), and talks about the relationship of each level,
he pointedly states that one cannot live in the afternoon of life according to the program of life's morning; the afternoon of life must
have significance of its own.

According to Boelen (3), personal maturity is never an accomplished fact, nor is it a state of being that can be captured once
and for all; neither can it be retained as a permanent possession.
On the contrary, as a person emerges from the "crises of limits,"
maturity is not a *thing* but a *happening*, a "coming to pass" that
dynamically continues, an occurrence which is always in the process of being achieved.

Kimmel (33) introduces the notion of change in relationship to the
adult life by identifying five areas in which change occurs during
adulthood:

1. Self concept and inner life
2. Family life
3. Environment
4. Interpersonal relationships
5. Working life

Kimmel further states that in the first half of life a person 1) does allow for expansion, 2) is open to change and 3) is outward in viewpoint, while during the second half of one's life a person is concerned about 1) contraction, 2) inwardness, and 3) rigidity (33). Neugarten (54) commented that inner life becomes altered over the life span but that it is doubtful that people change internally at regular intervals since the present always has the elements of the past contained within it.

Walz and Libby (67) concur with Neugarten in describing the connection between two stages as "fluid movement."

In commenting about change in relationship to the life cycle, Jung (29) suggests that the beginning of change in the human psyche occurs between 35-40 years of age. He states that if a person is not ready for change in his/her life there will be difficulty. Although it might occur later in one's life, one should be aware of his/her role changes, such as from being a parent to being a grandparent.

Gould (23) specifically looks at the way people view events that take place in their lives (consciousness). Co-existing with one's adult consciousness is an unsuspected childhood consciousness. Any person, as he/she views the prospect for change, needs to be aware that the childhood consciousness, with its "demons of fear, rage and frustration, powerfully restrict our capacity to be authentic adults."

Life experiences are learning experiences, and the field of *adult education* is based on the changing experience of the Adult Life Cycle. Probably the best known investigator in the areas of adult learning and teaching is Malcolm Knowles, who has pioneered in the differentiation of the patterns of adult learning and children's learning.

Knowles introduced the concept of "andragogy" to the field of education. Its focus is on self-directed learning, with strong emphasis on the self-motivation of the learner and the role of teacher primarily as enabler. Conceived originally as primarily for adult learning situations, *andragogy* is increasingly being seen as valid for all ages. Knowles contrasts *pedagogy* and *andragogy* in this way:

25

"PEDAGOGY: The role of the learner is, by definition, a dependent one. The teacher is expected by society to take full responsibility for determining what is to be learned, when it is to be learned, how it is to be learned, and if it has been learned.

ANDRAGOGY: It is a normal aspect of the process of maturation for a person to move from dependence toward increasing self-directedness, but at different rates for different people and in different dimensions of life. Teachers have a responsibility to encourage and nurture this movement. Adults have a deep psychological need to be generally self-directing, although they may be dependent in particular temporary situations."(35)

Traditionally education related to faith development has been primarily pedagogical; in recent years, more and more of it is becoming *andragogical*. This shift is highly significant for the current study.

A Separate Look at Women

For much of the work done on the Adult Life Cycle, most respondents for the investigators were men. This is the reality; however, most writers suggest that a complete picture of the Adult Life Cycle cannot take place until women play as important a role in the research as do men. For example, the reader should note that, in reference to the several sets of categories listed earlier, only one of them (DeBoy) considers different age periods in parallel studies of men and women.

Merriam (50) cautions against making general conclusions about women being involved in Adult Life Cycle research and suggests that even worse than neglecting the experience of women is the fact that women are judged by a male standard.

Gilligan (20) suggests that the conventions that shape women's moral judgments differ from those that apply to men. She states:

"Given the difference in women's conception of self and morality, it is not surprising that women bring to the life cycle a different point of view and that they order human experiences in terms of different priorities."(20)

Wylie (76) devotes her attention to widows. She indicates that after the death of her husband she, the widow, is expected to return to decision-making not unlike that which she had encountered in early adulthood. She states further that because widows abruptly get involved in this decision-making, it is inappropriate to categorize them with other adults when drawing conclusions from general adult life cycle research.

Baruch and Barnett (1) hypothesize that chronological age is not a core variable in organizing and understanding the events of the middle years for the women, as Levinson (42) perceived it to be for men. They conclude that women have tended to blame themselves for feelings of dissatisfaction and depression and that some other women now are attributing more positive feelings solely to person-internal factors, recognizing social, political and economic causes.

To explicate women's feelings about their experiences, Rubin (58) says that the empty nest is a myth. For most women the end of active mothering is a relief, although many experience some fear of new beginnings and some anger at lost time and capacities.

In Kahnweiler and Johnson's (31) study of women who were returning to college, a midlife developmental profile was created. The research indicates that the women returning to college tended to have a focus on the future and where it will take them. It was noted that each woman who returned had experienced a "culminating event" (e.g., divorce, marriage, etc.) as a significant point in midlife.

In summary, Gilligan (19) cautions that persons who expect to do research about adult developmental process must consider the evolution of women to be different from men. If this does not occur, it becomes inappropriate to make generalizations about overall adult development.

Summary

Much effort has been devoted to the idea of stages in human development. Most theories posit a loose sequence through which development occurs. Some of them are supported by empirical research which suggests that the theory describes a typical sequence of development. Others posit a normative progression from simpler, more infantile, less adaptable stages to more complex, adult, adaptable stages.

From children and teenagers, the developmental literature suggests that the ability to structure beliefs is age related. Not until persons reach their teens are they capable of developing a referent-state which includes a societal outlook or are they able to form "universal principles" (Kohlberg) or "universal faith" (Fowler). Adults, while they may not be in the more advanced stages of faith development, are not generally restricted by their cognitive ability. Rather, the stage they are in represents situational or emotional constraints.

Despite the number of different labels given by researchers to the various stages of human development, the initial stages reflect a dependence on authority and satisfaction of hedonistic desires. The later stages reflect the development of community awareness and autonomous values.

Virtually all the stage theories are based on the assumption that something happens cognitively, emotionally, and volitionally as the individual matures, which creates greater potential over time to reach higher stages of development.

All of the theories, however, recognize that individuals do not necessarily proceed successively through all stages. For example, individuals may stay at an intermediate stage, they may regress, or may advance faster than other individuals. The analogy between these theories and the idea of faith development is only loose and suggestive, but several observations appear warranted.

First, the idea of stages is a heuristic device. Development is actually gradual and continuous, though punctuated with spurts, setbacks, and plateaus. A particular stage may be characterized by a special set of problems. But these problems also confront people at earlier or later stages and may be resolved only temporarily. Much of what constitutes development actually occurs along a continuum.

Second, there appears to be general agreement that earlier stages of human development are characterized by rote learning, imitation, efforts to please, and adherence to simple (and sometimes rigid) rules and concepts. Later stages are characterized by greater capacities for abstract reasoning, by an ability to sort through concepts and come up with uniquely individual avenues of conduct.

Third, there is also agreement that development involves greater degrees of self-awareness, both as to who one is and what one thinks, feels and wants. Along with this awareness, there is supposed to be an enhanced ability to meet one's needs and, with growing recognition of the interdependence of life, to serve the needs of others.

Fourth, from a scaling perspective stages suggest a determinate model—one must pass through each stage before moving on to the next. Empirically this is suggestive of a Guttman scale with a single underlying dimension. However, any dimension of humanity, such as faith, may be multidimensional rather than strictly chronological. A person may have some of each dimension without having a total "score" on any dimension. Empirically this would be tested by probabilistic models such as multidimensional scaling techniques.

Fifth, the literature on human development is heavily biased toward purely cognitive, rationalistic conceptions of growth. It tells how to become a philosopher but not how to become an artist. Literature produced since the late '60's and early '70's has begun to challenge these biases. The newer literature forces attention to be paid to growth in feelings, intuition, expressivity, and centeredness. It gives greater attention to growth from experiences, meditation, and reflection and less to growth from purely rational learning. The pedagogy of life has begun to reassert itself over that of the classroom.

Sixth, the human development literature is also biased in the direction of liberalism. It champions tolerance and flexibility over conservative adherence to absolute truths. Again, recent discussions have challenged these assumptions, pointing out that the highest stages of development may involve an overlay of conviction and commitment that transcends simple libertarianism.

It is expected that the literature of the Adult Life Cycle will provide a framework for the study of Faith Development during the adult years. It is assumed that the entire span of adult life—from late adolescence to death—will be the scope of attention and that the differences based upon ethnic, sexual, social roles will be studied.

Definition

The Adult Life Cycle refers to the changing patterns of needs, interests, and responses which occur in adulthood from the transition out of adolescence through mid-life and older adulthood to death. Simpler concepts of the Adult Life Cycle refer to young, middle, and older adulthood; other, more complex constructions involve as many as nine identifiable stages of human development in adulthood. According to this literature, there are predictable physical, psychological, and social patterns that affect most, if not all, adults as they move through life.

II. FAITH DEVELOPMENT

"Faith"—What Does It Mean?

Understandably, the term "Faith" has many historic definitions, and when combined with the concept of "Development," suggests an even wider variety of interpretations. Increasingly, however, the concept of FAITH as being a static and unchanging concept is giving way to a more developmental definition.

Tillich indicates that

> "There is hardly a word in the religious language, both theological and popular, which is subject to more misunderstandings, distortions, and questionable definitions than the word 'faith.' " (65)

This section includes a selective review of the literature of Faith Development, presented as a basis for the working definition of "Faith Development" suggested for the purposes of this study.

Faith

Several persons have attempted to clarify the meaning of faith. For example, in his book *Dynamics of Faith*, Tillich defines faith as:

> " . . . the state of being ultimately concerned. The dynamics of faith are the dynamics of man's ultimate concern. . . . Faith as ultimate concern is an act of the total personality. It happens in the center of the personal life and includes all its elements. . . . Faith is more than trust in authorities, although trust is an element of faith."(65)

The dictionary definition of "faith" is "allegiance to duty or a person . . . a system or religious beliefs." Richard McBrien (46), in his article entitled "Faith, Theology and Belief," states that faith is "a way of perceiving reality." In "The Meaning of Faith Considered in Relationship to Justice," Avery Dulles (8) analyzes the three main theologies of faith operating in contemporary Christianity today: 1) Intellectual Approaches, 2) Fiducial Approaches, and 3) Performative Approaches. Even though faith is addressed primarily as it relates to justice, he indicates that faith can be viewed from a variety of perspectives, including the three mentioned above.

The scholar who has done the major work relating to faith and Faith Development is James Fowler. In *Life Maps*, he suggests that "... faith is not a *noun* but a *verb*" (18), meaning that it has an active, changing, developmental quality not usually associated with more traditional definitions of faith which relate primarily to belief systems and participation in religious activities. By this definition, faith is "... a *universal*, ... a feature of the living, acting, and self-understanding of all human beings, whether they claim to be 'believers' or 'religious' or not." (18)

Keen (32) looks at the developmental aspect of "faith as trust." He suggests that faith is a gradual or sudden yielding of the illusion of control and a concomitant loss of character and transformation of personality.

Westerhoff (70) defines faith as the expression of meaning revealed in a person's life style, or that foundation upon which persons live their lives—that point of centeredness or ultimacy that underlies and is expressed abstractly in a world view and value system or, more concretely, in the person's thought, feeling, and action. Jung (29) says that people call faith the true religious experience, but they do not stop to think that actually it is a secondary phenomenon arising from the fact that something happened in the first place which instilled trust and loyalty.

Groome (25), addressing the Christian faith in particular, suggests that faith is a lifelong developmental process involving the total person. Coughlin (6) states that if a person's faith remains "out there" or something that is only taken off the shelf for an hour on Sunday, it will seldom develop into anything meaningful for that person.

Westerhoff and Neville (69) suggest that a person's faith can expand, that is, become more complex, but that expanded faith is not greater faith and, therefore, one's style of faith is not to be judged. Neither is the style of our faith directly related to our age. From a Christian perspective, God's grace is freely given to all. Though it is our potential to expand in faith, we do not earn anything by so doing; indeed, the desire to expand in faith is, for Christians, only an act of gratitude for the gift given.

DeBoy (7) has found that "If a person makes a faith commitment at one stage of development, the commitment will have to be renewed or deepened at a later stage; faith commitments that are not renewed will gradually fade and die."

Stock (62) suggests that becoming involved in a life of faith means that there is continual growth and change; it could become ever deeper and more integrated into the fabric of one's life.

To conclude the consideration of "faith," we note Fowler's expansion of its many dimensions into a complex but comprehensive definition. Faith is:

> "The process of constitutive knowing

> Underlying a person's composition and maintenance of a comprehensive frame (or frames) of meaning

> Generated from the person's attachments or commitments to centers of supraordinate value which have power to unify his or her experiences of the world

> Thereby endowing the relationships, contexts, and patterns of everyday life, past and future, with significance." (17)

Religion

A logical extension of the concept of faith is the meaning of religion and its relationship to faith. The definition of religion that Belgum (2) advocates is the faith, values, and action whereby a person is bound in a comprehensive and integrating way to whom or what he/she considers fundamental in the universe, which includes relationship to nature, to society in historical perspective, to one's own psycho-physical experience, and to one's destiny.

Whereas Westerhoff and Neville (70) define religion as faith given shape, form and content, Knox (36) adds that society wants religion to be effective in providing 1) personal salvation, 2) a community dimension, and 3) institutional religion. Each person, according to Knox, feels a tension between the "I" and the "we," as well as between one's relationship with God and the demands made by the church. There is, therefore, an integral relationship between faith and religion.

Kohlberg's Stages of Moral Development

Fundamental to any study of Faith Development is the pioneering research of Lawrence Kohlberg in Moral Development. Kohlberg studied the responses made to a series of moral dilemmas by individuals of different ages, and later by the same individuals at an older age and found a definite progression of moral reasoning which he classifies by levels or stages. Building upon the stage theory concepts of Jean Piaget, the Swiss scientist, regarding the cognitive development of children and adolescents, Kohlberg projected a series of stages of moral development which apply to the entire life span. These are:

Preconventional Level
1. The punishment-and-obedience orientation
2. The instrumental-relativist orientation

Conventional Level
3. The interpersonal concordance or good boy–nice girl orientation
4. The law and order orientation

Post-Conventional Level
5. The social contract, legalistic orientation
6. The universal-ethical-principle orientation (37)

Related to his schema, Kohlberg (39) notes that cultural factors can speed up or slow down, but do not change, the sequence of Moral Development in the individual.

It is Kohlberg's comment about the relationship of faith and moral development which causes us first to take a serious look at his work and supportive research as well as at a sampling of critiques of his work. About the relationship of faith and moral development, he states:

> "We may expect parallel development of faith stages and moral stages. The critical question both psychologically and philosophically is whether moral development precedes (and causes) faith development or vice-versa. . . . We hypothesize that development to a given moral stage precedes development to the parallel faith stages. . . . Moral principles, then, do not require faith for their formulation or for their justification. In some sense, to ultimately live up to moral principle requires faith." (38)

Extensions of Kohlberg's Work

Sullivan (63) wondered whether there was an error in Kohlberg's sequence of stages; therefore, he replicated his study and found that the stages were seriated correctly in a continuum of human development. In addition, Kohlberg (40), in his 20-year study, found that his theory was supported in the area that in no case did a subject reach a stage without having gone through each preceding stage.

Miller (51) found that there is a significant relationship between Kohlberg's stages of moral development and the stages of religious thinking (using Goldman's test of religious thinking), between stages of moral development and age categories, and between stages of religious thinking and age categories.

Roberts (57) examines some of the theoretical assumptions of Kohlberg's work and states that a philosophical synthesis of his theories with other moral law concepts does produce valid theoretical foundation for adult moral education as well as for further experimentation and research.

At the present time, Wilcox (74), working in the area of moral development, refers to the work of Piaget, Kohlberg, Perry and Fowler as being important to the development of her efforts. She identifies five styles of reasoning; namely, 1) Imaginative Style, 2) Literal Style, 3) Conventional Style, 4) Reflective Style and 5) Integrative Style and notes that:

"1. We (the church) can accept and affirm the different way in which persons think and reason, encouraging them to develop skills in the Styles of Reasoning they are using. . . .
2. We (the church) can challenge by exposure to the next style in the sequence." (74)

Further, she and her colleagues, Snelling and Everding, are finding ways to make the moral development stages and processes theory practical for the local church or synagogue (75).

Wilcox (73) has identified three ways that the educative process presently responds to the development of values. They are:

"1. Leave values education to the home and church.
2. Teach the traditional values on which everyone agrees.
3. Help each person to discover what his/her own values are, making no judgments about them." (73)

She gives positive and negative aspects of the three processes and goes on to suggest a fourth way, a model for "teaching the whole person." What she says about this approach as a response to the need for moral development is consistent with her comments about the Styles of Reasoning.

These persons who have used Kohlberg's schemata demonstrate the variety of possible extensions of research in moral development.

Ott (56) stipulates that moral development should be seen in the context of total human development—social, emotional and rational. He calls his position "reasonable universalism" because it is formulated as a result of wide experience, insight, reflection and understanding rather than logic.

From another perspective, Schnurer (59) states that personality structures may have an effect on moral decisions that cannot be explained by cognitive development alone.

Even more specifically, Mullen (53) suggests that as one looks at Piaget and Kohlberg, it can be seen that they are biased in using the cognitive domain almost exclusively to explain moral behavior. He suggests that as one studies moral behavior, it is also necessary to look at Jung and Newman for the affective domain's part in explaining moral development.

Just as Mullen (53) spoke out against cognitive-developmental psychologists, Dykstra (9) states that juridical ethics are of little value to living a Christian life. Dykstra criticizes Kohlberg on three counts. First, people are more than what they know—it is not enough just to know what is just; one needs to care about justice also. Second, people's decisions and choices are rooted in our vision of the world. Dykstra takes Kohlberg to task a third time, saying his work is found wanting because Kohlberg limits morality to a juridical notion and a moral person is viewed as a detached rational agent. He also believes that Kohlberg's efforts are at variance with traditional Christian understanding of morality (namely, that morality is a response to God's revelation of a person sinful and in need of redemption). Dykstra further states that transformation of the whole self, not just the cognitive self, is required to be a mature, moral person.

Fowler's Stages of Faith Development

Early in his career, James Fowler began to study the change and growth that take place in the faith of people as they mature from childhood into and through adulthood. By asking persons, in an interview setting, to reflect on their "journey of faith" through the years, a pattern of responses began to take shape. Relating these responses to the stage theories of Piaget and Kohlberg, and the periods of the life cycle suggested by Erikson, Fowler developed a stage theory of Faith Development which he sees as hierarchical (increasingly complex and qualitative), sequential (they appear one after the other in the life span), and invariant (they follow the same order for all persons). It is one of the first and undoubtedly the most complete organization of concepts of faith within the framework of human development.

First developed in a single chapter of *Life Maps* (18), Fowler has recently published a comprehensive volume, *Stages of Faith* (16), which provides the full development of his research and theories. It is not possible here to develop in detail the multi-faceted factors of Fowler's design. A basic survey of his six stages of Faith Development must, however, be noted with a brief interpretation of each.

I. Intuitive-Projective Faith

Almost totally limited to children to about age 6, persons in Stage I reflect the faith attributes of parents and family as perceived by that child. At this time of his/her life, the preschool child accepts parental faith attitudes without question.

II. Mythic-Literal Faith

In later childhood, the person becomes aware of and begins to internalize the faith attitudes and views of persons, primarily adults, other than family members. She/he has an increasing awareness of different faith attitudes in society but still tends to hold to those of family and religious traditions. Some adults remain in this stage through much or all of their lives.

III. Synthetic-Conventional Faith

In the early teens, peer pressure becomes significant. The attitudes and values of the "gang" are major determinators of most of one's values, including those related to faith. Adherence to the "norm" is paramount as life's increasing complexities necessitate a set of values held securely in common by a significant number of other persons close to the individual. This need continues for many into adulthood, where a large percentage of people find a faith-security in their relationship with their church, synagogue, or other religious affiliation.

IV. Individuative-Reflective Faith

As the adolescent moves into adulthood and begins to take an adult responsibility—marriage and family, vocation, financial responsibility, etc.—he/she also often begins to question some of the faith assumptions of parents and/or religious tradition. For many, the need to doubt, question, and even reject elements of one's faith traditions is necessary for faith development. This phenomenon is not restricted to young adulthood, as an increasing number of persons in the middle and later years are faced with the need to rethink their faith.

V. Conjunctive Faith

Usually no earlier than the middle years, some adults are able to bring into meaningful reconciliation the variety of faith dynamics that have played important roles in previous stages of their faith development—their faith roots of family and church, the beliefs of others, the answers they have found to their own questions, all tempered with the maturity that comes only with the experiencing of life. Stage V individuals are able to identify beyond boundaries of race, class, or ideology to understand and integrate the views of others into their own expression of faith, arrived at individually as a mature expression of a faith that is wholly theirs.

VI. Universalizing Faith

Persons in Stage VI are rare. They are, however, those whose lives are so attuned to the ultimate meaning of life that their faith expression is beyond self-interest, taking on a truly universalizing quality. Fowler says of Stage VI that it "... represents the culmination of growth in faith, brought about by human fidelity and Divine grace and revelation."

Fowler develops each of the six stages in a variety of aspects such as "Locus of Authority," "Bonds of Social Awareness," and "Symbolic Function" in a horizontal dimension which combines with the vertical dimension of the stages to provide a framework for a holistic overview of his concept of Faith Development.

Although Fowler's faith stages follow each other chronologically and each is usually not found *before* a given age, they do not necessarily relate to precise age periods. Adults are found in all of the stages from II to VI, and the relationship between faith stages and life stages is general, not specific.

Fowler's work is the most comprehensive research-based exploration of this emerging field and has already served as the springboard for a number of related studies.

Extensions of Fowler's Work

Haunz (26) notes that Fowler describes faith as being rational and knowing, as the meaning of cognition and affection, and suggests that the most contemporary model of God is the process model, such as Fowler's, because it combines transcendence and immanence. Similarly, Erb (10) relates faith to a transcendent quality and process to develop a categorization concerning faith development:

1. Concrete Trust—Dependent
2. Doubtful Belief—Counter-Dependent
3. Autonomous Action—Independent
4. Committed Complexity—Interdependent
5. Synthesizing

Although Girzaitis' categories (21) may not be a direct extension of Fowler's work, her work may be considered a translation into practical application. She indicates that she has used Fowler, Gould, Sheehy, Levinson, and Good as bases for her stages of faith development:

1. Early Adulthood—Pulling up Roots
2. Provisional Adulthood—Making Choices
3. Searching Adulthood—Dealing with Crises
4. Rooting Adulthood—Settling Down
5. Crises Adulthood—Mid-year Explosion
6. Flowering Adulthood—Maturity
7. Peak Adulthood—Integration

She indicates that this practical approach to naming stages will help planners understand the importance of focusing on spiritual needs as these emerge through the various periods of adult life.

Summary

It has become increasingly clear that no one definition of "faith" will satisfy everybody. For some, faith is a universal of life ("I have faith that the sun will rise tomorrow"), while for others it may be related to a specific discipline ("I have faith in medical science"). For some, faith includes the humanistic "I have faith in the integrity of people," while for others, "faith" must be reserved for the Deity. Religious faith can be viewed as essentially cognitive ("The creed is my faith"), experiential ("A 'born again' Christian"), or essentially behavioral ("faith is meaningless without action"). These are but illustrative; the list could be endless.

The Project leadership is aware of the broad spectrum of scholarship which has addressed itself to the concept of faith over the centuries. However, the purpose of this study is not primarily a theological exploration of the meaning of faith, but rather an effort to relate a generally accepted meaning of the term to the dynamics of the Adult Life Cycle. The research design consciously involves the faith understandings and interpretations of "everyday people" as well as those of scholars in its effort to provide resources which speak to the real needs of the average person.

Recognizing, however, the need to provide a working definition of Faith Development for the purposes of the Project, that which is suggested is purposely expressed in broad and simple terms. *Not* included are many of the descriptive and definitive words and phrases which add richness and specificity to a definition but in so doing exclude a number of individuals who may not be able to accept, in good conscience, certain elements of that definition.

Definitions

Faith is seen as a dynamic element of the individual's total being which addresses issues of ultimate concern, such as the meaning of life and death, the nature of being, the existence and nature of Deity, and the like. One's faith is extremely personal and individual, focusing not so much on creeds and doctrines per se, but more on those perceptions and values of an ultimate nature which are a part of that individual's very being.

Faith Development reflects the changing nature of one's faith perceptions and understandings through the developmental journey of his or her life. It is through Faith Development that maturing adults function in increasingly complex and adequate responses to life's ultimate questions and issues.

III. THE INTERFACE

The paucity of research related to the Interface between Adult Life Cycle and Faith Development prompted the present study. Considerable investigation, as noted in the two previous sections, indicates the extent of work done in each of the disciplines separately, but it is difficult to identify much definitive research in the relationship between the two. However, on the basis of correspondence in Phase I, it is apparent that there is considerable interest in this Interface and that it is clearly an emerging area of academic discussion and research. Put another way, there is every indication that significant work in this field will probably be taking place throughout the '80's.

Meissner, in his article entitled "Notes on the Psychology of Faith," says, "Faith is not, therefore, an isolated act standing apart from the context of the believer's life cycle" (49). If one were to assume that faith has a relationship to consciousness, Gould (23) suggests that by striving for a fuller, more independent adult consciousness, we trigger the "angry demons of childhood consciousness." Growing and reformulating our self-definition, he continues, becomes a dangerous act because faith is an act of transformation.

The image that emerges from the literature of any Christian, according to Bouwsma, should be that of a "wayfarer" or "pilgrim" who has a direction to his journey, yet is on a "voyage" in the unknown. "As movement in a direction, it also implies progress, but a progress that remains incomplete in this life." For Bouwsma, ". . . faith begins . . . not in illusion, but in an absolute and terrifying realism," an experience of total helplessness, an admission and acceptance of one's creaturehood and limitations (4).

Shulik (61), in his study of 40 to 60-year-olds, uses Fowler's, Kohlberg's, and other instruments to explore issues related to the following areas: disengagement, life review, philosophical development, and preparation for death. His findings suggest that: engagement was *not* found to correlate significantly with any variable examined in the study; persons who have achieved a higher level of Faith Development are likely to be more sensitized to the internal or physiological changes which accompany the aging process than are persons at lower levels; and the higher maturational levels are associated with greater life satisfaction and with a stronger sense of emotional equilibrium.

In their study of the life cycle/faith relationship, Evelyn and James Whitehead see general patterns of adult growth involving crises which are predictable; these patterns and crises have religious dimensions and faith implications which must be recognized. From their perspective,

> "God's grace can be discovered at work within the structure of psychosocial development. The psychological challenges, crises, and tasks of human development present opportunities and invitations that a believer can recognize as graceful." (71)

In yet another statement, the Whiteheads suggest that the sacraments can be viewed as rites of passage helping people through crises in their lives, crises that can be breakdown or breakthrough. The parish can be viewed, so they indicate, as a sacrament responding to adults in crises and/or in transition and should help people see these acts as religious and sacramental events or times. (72)

Olson (55) implores us, as we consider ceremony (including the thought of sacrament and symbols), not to make it a copy of what the religious institution wants. He further observes that if you allow the people involved to construct their own ceremony, it helps them to examine what they really believe. Crises, as the Whiteheads (71) comment on Olson's concept, have characteristics that are common. Extending the Whiteheads' work, Goldbrunner identifies the following characteristics of a crisis:

1. a period of inner restlessness, followed by . . .
2. a period of inactivity, disorientation and inability to make decisions, even feelings of despair, meanwhile . . .
3. within the inner realm of the individual vital powers and energies become active and then . . .
4. more or less suddenly, these powers are set free and the individual regains the ability to act, and finally . . .
5. new vitality is assimilated, new rhythm fills life and new tasks are assumed. (22)

Thus it can be suggested that crises play a significant part conceptually in the Interface between Adult Life Cycle and Faith Development. As the present study proceeds, other concepts will no doubt emerge, but "crisis" appears to be a critical point of linkage between the two.

Summary

There is little research to date regarding the Interface between the Adult Life Cycle and Faith Development. It is for that reason that the present study has been undertaken. The design proposes to explore the relationships by the testing of hypotheses regarding this Interface. It is presumed that, on the basis of such testing, some of the basic components of the dynamics that relate Faith Development and the Adult Life Cycle can be determined.

IV. CONCEPTS

A study of the literature of the Adult Life Cycle, Faith Development, and their Interface suggests a number of concepts which stem from the research of a specific individual or group and are relatively widely accepted and / or appear in the work of several of the scholars studied. These concepts seem to be fundamental elements of each field.

Only a few such concepts are here suggested. There are, undoubtedly, many more. One of the tasks of the Symposium will be to suggest additional concepts, to critique them and those here stated, and to refine the total to a workable summary of the primary concepts within each area of focus.

Concepts of the Adult Life Cycle

Life Stages
A significant concept of adult development is the stage theory. This provides chronological subdivisions, each with specific characteristics typically found at that stage of life. Some are relatively simple: Erikson and Havighurst look at young, middle, and older adulthood, although by different names. Some are broadly defined in terms of age, while others, as in Levinson, are quite explicit in terms of a precise definition of the applicable years of each stage. Some appear, like Sheehy's, in convenient 10-year blocks of time, while others suggest differing time frames for each stage. Each scholar has a rationale for her/his stage structure and, to date at least, there appears to be no consensus on the number or duration of adult life stages. What is clear, however, is that the concept of *life stages* is a major way by which Adult Life Cycle is defined.

Most *life stage* theories are sequential and invariant. That is, there is a predictable sequence of stages through which each person must travel on life's journey. Although an individual may move through the psychological dynamics of one stage quite rapidly and tarry for an unusual period in another, all adults move through them in the same invariant order, albeit at different paces. Therefore, whereas some will face the mid-life crisis in their 30's, others may not deal with it until their 50's; for some it may be a significant dynamic of life for 5-10 years, while for others it is dealt with relatively easily in a few months.

A problem with the *life stages* concept is that it can too easily be interpreted as hierarchical—some stages more important than others, depending on one's perspective. Levinson resists this with his concept of the "seasons of life," one no better than another, and each with its particular beauty of significance and meaning.

Another problem for many is the scholar's sometimes rigid adherence to the qualities of sequentiality and invariance in *life stages*. Research may show these phenomena to be operative, but often individual adults, valuing their individuality and resisting the formula, argue that "it didn't work that way for me."

Life stages are undoubtedly helpful in clarifying general patterns of human experience usually related to particular periods of life. It can be dangerous when it becomes seen as a norm: "The book says I should have had an affair in my late 30's, but I didn't. What's wrong with me?" Nothing is wrong. Each of us is still a unique individual. *Life stages* help us understand what behavior is normally to be expected at certain times in the cycle, little more, and help us to predict what may be some of the life dynamics ahead of us, five years down the road. In this sense, they provide a context in which each of us can identify himself/herself within the complexity of our culture.

Developmental Task

Havighurst conceived the concept of the *developmental task* in the 40's, defining it as

> " . . . a task which arises at or about a certain period in the life of the individual, successful achievement of which leads to his happiness and to success with later tasks, while failure leads to unhappiness in the individual, disapproval by the society, and difficulty with later tasks." (28)

Developmental tasks relate to physical maturation, cultural pressures, and personal values and aspirations throughout the life span, with the tasks of childhood and youth focusing more on the first and those of adulthood more on the latter two. Specific tasks of adulthood suggested for young, middle, and older adulthood were reviewed in Section I.

Essential to the *developmental task* concept is that there are physical, psychological, and social experiences appropriate to the different periods of life. Therefore, "starting a family'" is an appropriate task of young adulthood, "reaching and maintaining satisfactory performance is one's occupational career" is of particular importance in middle age, while "adjusting to retirement and reduced income" relates primarily to later maturity.

Havighurst suggests 21 *developmental tasks* in adulthood, some of which seem dated in terms of contemporary life styles. The concept, however, is important in suggesting that healthy human development is, in fact, based on successfully dealing with a series of generally age-related tasks which occur from birth to death. The way we deal with these *developmental tasks* as they occur can well affect the senses of fulfillment and frustration that are a part of our lives in adulthood.

The "Learnable Moment"

Havigurst (28) suggests the educational concept of the "teachable moment" as the time of a person's maximum readiness to learn a specific body of knowledge. Since adult education is essentially self-directed, the concept of *learnable moment* seems more appropriate, referring to the optimum time for dealing with specific growth needs, often related to the adult developmental tasks with which one is dealing.

Thus, a young man may have little interest in personal budgeting until such time as he wishes to buy a car and, therefore, needs to learn everything he can about financing options. Similarly, the mid-life couple may pay little attention to magazine articles on chemical dependency until faced with drug-use problems on the part of their children, at which time they devour all they can on the subject. A widow who has always depended on her husband and family for companionship is faced with developing a new style of social life in her later years.

Issues that were of slight interest at one time become tremendously important at another, and vice-versa. The *learnable moments* of life are ever shifting and changing, and each contributes significantly to the individualization of each person's Adult Life Cycle.

Crisis

From its recurrent appearance in the literature, it would appear that the concept of crisis may well be one of the major keys to the individual's developmental pattern. "Crisis" is a strong word, usually connoting a tragic or near-tragic event. As used by developmental scholars, however, it more often connotes an experience of significant change—for better or worse—in life's patterns. Erikson defines it:

> ". . . not [as] a threat of catastrophe, but a turning point, a crucial period of increased vulnerability and heightened potential." (13)

It is the *crisis* experience that frequently leads to changes and transitions in life. Put objectively at least, without *crisis* life would be humdrum and monotonous. Most of us resist change and try to avoid the crises of life; yet these crises, be they marriage or divorce, a birth or a death, being hired or being fired, are the catalysts by which we grow. Life becomes better as we can see and accept the opportunity in every obstacle.

There are related concepts, often used in place of *crisis*. Levinson prefers "transitions," while Sheehy refers to "passages." Whatever the term, the basic concept remains much the same: life, particularly adult life, is made up of a succession of change dynamics—crises, transitions, passages—which reform our lives in sometimes subtle or often dramatic ways. Everyone has different crises with which he/she must deal, and we cope with them in a variety of ways. The net result, over the years, is the framework of each of our unique life cycles.

Social Roles

One of the intriguing complexities of human personality is the multiplicity of *social roles* we play, many at the same time, throughout the Adult Life Cycle. An individual can be a grandchild, parent, spouse, lover, wage earner, scout leader, cancer volunteer, member of the choir, Democrat, graduate student, chief cook and bottle-washer all at the same time, and that's only a few of them. Roles change through the Adult Life Cycle. We play different ones at different times, and by our later years, most of us have been involved in thousands of *social roles.*

The concept is important in reminding the individual that although she/he views herself/himself from inside this many-faceted personality, we are viewed and judged from the variety of perspectives our spouses, children, parents, fellow workers, and friends have of us. The Adult Life Cycle, therefore, is not merely the journey of a single *persona* through a span of time, but an intertwining matrix of many personalities, each moving at varying paces and different ways through life's complex structure. Recognition of this diversity of *social roles* is an important concept for adults in the life cycle.

Sexual Roles

A sensitivity to *sexual roles* has been growing in our society in recent years. "That's a sexist statement," whether spoken with a smile or with a frown, has become an accepted part of everyday conversation. As a people, we are becoming aware of the *sexual roles*, real and pseudo, we play out in all aspects of our lives.

Increasingly, sexual stereotypes are being questioned. For example, is aggressive behavior inherently more masculine than feminine, or really is it a product of traditional roles which root back to primitive times in which males hunted for food while females stayed home to cook and mind the children? Dozens of issues such as these are debated regularly on campuses, in offices, and on TV talk shows.

A typical phenomenon of mid-life, for example, often felt but not always understood by couples in their 40's, is the counter-dynamic of their changing lives: he is wearying of vocational pressure at the very time that she, emancipated from family responsibilities, may well see the world of work as exciting and challenging. He wants to spend more time in the garden; she wants to work overtime to establish an identity in her new career. Too often they are ships that pass in the night—in more ways that one—and they don't understand why their marriage has lost its spark.

Too little of the life-cycle literature has dealt with male/female differences. Much of the best-known research is male-oriented (Kohlberg, Levinson—although he is presently studying women), and yet, ironically, many of the popular articles on the subject are female-oriented (usually in women's magazines). What is particularly needed are more parallel comparative studies of male and female development throughout the life span.

Certainly the concept of *sexual roles* is particularly important to today's society, not only in the *un*learning of old assumptions, but also in the development of new and more adequate understandings of the social and psychological developmental differences between men and women as they, separately yet together, move through the life span.

Concepts of Faith Development

Faith, Religion, and Beliefs

These three concepts are, unfortunately, often used synonymously, and yet each has an identity and meaning of vital importance for Faith Development. In Chapter 2 of his new book, *Stages of Faith* (16), Fowler addresses the distinctive features of each with a scholarly development of the concepts. He credits Wilfred Cantwell Smith, who studied the major religions of the world for two decades, with many of the fundamental insights basic to Fowler's research. (What follows is essentially a paraphrase; the entire chapter is commended for its insight at this point.)

Religion refers to the cumulative traditions of the faith of a people in history. It includes the wide variety of sacred writings, symbols, liturgical expressions, creeds, artistic representations, ethical teachings, etc., that make up the *religion* of a given group or individual within that group. It is a relatively stable and formalized structure of relationships which bind people together in a common purpose.

Faith is much deeper and more personal than religion. It is a part of the inner dynamic of an individual and/or that unstructured and often verbally inexpressable bond of commonality in dealing with life's ultimate issues which may be shared by two or more individuals. Faith necessitates a fundamental alignment of the heart and will, a commitment of loyalty and trust.

Beliefs are ways by which faith expresses itself. They are the expressions of the human's need to communicate and to translate experiences into concepts or propositions. *Beliefs* usually take the form of words, sentences, statements, doctrines, and creeds by which they, of necessity, become something outside the individual which the person can only intellectually affirm, deny, or question.

Space does not permit further development of these concepts, and the serious student will want to pursue the semantic differences further by reading the chapter cited and its references and other similar studies. Suffice it here to suggest that care needs to be taken to understand and communicate the differences between *religion, faith,* and *belief* when discussing Faith Development. Each has its own uniqueness too often lost in casual conversation but vitally important for meaningful communication within the field.

Faith Stages

Piaget and Erikson pioneered the concept of life stages. Kohlberg utilized their theories as a basis for his definition of the stages of moral development. Fowler, Erb, Westerhoff and Neville, and others expand the concept to suggest stages of Faith Development. These are noted in the literature review in Section II.

Faith stages is a controversial concept. Despite concerted efforts to disavow the connotation that "higher is better," the implication is always there. Educators and clergy are quick to reject the idea of what appears to be the manipulation of people toward higher *faith stages.* The classification of people into stages ("Stage 3 class in the Auditorium, Stage 4 in the Lounge, and Stages 5 and 6 in the Library") can also seem most distasteful. And the suggestion that "our congregation's goal for next year is to move everybody up one *faith stage*" is downright obnoxious.

And yet, these same leaders of people are also the first to affirm their vocational calling and responsibility: to help people grow and mature spiritually as well as mentally. Viewed in a different context, the concept of *faith stages* is positive, acceptable, and helpful. An understanding of the stages of Faith Development members of his/her group are in can help the leader better understand the dynamics of the discussion. When Walt questions the authenticity of a Bible story, Audrey tells him he has to "take it on faith," and feelings run tense, the fact of two individuals at different stages of Faith Development is obvious.

The concept of *faith stages* is helpful when used thoughtfully and non-judgmentally. In an increasingly multiverse culture, a concept of faith which permits a variety of interpretations and the opportunity for growth is a necessity.

Faithing

Fowler surprises his reader with the assertion that "faith is a *verb*" (18). Westerhoff and Neville (70) echo the same phrase, and the reader is taken aback, for we all know that "faith" is a noun: "Faith of our Fathers," "Your faith has made you whole," and countless other phrases we have known since childhood. How can "faith" be a *verb*?

These writers, and others, are not trying to rewrite the grammar books. They are suggesting an important point. They are helping the reader understand that faith is not a thing, not a static, unchanging entity. Rather, faith is a dynamic, changing dimension of the human personality. Better, refer to *faithing*, a gerund, a noun derived from a verb. I am running, you are laughing, he is walking, she is thinking, they are praying, we are *faithing*. Not yet a part of common vocabulary, perhaps its time has come.

The concept of *faithing* emphasizes the changing, growing, emerging, developing nature of faith. It is ever in transition. Doctrines, creeds, beliefs may be set in words, but faith cannot.

> "Faith is . . . a way of behaving which involves knowing, being, and willing; it is . . . a centered act of personality encompassing our hearts, minds, and wills according to our growth and development." (70)

The concept of *faithing* is fundamental to Faith Development. Those persons for whom faith is an unchanging absolute often cannot understand Faith *Development*. Developmental faith is an anachronism for them. It is sacrilegious to speak of faith and change in the same breath. Yet, for many people, it is a new and challenging concept, worth serious consideration. *Faithing* may be one of the most significant concepts contributed by the faith developmentalists. Taken seriously, the idea of a growing, maturing faith has the potential of changing countless lives, regardless of religious persuasion.

48

Conversion

Probably no concept appears in the literature of Faith Development more than *conversion.* Countless definitions are to be found, most of which contain such key phrases as "about-face," "new beginning," "new selfhood," "new life," and "a turning." Historically, the *conversion* experience has been seen as an identifiable moment or period of time in which a person's faith-life undergoes a significant change. It has often carried with it the imagery of the revival meeting and the testimonial and a seemingly instantaneous quality suggesting an immediate about-face of faith values and ethical behavior.

In the context of the Faith Development literature, *conversion* is often, if not usually, a developmental experience occurring over a relatively long period of time. Griffin suggests four stages:

—desire or longing
—argument and reasoning
—struggle or crisis
—surrender (24)

Tiebout, writing in the context of his research on alcoholism, suggests a similar, developmental pattern:

—crisis
—hitting bottom
—surrender
—conversion switch
—release of power
—harmony and peace (64)

Fowler, however, (16) differentiates between the stages of Faith Development and *conversion* by suggesting that the latter occurs primarily in terms of change in the *content* of one's faith—i.e., the acceptance of a new set of beliefs and values such as might happen to a Christian who accepts the Buddhist faith. In making such a lateral change, the individual may or may not change the stage of his/her Faith Development. Movement through the stages of faith, however, do not necessarily imply such change in belief, but rather the way by which the person views and deals with his/her faith experience.

It is probable that it is and will continue to be around the concept of *conversion* that there will be a significant divergence of interpretation by various persons and groups. At a time when both the "born again" and Faith Development positions have high visibility, their seeming incongruity yet potential interdependence may offer a chance for future scholarship of integration.

Concepts of the Interface

Life Cycle and Ceremonial Events

Westerhoff and Neville (69) suggest an important relationship between the development of faith and life's ceremonial events—ranging from baptism, through confirmation/bar and bas mitzvah and marriage, to the funeral.

In a culture in which the ties and rituals of family and tradition are increasingly diluted by distance and secularity, a renewed emphasis on the *ceremonial* expressions of life as symbols of the relationship between a developing faith and the changing dynamics of the Adult Life Cycle is needed. In addition to their significance for children and youth, the rituals of baptism, circumcision, confirmation, bar and bas mitzvah, and the like can have meaning for participating adults also.

Thus, the baptism of a baby focuses on the nurturing role of grandparents and the commitment of parents *as well as* on the baby. The bar mitzvah of a young man not only recognizes his coming of age, but also celebrates the heritage of those who have gone before him in the same tradition.

In addition, new ceremonials for life's adult events are important. Can we celebrate a job promotion as we do a new child? Is it not possible for some couples, at least, to participate in a ceremonial recognition of the dissolution of their marriage as they did its foundation? Or, what about the mother whose children have grown and who begins a "new life at 40"? The person who retires may be given a luncheon and the traditional watch, but is there not a place for a ceremony involving his or her family and the faith community to celebrate this important transitional event? These are but a few of the stepping stones of life. They are important "marker events" of life that have an impact on the development of faith. They have the potential of playing significant roles not only in the Faith Development of the central figure, but also in the lives of family and friends because of the experience.

Faith and Change

Evelyn and James Whitehead in *Christian Life Patterns* (71), provide one of the first attempts to effect an interface between faith and life cycle issues. The authors suggest three concepts of interface related to *faith and change.* Although their concepts are admittedly Christian, and are presented as such by them, the implications for those of other faith persuasions are significant.

Conversion and Development. "Conversion" is seen as preliminary to "development." The former is the primary commitment in the faith–change process, but its significance is minor if there is not a continuing process of development and change in the pursuit of the fullest dimension of the new-found way of life. Thus, both conversion and development are necessary elements of growth in faith.

Sin and Maturity. The theological concept of "sin" manifests itself in the variety of frailties that plague the human animal. Psychologically, "maturity" is seen as the individual's ultimate ability to accept and cope with his/her faults. Therefore, *sin* and *maturity* provide a counterpoint between negative and positive dynamics in the individual's growth through the Adult Life Cycle.

Religious Development and Edification. The images of "building up" and construction are intrinsic to the concept of *edification* as it appears in the scriptures. They relate positively to a concept of *religious development* which is continually in pursuit of an increasingly more mature faith. It sees *edification* as a key element in the process of faith development in individuals.

Developmental Tasks of Faith

Havighurst's (28) concept of the developmental task was written from the perspective of human development with little specific reference to the dimension of faith. And yet, its fundamental concept of tasks which need to be dealt with at specific times in the life span may well be an important concept for Faith Development.

Are there, in fact, developmental tasks *of faith?* Are there not specific challenges which relate to our faith growth that must be dealt with successfully in adulthood if one's faith is to have its fullest meaning? To what extent are the experiences of establishing a family or dealing with one's singleness important elements of one's Faith Development in young adulthood? What about seeing one's vocation in perspective as an expression of faith as a person turns 30 or as the mother finds new fulfillment in further education or a new vocation beyond the home? Is it not the re-establishing of a marital relationship when "family" means "just the two of us again" a central expression of faith? And, as the years pass, the body slows, and the deaths of an increasing number of loved ones and friends remind us of our own mortality, does not the individual's need to work through for herself or himself an adequate theology of death become a very real part of Faith Development?

Perhaps the concept of these and other faith tasks may be funda-

51

mental to the interface between the Adult Life Cycle and Faith Development. It is a concept worthy of consideration.

Crisis and Faith

Earlier in this section, *crisis* was suggested as a concept under Adult Life Cycle. The review of the relatively small body of Interface literature available suggests that this concept may well be a major key to Faith Development in the Adult Life Cycle. The data suggest that the patterns of Faith Development in an individual appear to have a relationship to the crises in his/her life. At this point, this is but an untested possibility, but it certainly is a concept that needs to be studied further, both on the basis of existent literature and by means of the Phase II testing process.

V. HYPOTHESES

The Role of Hypotheses

A hypothesis is a statement which, on the basis of research and observation, could well be a statement of fact but is not yet tested and proven to be fact. It brings two or more concepts together into one statement that can be tested by means of empirical research. Assuming that such evaluation utilizes proven and established procedures of statistical measurement, the results of such testing can indicate whether or not the predicted relationships occur more often than would be expected by chance alone.

It is our purpose here to suggest a number of hypotheses which are suggested by the review of the literature. The major responsibility of the SYMPOSIUM will be to discuss these hypotheses, to suggest and discuss other possible hypotheses, then determine which ones of the total number are the most significant to be tested in Phase II.

No specific number of hypotheses to be chosen has been set. For that matter, the definition of such a number presents a paradox for the Phase II research. On the one hand, the larger the number of hypotheses, the more dimensions of the Faith Development/ Adult Life Cycle interface that can be addressed. On the other hand, however, it is important to correlate statistically the responses to the various hypotheses of those interviewed in Phase II. Therefore, as the number of hypotheses increases numerically, the number of correlations increases *geometrically*—and with it the proportional cost of the Phase II study. Therefore, the process of refining and focusing the hypotheses involves the need to develop relatively few hypotheses which, however, carry in their expression as broad a range of testable variables as possible. Defining the final set of hypotheses will involve surgical precision rather than literary excavation.

The proposed hypotheses are not necessarily assumed to be provable. There may be some which, on the surface, appear to be true but, in the process of testing, will be disproven. Such negative findings are as important as the confirmation of the hypotheses. Therefore, it is not the purpose of this Project to prove each hypothesis, but rather to *test* the relationship between specified variables to provide a better understanding of the dynamics of relationship between the Adult Life Cycle and Faith Development.

Some Hypotheses Which Might Be Tested

1. *Faith Development (positive and / or negative) occurs naturally as a part of the aging process.*

   The very process of moving through life's stages with the changing values systems related to each succeeding period has an effect on faith development wholly apart from cultural, psychological, and other factors.

2. *Young adults are less concerned with Faith Development than are those over 35.*

   Young adults, preoccupied with establishing themselves in terms of vocation and marital status, are not as concerned with matters related to life's ultimate values as are their elders or as they themselves will be in later years.

3. *The amount and nature of one's formal education is a positive factor in one's Faith Development.*

   The experience of undergraduate and graduate education stimulates a person's critical faculties in such a way that he/she also re-examines his/her faith concepts. Although such reflection often results in a diminuition of one's traditional religious relationships, it may well lead to a higher degree of faith development.

4. *The extent of one's Faith Development in young adulthood has a significant impact on that person's vocational values during young and middle adulthood.*

   The vocational world of the young adult is one in which values can be severely tested. He/she may be asked to compromise ethical principles as a part of his/her job. The basic question of vocational values—"What do I really want to do with my life?"—may well be sensitized by one's faith. To what extent does the young adult's faith development affect his/her adherence to such values?

5. *The extent of one's Faith Development in young adulthood has a significant effect on her/his values related to family and close interpersonal relationships during young and middle adulthood.*

   This hypothesis would suggest that faith development and sensitivity to one's family and close friends in young and middle adulthood are closely and positively related.

6. *The dynamics of mid-life change affect the Faith Development of adults.*

   Most of the adult life cycle literature suggests significant changes occurring in mid-life. To what extent, if any, do such changes affect an individual's faith development?

7. *Older adults are more concerned with Faith Development than are those under 65.*

   As they age and become increasingly conscious of their own mortality, individuals focus more of their concern on issues of ultimate meaning—life and death—which are basic elements of one's faith.

8. *There are developmental tasks of faith that occur throughout the Adult Life Cycle which, when dealt with responsibly, contribute to Faith Development.*

   One of the concepts suggested is the developmental task of faith. Can it be shown that faith development is related to the degree in which an individual is able to handle such tasks as they present themselves during the life cycle?

9. *Faith Development in adults is increased as they can see its significance in their personal/professional lives (cf. the "learnable moment").*

   A fundamental axiom of adult education is the adult's need to see the significance of the learning experience immediately. If this is valid for faith development also, the concept of the "learnable moment" becomes extremely important.

10. *There are significant differences in Faith Development patterns based on ethnic factors.*

Because of heritage, tradition, and culture, it is suggested that differences in patterns of faith development related to ethnic factors may exist. For example, to what extent, if any, does an Oriental or African background and/or deep roots in a highly ethnic community or neighborhood affect the individual's faith development? If a significant relationship is found to exist, an exploration of its meaning would be an important extension of the hypothesis.

11. *There is a positive correlation between higher socio-economic status and more advanced Faith Development.*

The research of Kohlberg suggests that there may be a positive correlation between higher socio-economic status and the more advanced stages of moral development. There is some question whether such relationship is based on actual socio-economic factors or on corollary ones like ability to verbalize ideas and concepts. This hypothesis questions whether, in fact, such a correlation exists in relation to faith development and, if so, what factors are most significant in establishing it.

12. *Women are more concerned with their Faith Development than are men.*

The traditional image of the female role suggests a greater sensitivity to faith issues than that exemplified by the male. In a time of changing sexual roles, is this hypothesis a valid one?

13. *The variety and complexity of a person's social roles (spouse, parent, vocation, community member) has a positive effect on his/her Faith Development.*

It is suggested that the individual who must function in a wide variety of social roles may have a broader perspective on life and, therefore, develop more fully in his/her faith.

14. *Significant Faith Development can occur best around ceremonial events related to faith (such as baptism, bar mitzvah, confirmation, marriage, death, etc.).*

Ceremonial events related to one's religion are times when there is a greater-than-usual reflection upon issues of faith which leads to the development of new concepts and/or values.

15. *Adult Faith Development takes place more fully in the context of participation in a faith community (church, parish, synagogue, small group).*

There is some disagreement whether faith development is essentially personal or social in its context. The role of participation in a faith community needs to be tested.

16. *Faith Development in some form is taking place in all adults throughout the Adult Life Cycle, regardless of their religious persuasion or affiliation.*

Although we usually think of "faith" in the context of one's religious relationship, this hypothesis suggests that faith development is something intrinsic to the human animal, regardless of his/her formal affiliation.

17. *One's adult Faith Development is positively influenced by the faith development of one's significant others (spouse, parents, mentor, close friends).*

The faith attitudes of important people in a person's life cannot help but affect that person's faith development, but whether it is in a positive or negative way needs to be tested.

18. *A relationship with a mentor figure influences Faith Development positively.*

Levinson suggests the importance of a mentor figure in the development of the young adult. Can it be shown that there is a similar positive relationship between the participation of a mentor figure in a person's life and his/her faith development?

19. *Faith Development occurs only in the context of questioning and reforming religious ideals and values.*

If faith is seen as a developmental process, change must be taking place. Change can occur only in the context of a desire to question and rethink one's ideals and values.

20. *Faith Development occurs more during periods of crisis than during periods of stability.*

It is in these periods of crisis in one's life that the individual faces more directly the ultimate questions of life's meaning and the relationship of his/her faith to them.

21. *Persons in the higher stages of Faith Development have greater faith resources for meeting the crisis of adult life than those in the more basic stages.*

This hypothesis seeks to test an assumption often made, but open to question, that faith development leads to greater ability to deal with life crises.

Bibliography

1. Baruch, Grace, and Rosalind Barnett. "If the Study of Midlife Had Begun with Women." U.S. Educational Resources Information Center, ERIC Document ED. 186 834, 1979.
2. Belgum, David. *Religion and Personality in the Spiral of Life.* Washington, D.C.: University Press of America, 1979.
3. Boelen, Bernard J. *Personal Maturity: The Existential Dimension.* New York: Seabury, 1978.
4. Bouwsma, William. "Christian Adulthood," *Adulthood.* ed. Erik Erikson. New York: W.W. Norton and Company, 1978.
5. Bromley, D.B. *The Psychology of Human Aging.* London: C. Nichols and Company, 1974.
6. Coughlin, Kevin. "Motivating Adults for Religious Education." *Living Light,* 13 (Summer, 1976) 269-298.
7. DeBoy, James J., Jr. *Getting Started in Adult Religious Education.* New York: Paulist Press, 1979.
8. Dulles, Avery. "The Meaning of Faith Considered in Relationship to Justice." *The Faith That Does Justice,* ed. John C. Haughey. New York: Paulist Press, 1977.
9. Dykstra, Craig. *Christian Education and the Moral Life: An Evaluation of an Alternative to Kohlberg.* PhD. Dissertation, Princeton Theological Seminary, 1978.
10. Erb, David. "Faith Development." *Faith Development.* Prepared by the Task Force of Faith Development, Department of Christian Education, Synod of Alaska-Northwest, the United Presbyterian Church in the U.S.A., Seattle, Washington, Spring, 1978.
11. Erikson, Erik, ed. *Adulthood.* New York: W.W. Norton and Company, 1978.
12. Erikson, Erik. *Childhood and Society.* New York: W.W. Norton and Company, 1950.
13. Erikson, Erik. *Identity: Youth and Crises.* New York: W.W. Norton and Company, 1968.
14. Erikson, Erik. "Reflections on Dr. Borg's Life Cycle." *Daedalus,* 105 (Spring, 1976) 1-28.

15. Fowler, James. "Stage Six and the Kingdom of God." *Religious Education*, 75 (May/June, 1980) 231-248.
16. Fowler, James. *Stages of Faith: The Psychology of Human Development and the Quest for Meaning*. New York: Harper and Row, 1981.
17. Fowler, James, and Antoine Vergote, senior authors. *Toward Moral and Religious Maturity*. Morristown, New Jersey: Silver Burdett Company, 1980.
18. Fowler, Jim, Sam Keen, and Jerome Berryman, ed. *Life Maps: Conversations on the Journey of Faith*. Waco, Texas: Word, Inc., 1978.
19. Gilligan, Carol. "In a Different Voice, Women's Conception of the Self and Morality." *Harvard Educational Review*, 47 (November, 1977) 481-517.
20. Gilligan, Carol. "Woman's Place in Man's Life Cycle." *Harvard Educational Review*, (November, 1979) 431-446.
21. Girzaitis, Loretta. *The Church as Reflecting Community: Models of Adult Religious Learning*. West Mystic, Connecticut: Twenty-Third Publications, 1977.
22. Goldbrunner, Josef. *Realization: The Anthropology of Pastoral Care*. Notre Dame, Indiana: University of Notre Dame Press, 1966.
23. Gould, Roger. *Transformations: Growth and Change in Adult Life*. New York: Simon and Schuster, 1978.
24. Griffin, Emilie. *Turning: Reflections on the Experience of Conversion*. Garden City, New York: Doubleday, 1980.
25. Groome, Thomas. *Christian Religious Education*. New York: Harper and Row, 1980.
26. Haunz, Ruth A. "Development of Some Models of God and Suggested Relationship to James Fowler's Stages of Faith Development." *Religious Education*, 73 (November/December, 1978) 640-655.
27. Hauser, Stuart. "Loevinger's Model and Measure of Ego Development: A Critical Review." *Psychological Bulletin*, 83 (September, 1976) 928-955.
28. Havighurst, Robert. *Developmental Tasks and Education*. New York: David McKay Company Inc., 1972.
29. Jung, Carl J. *Modern Man in Search of a Soul*. New York: Mentor Book, 1958.
30. Jung, Carl J. *The Undiscovered Self*. New York: Mentor Book, 1958.

31. Kahnweiler, Jennifer, and Patricia Johnson. "A Mid-Life Development Profile of the Returning Woman Student." *Journal of College Student Personnel,* 21 (September, 1980) 414-419.

32. Keen, Sam. "Body/Faith: Trust, Dissolution and Grace." *Life Maps: Conversations on the Journey of Faith.* Jim Fowler, Sam Keen, and Jerome Berryman, ed. Waco, Texas: Word, Inc., 1978.

33. Kimmel, Douglas C. *Adulthood and Aging: An Interdisciplinary, Developmental View.* New York: John Wiley and Sons, Inc., 1974.

34. Knowles, Malcolm. *The Adult Learner: A Neglected Species.* Houston: Gulf Publishing Company, 1973.

35. Knowles, Malcolm. *The Modern Practice of Adult Education: From Pedagogy to Andragogy.* Chicago: Association Press/Follett Publishing Company, 1980.

36. Knox, Ian. "Religion and the Expectations of Modern Society Toward the Adolescent." *Religious Education,* 70 (November/December, 1975) 649-660.

37. Kohlberg, Lawrence. "The Cognitive-Developmental Approach to Moral Education." *Phi Delta Kappan,* 56 (June, 1975) 670-677.

38. Kohlberg, Lawrence. "Education, Moral Development and Faith." *Journal of Moral Education,* 4 (October, 1974) 5-16.

39. Kohlberg, Lawrence. "The Implications of Moral Stages for Adult Education." *Religious Education,* 72 (March/April, 1977) 183-201.

40. Kohlberg, Lawrence, et al. *Assessing Moral Stages—A Manual.* Unpublished manuscript. Harvard University, 1978.

41. Kummerow, Jean M., and Thomas Hummel. "Adult Development: Life Stages and Age-Group Characteristics of Adults, Ages 23-38." *Measurement and Evaluation in Guidance,* 13 (April, 1980) 8-19.

42. Levinson, Daniel J., et al. *The Seasons of a Man's Life.* New York: Knopf, 1978.

43. Loevinger, Jane. "The Meaning and Measurement of Ego Development." *American Psychologist,* 21 (March, 1966) 195-206.

44. Loevinger, Jane, and Ruth Wessler. *Measuring Ego Development.* San Francisco: Jossey-Bass, Inc., 1970.

45. Loevinger, Jane, with the assistance of Augusto Blasi. *Ego Development.* San Francisco: Jossey-Bass, Inc., 1976.

46. McBrien, Richard. "Faith, Theology and Belief." *Commonweal,* 101 (November 15, 1974) 134-137.

47. McCoy, Vivian R. "Adult Life Cycle Change." *Lifelong Learning: The Adult Years,* 1 (October, 1977) 14-18, 31.
48. McCoy, Vivian Rogers. "Adult Life Cycle Tasks/Adult Continuing Education Program Response." *The Adult Life Cycle: Training Manual and Reader.* Vivian Rogers, McCoy, ed., et al. Lawrence, Kansas: Adult Life Resource Center, University of Kansas, 1978.
49. Meissner, W. W. "Notes on the Psychology of Faith." *Journal of Religion and Health,* 8 (January, 1969) 47-75.
50. Merriam, Sharan. "Linking Adult Development and Adult Education through Research." Paper presented at Northern Illinois University, DeKalb, Illinois, Summer, 1980.
51. Miller, Kenneth. "The Relationship of Stages of Development in Children's Moral and Religious Thinking." PhD. Dissertation, Arizona State University, 1976.
52. Moran, Gabriel. *Education Toward Adulthood.* New York: Paulist Press, 1979.
53. Mullen, Peter. "Education for Moral and Spiritual Development." PhD. Dissertation, University of Massachusetts, 1977.
54. Neugarten, Bernice, ed. *Middle Age and Aging.* Chicago: The University of Chicago Press, 1976.
55. Olson, Wayne. "Ceremony as Religious Education." *Religious Education,* 74 (November/December, 1979) 563-569.
56. Ott, Helmut. "Reasonable Universalism as an Approach to Moral Values and Some Implications for Moral Education." PhD. Dissertation, University of Toronto, 1976.
57. Roberts, David. "Foundations and Implications for Adult Moral Development in Lawrence Kohlberg's Theory of Moral Development and Walter G. Muelder's Concept of Moral Laws." PhD. Dissertation, Boston University, 1977.
58. Rubin, Lillian. *Women of a Certain Age: The Midlife Search for Self.* New York: Harper and Row, 1979.
59. Schnurer, Greeta. "Sex Differences and Personality Variables in the Moral Reasoning of Young Adults." PhD. Dissertation, University of Pittsburgh, 1976.
60. Sheehy, Gail. *Passages.* New York: E. P. Dutton and Company, Inc., 1976.
61. Shulik, Richard. "Faith Development, Moral Development and Old Age: An Assessment of Fowler's Faith Development Paradigm." PhD. Dissertation, University of Chicago, 1979.
62. Stock, Michael. "Spiritual Direction from a Dominican Perspective." *Spirituality Today,* 33 (March, 1981) 4-33.

63. Sullivan, Arthur. "Scaling Five Steps of Moral Development." PhD. Dissertation, Fordham University, 1978.

64. Tiebout, Harry. "Conversion as a Psychological Phenomenon." *Pastoral Psychology* 2 (April, 1951) 28-34.

65. Tillich, Paul. *Dynamics of Faith.* New York: Harper and Row, 1957.

66. Vaillant, George. *Adaptation to Life.* Boston: Little, Brown and Company, 1974.

67. Walz, Garry, and Benjamin Libby. "Counseling Adults for Life Transitions." U.S. Educational Resources Information Center, ERIC Document ED.190 769, 1980.

68. Warnat, Winifred. "Building a Theory of Adult Learning." U.S. Educational Resources Information Center, ERIC Document ED. 190 769, 1980.

69. Westerhoff, John H., III, and Gwen Neville. *Generation to Generation.* Philadelphia: United Church Press, 1974.

70. Westerhoff, John H., III, and Gwen Neville. *Learning Through Liturgy.* New York: Seabury, 1978.

71. Whitehead, Evelyn Eaton, and James D. *Christian Life Patterns: The Psychological Challenges and Religious Invitations of Adult Life.* Garden City, New York: Doubleday, 1979.

72. Whitehead, James and Evelyn. "The Parish and Sacraments of Adulthood." *Notre Dame Journal of Education,* 5 (Spring, 1974) 22-34.

73. Wilcox, Mary. *Developmental Journey.* Nashville: Abingdon, 1979.

74. Wilcox, Mary. "Styles of Reasoning." *Church School Today,* (Summer, 1982), 20-23.

75. Wilcox, Mary, Clarence Snelling, and Edward H. Everding. "Interpretation and Truth in Adult Development." Paper presented at the Association of Professors and Researchers in Religious Education, November, 1979.

76. Wylie, Betty Jane. *Beginnings: A Book for Widows.* Toronto: McClelland and Stewart Ltd., 1977.

Malcolm Knowles

(ADULT LEARNING), Emeritus Professor of Adult and Community College Education, North Carolina State University, Raleigh, is probably the best known person in his field through his writing, lectures, and workshops. His high visibility and personal charisma have played an important part in the growing public consciousness of adult education in recent years. Dr. Knowles' book, *The Modern Practice of Adult Education* (revised 1980) is considered by many to be the most comprehensive text on the nature of adult learning. He brings to this dialogue a practical perspective that helped SYMPOSIUM participants and the current reader better understand the very real educational possibilities of the topic.

4

An Adult Educator's Reflections on Faith Development in the Adult Life Cycle

Introduction

This critique of the *Hypotheses Paper* begins with commentary on the relationship between adult education and faith development in the adult life cycle. Then it offers some reflections on specific sections of the Paper. It concludes with a brief postscript and two appendices ("Life Tasks of American Adults" and "Dimensions of Maturation").

I. The Relationship Between Adult Education and Faith Development in the Adult Life Cycle

Perhaps a necessary starting point in writing a critique of the *Hypotheses Paper* is to make clear what I mean when I talk about "adults" and "adult education," and then I can say something meaningful about their relationship with faith development in the adult life cycle.

What Is an Adult?

As I see it, there are four definitions of "adult":

1. The **biological** definition: people become adult biologically at the point at which they can reproduce.
2. The **legal** definition: people become adult legally when they reach the age at which the law states that they are eligible to get drivers' licenses, buy liquor, enlist in the military services, marry without parental consent, stand trial as an adult, and the like. This definition varies geographically.
3. The **social** definition: people become adult socially when they start performing the roles their culture assigns to the

adult years, which in our culture include the roles of full-time worker, spouse, parent, voting citizen, and the like.

4. The **psychological** definition: people become adult psychologically at that point at which they perceive themselves as being essentially responsible for their own lives. This self-concept of adultness evolves gradually, largely as a result of influences from the first three definitional sources. For example, I started moving toward a self-concept of adultness in early adolescence when I became aware of the fact that I could now reproduce; I moved a step further in later adolescence when I got a part-time job managing a paper route in which I employed several helpers and had to file IRS returns; and I moved another step when I got a driver's license in order to deliver papers. But I do not think I came to see myself as wholly adult until I graduated from college, got a full-time job, got married, and started raising a family.

From the point of view of education, the psychological definition is the most significant and the most troublesome. It is significant because at the point at which I come to see myself as responsible for my own life, I also develop a deep psychological need to be seen by—and treated by—others as being capable of being self-directing. It is troublesome because adults have been conditioned by all of their previous school experiences to see the role of learner as a dependent role. Teachers have always told them what they will learn, when they will learn it, how they will learn it, and if they have learned it. So when they enter into any institution or activity that they perceive to be educational, they expect to take the dependent role of learner and be taught; and, in fact, they will put a lot of pressure on teachers to treat them as dependent. The problem is that if teachers do start treating them like children, the adults experience—albeit often unconsciously—an internal conflict between their intellectual definition of student as dependent and their deeper psychological need to be self-directing. And the way people usually respond to psychological conflict is to flee from it, which I think accounts in large measure for the high drop-out rate in much voluntary adult education.

What Is Adult Education?

The term "adult education" is used in our society with at least three different meanings:

1. **As a process.** In its broadest sense the term describes the process of adult learning. In this sense it encompasses prac-

tically all experiences of mature men and women that result in gaining new knowledge, understanding, skills, attitudes, values, and interests. It is a process that is used by adults for their self-development, both alone and with others, and by institutions of all kinds for the growth and development of their members, employees, and clients.

2. **As a set of organized activities.** In its more technical meaning, "adult education" describes a set of organized activities carried on by a wide variety of institutions for the accomplishment of specific educational objectives. In this sense it encompasses all the organized classes, study groups, lecture series, planned reading programs, guided discussions, conferences, institutes, seminars, workshops, retreats, educational television programs, computer-assisted instruction programs, and correspondence courses in which American adults engage.

3. **As a movement.** A third meaning combines all of these processes and activities into the idea of a social movement. In this sense "adult education" brings together into a discrete social system all the individuals, institutions, and associations concerned with the education of adults and perceives them as working toward the common goals of improving the programs, methods, and materials of adult learning, extending the opportunities for adults to learn, and advancing the general level of our culture.

What Is the Relationship with Faith Development in the Adult Life Cycle?

Insofar as faith development involves adults in the process of learning, adult education has something to contribute to it. During the past several decades there has been an accelerating accumulation of research-based knowledge, theoretical frameworks, and techniques regarding the unique characteristics of the adult learning process. As is pointed out in Section I of the *Hypotheses Paper,* this system of thought has been labeled "andragogy," and it provides guidelines for helping adults learn more effectively.

The difference in assumptions about learning between the traditional pedagogical model and the andragogical model can be summarized as follows:

A Comparison of the Assumptions of Pedagogy and Andragogy[1]

Regarding:	Pedagogy	Andragogy
Concept of the learner	The role of the learner is, by definition, a dependent one. The teacher is expected by society to take full responsibility for determining what is to be learned, when it is to be learned, how it is to be learned, and if it has been learned.	It is a normal aspect of the process of maturation for a person to move from dependency toward increasing self-directedness, but at different rates for different people and in different dimensions of life. Teachers have a responsibility to encourage and nurture this movement. Adults have a deep psychological need to be generally self-directing, although they may be dependent in particular temporary situations.
Role of learners's experience	The experience learners bring to a learning situation is of little worth. It may be used as a starting point, but the experience from which learners will gain the most is that of the teacher, the textbook writer, the audiovisual aid producer, and other experts. Accordingly, the primary techniques in education are transmittal techniques—lecture, assigned reading, AV presentations.	As people grow and develop they accumulate an increasing reservoir of experience that becomes an increasingly rich resource for learning— for themselves and for others. Furthermore, people attach more meaning to learnings they gain from experience than those they acquire passively. Accordingly, the primary techniques in education are experiential techniques.

Readiness to learn	People are ready to learn whatever society (especially the school) says they ought to learn, provided the pressures on them (like fear of failure) are great enough. Most people of the same age are ready to learn the same things. Therefore, learning should be organized into a fairly standardized curriculum, with a uniform step-by-step progression for all learners.	People become ready to learn something when they experience a need to learn it in order to cope more satisfyingly with real-life tasks or problems. The educator has a responsibility to create conditions and provide tools and procedures for helping learners discover their "needs to know." And learning programs should be organized around life-application categories and sequenced according to the learners' readiness to learn.
Orientation to learning	Learners see education as a process of acquiring subject matter content, most of which they understand will be useful only at a later time in life. Accordingly, the curriculum should be organized into subject-matter units (e.g., courses) which follow the logic of the subject (e.g., from ancient to modern history, from simple to complex mathematics or science). People are subject-centered in their orientation to learning.	Learners see education as a process of developing increased competence to achieve their full potential in life. They want to be able to apply whatever knowledge and skill they gain today to living more effectively tomorrow. Accordingly, learning experiences should be organized around competency-development categories. People are performance-centered in their orientation to learning.

The andragogical model also provides the following guidelines regarding the conditions of learning and principles of teaching[2]:

Conditions of Learning

The learners feel a need to learn.

Principles of Teaching

1) The teacher exposes the learners to new possibilities for self-fulfillment.
2) The teacher helps the learners clarify their own aspirations for improved behavior.
3) The teacher helps the learners diagnose the gap between their aspirations and their present level of performance
4) The teacher helps the learners identify the life problems they experience because of the gaps in their personal equipment.

The learning environment is characterized by physical comfort, mutual trust and respect, mutual helpfulness, freedom of expression, and acceptance of differences.

5) The teacher provides physical conditions that are comfortable (as to seating, smoking, temperature, ventilation, lighting, decoration) and conducive to interaction (preferably, no person sitting behind another person).
6) The teacher accepts the learners as persons of worth and respects their feelings and ideas.
7) The teacher seeks to build relationships of mutual trust and helpfulness among the learners by encouraging cooperative activities and refraining from inducing competitiveness and judgmentalness.
8) The teacher exposes his or her own feelings and contributes resources as a colearner in the spirit of mutual inquiry.

The learners perceive the goals of a learning experience to be their goals.

9) The teacher involves the learners in a mutual process of formulating learning objectives in which the needs of the learners, of the institution, of the teacher, of the subject matter, and of the society are taken into account.

The learners accept a share of the responsibility for planning and operating a learning experience, and therefore have a feeling of commitment toward it.

The learners participate actively in the learning process.

The learning process is related to and makes use of the experience of the learners.

The learners have a sense of progress toward their goals.

10) The teacher shares his or her thinking about options available in the designing of learning experiences and the selection of materials and methods and involves the learners in deciding among these options jointly.

11) The teacher helps the learners to organize themselves (project groups, learning-teaching teams, independent study, etc.) to share responsibility in the process of mutual inquiry.

12) The teacher helps the learners exploit their own experiences as resources for learning through the use of such techniques as discussion, role playing, case method, etc.

13) The teacher gears the presentation of his or her own resources to the levels of experience of particular learners.

14) The teacher helps the learners to apply new learnings to their experience, and thus to make the learnings more meaningful and integrated.

15) The teacher involves the learners in developing mutually acceptable criteria and methods for measuring progress toward the learning objectives.

16) The teacher helps the learners develop and apply procedures for self-evaluation according to these criteria.

II. Reflections on the Hypotheses Paper

Section I, "Adult Life Cycle"

A general observation that cannot be avoided in surveying the very skillfully condensed overview on the literature of life stages in Section I is that this area of research is in a very primitive stage of development. I found myself reacting to it out of Erikson's first stage, Trust vs. Basic Mistrust, with the wide variation among the taxonomies of stages presented by the different writers and the complexity of language they use. And none of them addresses the question, "What are the stages of faith development?"

I wonder if the most productive way for the Symposium to deal with this problem would not be to pick one of the lists and try to build stages of faith development onto it. Since from the point of view of providing guidance for learning, the most useful aspect of the concept of developmental stages is the identification of developmental tasks, which in turn provide the chief stimuli (or motivations) to learn, I find Havighurst's list the simplest to apply. In Appendix A I have attempted to list the "Life Tasks of American Adults" based on Havighurst's categories. It lists six sets of tasks: 1) Vocation and Career, 2) Home and Family Living, 3) Personal Development, 4) Enjoyment of Leisure, 5) Health, and 6) Community Living. I would like to add a seventh column to the chart, Faith Development, and see if we could brainstorm some of the developmental tasks associated with this aspect of human development.

Another observation that I am bursting to make is that developmental stage theory has some real risks attached to it. One risk is to see the stages as hierarchical when they may only be different. But the main risk is the temptation to use them for stereotyping. I would like to underline the caution by Kummerow and Hummel within the Paper and reinforce it with a more explicit statement:

> . . . individual differences are probably greater among the old than among the young. One does not need much data to see why individual differences increase with age. Consider, for example, that most adults in their twenties are married, have children, are employed (if they are males), and are in reasonably good health. Some older people are married, too, and many are divorced or separated or widowed. Most older people have children and grandchildren and some have great-grandchildren. Some have outlived their own children. Many older males are still employed, some are em-

ployed only part time, some are fully retired, and some have entered second or third careers. Many older people are in excellent health, some are in fair health, some in poor health, and some in very poor health. As life experience accumulates, the chances that any two people will have the same history continue to diminish. It is, therefore, predictable that personality and cognitive function will vary more from one person to another in a group of elderly people than in a group of young adults or children. (Stevens-Long, 1979, pp. 327–328)

To move to a more concerete level of critique, I have a problem with Moran's definition of "adult" as "the ideal of maturity" (page 18). I simply do not understand how it can be made operational, but perhaps I can be made to understand with further elaboration of his ideas. I have somewhat the same problem with Boelen's definition of "maturity" (page 24). It reminds me of Overstreet's observation:

A mature person is not one who has come to a certain level of achievement and stopped there. He is rather a *maturing* person—one whose *linkages with life* are constantly becoming stronger and richer because his attitudes are such as to encourage their growth rather than their stoppage. A mature person, for example, is not one who knows a large number of facts. Rather, he is one whose mental habits are such that he grows in knowledge and the wise use of it. (Overstreet, 1949, p. 43)

As I see it, both of these treatments of maturity are more philosophical than operational propositions. Some years ago I attempted to translate Overstreet's proposition into operational terms in the form of "Dimensions of Maturation," which I am reproducing in Appendix B. I wonder if the Symposium could identify one or more dimensions of spiritual (or faith) maturation.

I have given my own definition of "adult" in the opening section of this critique and simply acknowledge at this point that, for educational purposes, people are adult when they perceive themselves to be adults.

Section II, "Faith Development"

It is with this section that, as a secular adult educator, I have the most difficulty. I can grasp the notion that there is a theological definition of "faith," but I cannot yet grasp its educational definition. In the literature of developmental psychology or adult education (or of education generally) I can find no references to faith. I find many references to "moral values" and "character traits," with such measurable correlates as honesty, kindliness, friendliness, generosity, modesty, fidelity, respect for law, and the like. And I find many references to "religiousness" and "religious beliefs," with such measurable correlates as belief in God, belief in heaven and hell, participation in prayer, attendance at church, acceptance of the Bible as the literal word of God, and the like. We educators know how to formulate educational objectives that describe desirable values, traits, and beliefs, and we know how to design learning experiences that will help people develop values, traits, and beliefs. But I take it that faith development is something more than the development of values, traits, and beliefs.

What I do not understand is what the "something more" is. What are the observable and measurable behavioral correlates of faith? In the summary of Fowler's stages of faith (pages 36-37), mention is made of "faith attitudes," but they are not defined. Perhaps they are in his *Life Maps* and *Stages of Faith*, in which case those definitions should be made available, since attitudes can be detected and, at least to some degree, measured. The definitions given in the final paragraphs of Section II (page 39), "the meaning of life and death, the nature of being, the existence and nature of Deity, and the like," I do not find any more helpful in terms of providing guidelines for educational objectives and learning experiences. Perhaps faith cannot be nutured by education, but only by the grace of God; and if this is the case, the nature of the research in Phase II and of the strategies in Phase III would take on an entirely different character from that planned in the Proposal.

As I see it, for the final two phases of the project to be viable we shall somehow have to identify what the measurable correlates of faith are at each stage of faith development.

Section III, "The Interface"

I have just two comments about this section. The first is that I am not surprised that there is a "paucity of research related to the interface between adult life cycle and faith development," since faith development has not been operationally defined. And I do not see how there can be research—in contrast to philosophizing—about the interface until we know what we are talking about operationally.

The second is that I have some strong reservations about all stage developments being classified as "crises," as Goldbrunner and Sheehy classify them. I suspect that Gould's "transformations" and Levinson's "transitions" are more descriptive of what most people moving from one stage to another really experience. I am afraid that if the research questions emphasize crises, many respondents will be thrown off the track, and we will miss a lot of useful data.

Section IV, "Concepts"

Regarding "Life Stages," see my earlier comments. Regarding "Crisis," see my comments above. Regarding "Faith Development," "Faith Stages," and "Faithing," see my comments on Section II. I find the concept "faithing" to be especially promising, since it implies that we might be talking about some activity that a person engages in that can be observed—or at least described. Perhaps the Phase II research could investigate what that activity is.

I feel that the paragraphs under "Developmental Tasks of Faith" are moving in this direction. If we could discover what the developmental tasks of faith development at various life stages are, we would have some clear guidelines for designing adult educational experiences that would facilitate the developmental process.

Another concept that I have mentioned previously is "dimensions of maturation," and I suggested that it might be possible to identify the various dimensions of maturation in faith development.

A key concept that I find missing in Section IV is "learning"—or, more specifically, "adult learning." Educational psychology has long made a distinction between those competencies that are developed naturally in the process of maturing (such as walking and talking) and those that are learned from the external environment (such as moral conduct). For adult education to be relevant to faith development, we need to know what "faithing" competencies need to be learned and how they are learned. When we know these two things, then we can apply concepts of adult learning to facilitate the development of faithing abilities.

73

Which leads to another concept that may be worthwhile investigating—the concept of "competency." A substantial body of literature now exists regarding the competencies required for performing various roles, and entire educational programs have been constructed with their focus specifically on the development of these competencies. One of the best overviews of recent developments in competency-based education is Kay P. Torshen's *A Mastery Approach to Competency-Based Education* (New York: Academic Press, 1977). It would be useful to know what competencies are involved in faithing.

Section V, "Hypotheses"

I seriously question whether we are at a point in the state of the art of investigating faith development at which hypothesis-testing research is appropriate. I feel that we need to know much more about the phenomena we are concerned with and that, therefore, hypothesis-generating research would be more productive.

During the past few years there has been a decided turn in social science research away from an almost exclusive emphasis on quantitative research, especially correlational studies, toward more holistic research (Cronbach, et al., 1980). We now have much more sophisticated designs and methods for using grounded theory (Glaser and Strauss, 1967), qualitative methods (Patton, 1977, 1980), and naturalistic approaches (Guba and Lincoln, 1981).

I would like to urge my colleagues in the FAITH DEVELOPMENT IN THE ADULT LIFE CYCLE Project at least to consider adding some more holistic research questions to the Phase II design and pursuing them, perhaps through in-depth interviews with a smaller sample of respondents. This approach has resulted in the major breakthrough in our understanding of the dynamics of adult learning (Tough, 1979).

Some of the research questions that occur to me are:

—How do people perceive faith as it makes itself manifest in their daily lives?
—How do they describe the experience of "having faith"? In what situations does it express itself?
—What knowledge, understandings, skills, attitudes, values, and interests do they perceive facilitated or inhibited their "having faith"?
—In what ways do they feel they would like to be more open

to faith?

—In what ways do they feel that their faith has been misguided or unrealistic? In what situations?

—Have they ever sought to help others make use of faith? How? With what results?

—Can they trace the role that faith has played in their lives up to this point?

—With whom do they discuss their faith? What do they say about it?

—Can they identify specific actions they have taken as a result of faith? With what effects?

As I see it, the data obtained through naturalistic questions like these can then be subjected to correlational analysis with such variables as sex, age, educational level, socioeconomic status, and other variables contained in the twenty-one hypotheses in the *Hypotheses Paper*.

Notes

1. Malcolm S. Knowles, *The Modern Practice of Adult Education.* Chicago: Follett Publishing Co., 1980, pp. 43-44.
2. Op. cit., pp. 57-58.

References

Cronbach, Lee J., et al. *Toward Reform of Program Evaluation.* San Francisco: Jossey-Bass, 1980.

Glaser, Barney G., and Anselm L. Strauss. *The Discovery of Grounded Theory.* Chicago: Aldine Publishing Co., 1967.

Guba, Egon G., and Yvonna S. Lincoln. *Effective Evaluation.* San Francisco Jossey-Bass, 1981.

Overstreet, Harry A. *The Mature Mind.* New York: W.W. Norton, 1949.

Patton, Michael Q. *Utilization-Focused Evaluation.* Beverly Hills, CA: Sage Publications, 1977.

———. *Qualitative Evaluation Methods.* Beverly Hills, CA: Sage Publications, 1980.

Stevens-Long, Judith. *Adult Life: Developmental* Processes. Palo Alto, CA: Mayfield Publishing Co., 1979.

Tough, Allen. *The Adult's Learning Projects.* Toronto: Ontario Institute for Studies in Education, 1979.

Postscript

In reflecting on my Critique Paper since writing it, I have had another issue occur to me that I think the SYMPOSIUM might consider. It has to do with the research design and the dangers involved in generalizing about developmental processes from cross-sectional research in which age cohorts are compared with one another at one point of time.

One of the classic fallacies in developmental psychology—the disengagement theory—is a result of this error in design.

Although longitudinal studies would not be possible within the time frame of this Project, some safeguards against erroneous conclusions from cross-sectional data are available. See: Paul B. Baltes and L. R. Goulet, *Life-Span Developmental Psychology* (New York: Academic Press, 1970), pages 150-191; Paul Baltes, Hayne Reese, and John Nesselroade, *Life-Span Developmental Psychology: Introduction to Research Methods* (Monterey, CA: Brooks/Cole Publishing Co., 1977); and Judith Stevens-Long, *Adult Life: Developmental Processes* (Palo Alto, CA: Mayfield Publishing Co., 1979), pages 18-39.

APPENDIX A

LIFE TASKS OF AMERICAN ADULTS

Early Adulthood (18 to 30)	Vocation and Career	Home and Family Living	Personal Development
	Exploring career options	Courting	Improving your reading ability
	Choosing a career line	Selecting a mate	Improving your writing ability
	Getting a job	Preparing for marriage	Improving your speaking ability
	Being interviewed	Family planning	Improving your listening ability
	Learning job skills	Preparing for children	Continuing your general education
	Getting along at work	Raising children	Developing your religious faith
	Getting ahead at work	Understanding children	Improving problem-solving skills
	Getting job protection	Preparing children for school	Making better decisions
	Dealing with the issue of military service	Helping children in school	Getting along with people
	Getting vocational counseling	Solving marital problems	Understanding yourself
	Changing jobs	Using family counseling	Finding your self-identity
		Managing a home	
		Financial planning	
		Managing money	
		Buying goods and services	
		Making home repairs	
		Gardening	

Middle Adulthood (30 to 65)			
Learning advanced job skills	Helping teenage children to become adults	Discovering your aptitudes	Finding new interests
Supervising others	Letting your children go	Clarifying your values	Keeping out of a rut
Changing careers	Relating to one's spouse as a person	Understanding other people	Compensating for physiological changes
Dealing with unemployment	Adjusting to aging parents	Learning to be self-directing	Dealing with change
Planning for retirement	Learning to cook for two	Improving personal appearance	Developing emotional flexibility
Making second careers for mothers	Planning for retirement	Establishing intimate relations	Learning to cope with crises
		Dealing with conflict	Developing a realistic time perspective
		Making use of personal counseling	

Later Adulthood (65 and over)		
Adjusting to retirement	Adjusting to reduced income	Developing compensatory abilities
Finding new ways to be useful	Establishing new living arrangements	Understanding the aging process
Understanding Social Security, Medicare, and welfare	Adjusting to death of spouse	Re-examining your values
	Learning to live alone	Keeping future-oriented
	Relating to grandchildren	Keeping up your morale
	Establishing new intimate relationships	Keeping up to date
	Putting your estate in order	Keeping in touch with young people
		Keeping curious
		Keeping up personal appearance
		Keeping an open mind
		Finding a new self-identity
		Developing a new time perspective
		Preparing for death

	Enjoyment of Leisure	Health	Community Living
Early Adulthood	Choosing hobbies Finding new friends Joining organizations Planning your time Buying equipment Planning family recreation Leading recreational activities	Keeping fit Planning diets Finding and using health services Preventing accidents Using first aid Understanding children's diseases Understanding how the human body functions Buying and using drugs and medicines Developing a healthy life style Recognizing the symptoms of physical and mental illness	Relating to school and teachers Learning about community resources Learning how to get help Learning how to exert influence Preparing to vote Developing leadership skills Keeping up with the world Taking action in the community Organizing community activities for children and youth
Middle Adulthood	Finding less active hobbies Broadening your cultural interests	Adjusting to physiological changes Changing diets Controlling weight	Taking more social responsibility Taking leadership roles in organizations

	Learning new recreational skills Finding new friends Joining new organizations Planning recreation for two	Getting exercise Having annual medical exams Compensating for losses in strength	Working for the welfare of others Engaging in politics Organizing community improvement activities
Later Adulthood	Establishing affiliations with the older age group Finding new hobbies Learning new recreational skills Planning a balanced recreational program	Adjusting to decreasing strength and health Keeping fit Changing your diet Having regular medical exams Getting appropriate exercise Using drugs and medicines wisely Learning to deal with stress Maintaining your reserves	Working for improved conditions for the elderly Giving volunteer services Maintaining organizational ties

APPENDIX B

Dimensions of Maturation*

The essential characteristic of these dimensions of maturation is that they define directions of growth, not absolute states:

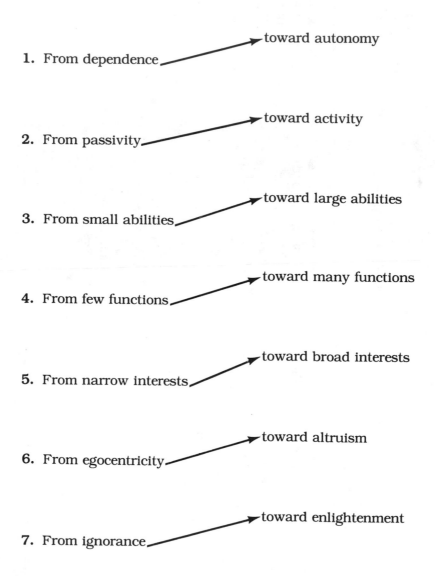

1. From dependence   toward autonomy

2. From passivity   toward activity

3. From small abilities   toward large abilities

4. From few functions   toward many functions

5. From narrow interests   toward broad interests

6. From egocentricity   toward altruism

7. From ignorance   toward enlightenment

8. From subjectivity → toward objectivity

9. From self-rejection → toward self-acceptance

10. From focus on particulars → toward focus on principles

11. From amorphous self-concept → toward integrated self-concept

12. From static concerns → toward expanding concerns

13. From imitation → toward originality

14. From need for certainty → toward tolerance for ambiguity

15. From irrationality → toward rationality

*Charles W. Merrifield (ed.) *Leadership in Voluntary Enterprise.* New York: Oceana Publications, 1961, pp. 149-153.

Winston Gooden

(DEVELOPMENTAL PSYCHOLOGY), Assistant Professor of Psychology, University of Illinois at Chicago Circle, brings to the investigation a unique combination of a seminary degree, doctoral study with Daniel Levinson at Yale, and personal, professional, and research roots in the black community. Although the youngest of the Subject Matter Consultants at the SYMPOSIUM, Dr. Gooden utilized this broad professional background in his reflection on the psychological dynamics of the faith experience. His soon-to-be-published dissertation, *Adult Development in the Black Man*, is a cross-ethnic study based on the Levinson human development model.

5

Responses and Comments from an Adult Development Perspective

Introduction

This critique responds to the literature review and the hypotheses presented in the *Hypotheses Paper* on Faith Development in the Adult Life Cycle. I have had the benefit of revising my original response after attending the SYMPOSIUM. While the revision is not extensive, it includes a discussion of the concept of "faith-work" that was only hinted at in the first version. The discussions, comments, questions, and suggestions made to me at the SYMPOSIUM were very helpful; unfortunately, this revision could not make use of all of them.

The response begins with an introductory statement of my view of the relationship between adult development and faith. Then it responds to the adult development issues, faith development issues, and the interface issues raised by the *Hypotheses Paper*. My response attempts three things: a critical look at the theoretical constructs reviewed; a critique of the theoretical links between faith and adult development discussed; and a critique of the methodological problems raised particularly by the proposed hypotheses.

Adult Development and Faith

The area of adult development, my major academic concern, is particularly germane to Faith Development in the Adult Life Cycle. While much of the literature in this field has looked at the changes of basic capacities, attributes, or skills after childhood and adolescence, very little has been done from the perspective of psychology on the role of religion in adult development. Yet for many reasons this topic is ripe for study. The relationship between faith and adult life emerges from several angles.

1. Adulthood is characterized by commitment in various areas

of life, commitment to family, occupation, and community. These commitments bind persons to their objects while providing returns in the form of money, prestige, affection, and gratitude. The commitments of adult life provide the structure through which a person engages life, acts upon the world, and becomes a definite part of a social group. Important aspects of the meaning of life and one's sense of purpose are appropriated through these relationships of commitment. Commitment implies both choice and investment. The person by the act of commitment entrusts himself/herself to the situation of commitment.

Definitions of faith often include the concept of commitment. Tillich's formulation, that faith is commitment to ultimate concern, is a good example. The commitment implied in faith also includes trust, investment, and choice. The connection between adult development and faith here is in the fact that the major commitments of adulthood are paradigmatic of the faith situation. The choice of person or occupation is made without firm knowledge of how things will turn out. This then demands trust, or better still, an entrusting of self and future to the object or person. The bargain is two-sided; the individual also pledges fidelity, i.e., to be trustworthy. This paradigmatic element of all adult commitment suggests that faith, understood as trust, fidelity, and commitment, is a central dynamic of all adult life.

2. Adult concerns go beyond the major responsibilities adults undertake. These responsibilities or commitments, of themselves, would be boring or suffocating if the individual did not reap from them a sense of worth, importance, and well-being. This adult need to have an overarching sense of purpose and meaning that embraces yet transcends the specific commitments of daily life is also related to the question of faith. The commitments made must be invested with value so that they in turn will make the committed worthy. A sense of necessity and significance is placed on the central concerns of the adult, thus giving them the quality of vocation or calling. The meaning of individual acts of commitment become significant within this framework of value. Uncomfortable, distasteful, or otherwise painful acts can be transformed by the overarching framework and so become acts of sacrifice, thus providing the person even greater sense of worth. This overarching sense of meaning, which is necessary to sustain a sense of well-being and which makes

it possible to sustain even difficult commitments, is again an act of faith both because one lives within the frame of meaning in a trustful, committed way and because its verity is accepted without proof. In both points raised so far, "self-giving" or entrusting one's self to someone or something are basic to adult life and indicate the necessity of faith. One of the paradoxes of adult life that makes faith necessary is that even after one has made the greatest achievement, one can only appreciate its value, and with it one's own value, by giving that achievement to a community, others, the gods. It is through the other's acceptance of this gift that one becomes verified and fully accepted.

3. The adult has the burden of relating to his/her past and living toward the future. Self-understanding and insight are necessary if the adult is to have productive, responsible relations with others. This requires an understanding of his/her own drives, motivation, instinctive urges, and patterns of defense. Going into one's past often entails confronting old hurts, unsettled conflicts, and images of self that are unflattering. These encounters often challenge present self-configuration. Yet an important aspect of adult life is some degree of self-knowledge. The adult must integrate this relearned information into a more balanced view of self. Additionally, there are inevitable crises of life that shatter one's old self-image and one's beliefs about how things are. These shattering experiences typical of adulthood require reimaging of self and world. The process of reimaging requires new choices, new investment, new self-giving, in spite of the pain. Faith must be operative at these times of self-transformation and reimaging.

4. Perhaps the most painful awareness that emerges in adult life is the reality of personal mortality and the attendant meaning of death. Not only must the adult deal with the death of relatives, parents, and friends; he/she must deal also with his/her own impending death. Along with the knowledge of death are issues of destructiveness, evil, hurt, rot, decay, infidelity tied to one's own life. This knowledge must be held in tension with a sense of the goodness of one's own life and its worth. If this sense of worth is not maintained, one may become despairing and feel that life is absurd. Perhaps the most difficult act of faith is this maintenance of commitment, this continued reimaging and giving of self in spite of the skulls and grave dust evident in daily

life. The need of the adult to transcend his/her bodily self, to feel that the pain of present life and the injustice of human society are not all there is, and that life is ultimately significant, reflects the need of faith.

Typically, the academic psychologist does not study this area of transcendent meaning. Yet adult life is flat and gray if it is not seen through the lens of meaning, commitment, and transcendence. The transcendence of the daily grind, the cultivation of a self beyond body and roles are the bases of a spiritual identity.

The Concept of Development

There are several ways of understanding development so that the one chosen for this work should best fit the task of conceptualizing both adult development and faith development. While every developmental theory involves the idea of change, change is not sufficient to understand the concept fully. Biologists, for instance, suggest that development involves permanent, structural change that is progressive and cumulative, requiring long periods of the organism's history (Ebert and Sussex, 1970; Anderson, 1957). Development involves, moreover, increased organization which leads to increased complexity and greater functional capacity. This latter definition is shared by psychologists. A further extension of the idea of development is Werner's (1957) orthogenetic principle, which views development as change from syncretic, global functioning to differentiated and articulated functioning.

An important question for this conference and the whole area of faith development is whether these types of images of development are appropriate for our task. These conceptions are used by theorists working with physical development, e.g., cell biology or nervous system, and with childhood development. Many theorists deny that concepts of development are applicable to adulthood.

A related issue of importance is our view of what develops. It is important to note that the area of life-span development focuses on variety of skills, attributes, and processes. Some theoreticians focus on personality development, using a variety of concepts; others focus on development of cognitive capacities, e.g., memory, perception, intelligence. Other theorists attend to development of career, marriage, or other roles, while still others focus on coping skills. One preliminary task is to narrow our focus by deciding what aspects and issues of the adult life cycle are critical to faith development.

We should also be clear on our assumptions about the process of development. The *Hypotheses Paper* does not speak to this issue in depth. What makes development happen? Why is there development? What are the mechanisms of development? These questions are to some extent the ultimate questions of the field and will not be conclusively answered. However, there are some assumptions that developmental theorists make that shed some light on the meaning of development for them.

Piaget, for instance, sees "Equilibration" as the basic dynamic of cognitive development. The organism is thrown off balance, so to speak, when it confronts a problem or situation it cannot assimilate. It must accommodate itself to the new situation and reestablish equilibrium by this new learning via accommodation.

Adaptation is another way of conceptualizing development. In this view, the personality develops by adaptively mastering various problems that are either environmentally or internally produced. Vaillant's work, *Adaptation to Life*, is a good example of this approach to development. Vaillant suggests a progressive maturation of adaptive mode (defense mechanisms) such that as adolescent men in his study were twice as likely to use immature defenses as they were to use mature ones. In mid-life, they were four times as likely to use mature defenses as they were to use immature ones. While the adaptation perspective takes the environment seriously, it is the maturation of personality or adaptive style that is essential.

The socialization perspective accounts for change in adulthood less by the maturation of the person and more by the socializing impact of occupation and family. A major portion of a man's life is spent at work, and work provides the central social and psychological framework for forty or fifty years of life (Henry, 1971). One is also socialized to age-appropriate behavior in adulthood.

Neugarten (1968) suggests that there is a prescriptive timetable for ordering life events. There is a time to marry, a time to have children, and a time to retire. The society encourages age-appropriate behaviors and discourages age-inappropriate ones. The convergence of role status and age status is a valuable perspective for understanding how periodic life events change the individual by changing his self-concept, skills, and roles as he adapts to these events.

Levinson's "seasons" perspective views development as the evolution of the life structure. Both internal psychological factors and external social ones account for emergence and evolution of life structure. The individual, to function in the adult world, makes critical choices and invests in those choices which form the basic structure of his/her adult life. Concepts central to this evolutionary view are "viability," the degree to which the life structure allows the person to function successfully in the society, thus finding a valuable and rewarding place for self; and "suitability," the degree to which the life structure allows the person to live out his/her most cherished dreams. A suitable balance between "viability" and "suitability" defines the "satisfactoriness" of the life structure.

What we have then are several images of development, each suggesting some level of interaction between the individual and the environment that results in the individual's increased capacities in one or another area. When we think about faith development in the life cycle, we should be aware of these various images of development and attempt to discover which ones are more appropriate to our task.

Several other studies relevant to our task should be mentioned. They are inspired primarily by psychoanalytic notions such as ego development. They include Vaillant's adaptation perspective already mentioned, a seminal discussion of the mid-life crisis by Jacques (1965), and Lovenger's work on ego development. The importance of attending to more systematic work on ego development rests with our conception of the relationship between the conscious, organizing, adapting aspect of the self (ego) and faith. What theoretical relationship do we perceive to exist between faith and ego? Is faith an instrument or attribute of ego, or vice versa? Obviously, we recognize a fundamental relationship between the two. Not only do we have to think about how the maturity of faith depends on the maturity of the ego but also what the status of faith is or can be when there is partial or complete disintegration of the ego, e.g., in psychosis. A discussion of the practical and theoretical relationship between ego development and disintegration on the one hand and faith development on the other is potentially fruitful.

Jacques' and Vaillant's studies raise the issue of unconscious forces and drives and their fate in the adult life cycle. Jacques theorizes that the mid-life crisis is brought about in part by a reawakening of issues first encountered in infancy, what is known as the depressive position. Archaic fantasies of destruction, hate, and rejection based on separation from Mother must be reworked as the individual confronts his/her mortality, time limits, and destructiveness. A new balance of love over hate must be established. Vaillant's concept of the maturation of ego defenses addresses not only how the individual deals with the external world and its demands but also how she/he handles internal instincts, wishes, desires, and the like. Both these studies raise the question of how faith may be related to an inner world with its history of childhood frustrations, its potential for decompensation and aggression and an unconscious life that, if given expression, may disrupt the conscious but, if totally ignored, may erupt into consciousness with an even greater vengeance.

Stages of Adulthood

In addition to looking at the description of stages and the relative differences between normative ages presented by each theorist, we can note the underlying bases on which stages are posited. Underlying Erikson's eight stages, for example, is a maturational concept. A given stage emerges at a maturationally given time. The transition from one stage to the next occurs after resolution of a particular developmental crisis. The result of this crisis, if successfully resolved, is the emergence of a new ego virtue. Erikson calls this an epigenetic theory. For instance, out of the crisis of "Generativity vs. Stagnation" emerges the virtue of care. Basic to Erikson's view, then, is a maturational timetable, an appropriate timing, not very age-restricted, and the emergence of a new strength. The new stage then is exemplified by this new ego quality and its contribution to personality functioning.

Levinson's theory differs in important ways from Erikson's. Not only is Levinson's more age-restricted, but Levinson conceptualizes development as the evolution of the life structure, not the maturation of ego or personality. Levinson uses periods rather than stages and posits transitional periods, while Erikson does not delineate a specific stage for transitions. The character and flavor of Levinson's period is not defined by a virtue, new strength, or qualitatively better functioning, but rather by the new tasks of the period, the physical vitality available, and the social expectations by society. Thus the image of "seasons" speaks more to a particular time of life than to a developmental stage.

Another basis for division into stages or periods is the notion of developmental tasks. This is shared by most theorists of development. It is not explicit why certain tasks emerge at certain ages, but most theorists posit high correlation between tasks and age.

An important distinction should be made on the qualitative distinctions of tasks. For example, Havighurst's task of "selecting a mate" shares some similarity with Erikson's task of resolving "Intimacy vs. Isolation." However, "selecting a mate" is only the first step in a sequence which includes "learning to live with a marriage partner," "starting a family," "raising children." These tasks, from Havighurst's point of view, are to be done in early adulthood. His definition is primarily social. While Erikson's task shares obvious similarity, his are more concerned with the ego's capacity to be intimate as an inner personality attribute. His view of tasks then is more psychological than social—the resolution of which is not becoming a married man or attaining some important adult social status but rather having the capacity to love.

Levinson's discussion of tasks is within the context of the overarching task of building, modifying, or changing the life structure. So, for instance, starting a family is a critical task of early adulthood and the period of "entering the adult world," but that task is embedded in the larger issues of the period, namely, creating the first provisional life structure. Thus, while psychosocial or life tasks may be a way of differentiating various stages or periods of the life cycle, what theorists mean by "task" is not homogeneous. Despite these differences, the notion that a stage is defined by certain tasks, primarily psychosocial, which have age-appropriateness, is very useful.

Age as a basis of stage or period has a complex if controversial role in the literature and discussion of development. While I cannot go into all the difficulties here, e.g., how time structures life, one important issue should be highlighted. There is both a macro-theory of adult development and a micro-theory regarding age. Levinson indicates, for example, that there are eras in the life cycle—pre-adulthood, early adulthood, middle adulthood, late adulthood, and late-late adulthood. Erikson's adult stages conform to this macro-view, so that "Intimacy vs. Isolation" is the primary issue of early adulthood, "Generativity vs. Stagnation" the primary issue of middle adulthood, and "Integrity vs. Despair" the primary issue of later adulthood or old age. Neugarten's division of the life cycle also fits this macro-model. Progressive growth is primarily the early adult phase, while stability of growth is the middle adult phase and decline or regressive growth is primarily in old age. Jung's division of the life cycle of childhood, young adulthood, mature adulthood, and extreme old age fits this macro-model. So does Havighurst's tripartite division of early adulthood, middle age, and later maturity.

The micro-theory attempts to study development within the larger time frame defined by the macro-theories. Levinson's periods are within the larger eras and are in part governed by their dynamics. Gould and Vaillant also study development in adulthood within smaller time frames; so does White (1952). What implications does this era/period split have for faith development?

Women in Adulthood

The *Hypotheses Paper* points out that much of the work done on adult development excludes women. There are, however, a few exceptions. Wendy Stewart did a doctoral dissertation at Columbia University using Levinson's theory and a sample of women. Gould included women in his studies and discussion of transformations. Marjorie Fisk Lowenthal's discussion of commitment in adulthood includes women. Levinson is currently studying the adult development of women. I have participated in the preliminary aspects of this study. While it is far from complete, some patterns emerge from some of the early interviews. This segment of the sample was primarily women who were married and had families. The career women are now being interviewed.

The life structure of family-centered women was more relationally defined than those of men studied. In talking to women about their lives, for instance, we found that the moves made were tied to spouses' moves and that work was typically secondary to home and family, particularly in their twenties and early thirties, so that the women typically went back to work when their children started school.

Another important observation is that those women who started families in their early twenties were eager to get to work in their late twenties and early thirties. Their age-thirty transition involved questioning the family-centered life and modifying it by going to work. Women who worked during their twenties seemed anxious to start families in their late twenties and early thirties. They seemed to feel it was time to get started on having children.

Another interesting trend is that women in their mid-to-late thirties experienced intense desire to become their own persons. This parallels the period Levinson defines as "Becoming One's Own Man." Men in their late thirties feel strong urges to gain more authority, speak with their "own voices," and move into more senior positions.

93

Other discussion of the development of women at mid-life suggests that while men become less power-oriented and often allow the more feminine aspect of the self to emerge at mid-life, the change is in the opposite direction for women. Long suppressed, more masculine characteristics find expression as women at mid-life become less tied to more nurturant mothering roles.

The consequences for theories of adulthood seems to be that the mothering role helps to accent the development of nurturant capacities in women in early adulthood. Family-centered women have life structures that share the man's dream or have family as the central component. This begins to change in the mid-to-late thirties as women become increasingly freed from day-to-day care of children and begin to explor roles in other areas of life. At mid-life the shift from the nurturant stance may be even greater, with women taking on more executive and power-oriented roles while men begin to question these roles and styles of being.

Crisis

A distinction should be made between developmental crisis and crises in general. The death of a loved one or the loss of a job can be so stressful that it threatens the functioning of the individual and so becomes a crisis. Yet there is an opportunity in every crisis, and, like the broken bone that gets stronger in healing, the person may overcome the crises and become stronger psychologically. Yet these event-related crises may not be strictly defined as developmental crises.

Developmental crises are more likely to occur during a period of transition and usually indicate that the tasks of the transition or period close to it are in serious jeopardy. A developmental crisis goes far beyond a single event or coping with a single event. Its basis is in the internal and life changes the individual is attempting to make and the difficulty he/she is having with those changes. Particular events in the life course have to be placed in context of the period before their meaning and full impact on the life can be fully understood. Transition is not synonymous with crisis. Transitions can be fairly smooth or extremely turbulent and crisis-filled. The transition or passage begins with a phase of termination, when the old status and/or roles are terminated. Next is the phase of separation, when some distance is gained. Finally, there is the phase of initiation, when the person initiates or is initiated into new status, role, or life structure. The transitional process takes some time, in Levinson's perspective 3 to 5

94

years, and typically begins with questioning and reappraisal. The first two phases are likely to be the most painful aspects of the transition.

Roles

We should not confuse role and personality. Roles are predetermined and predefined with rules, rewards, and obligations. The individual in the role may exercise some individuality within it, but the role governs behavior and provides norms for acting. The assumption of specific roles at various points in the life cycle demands preparation, readiness, commitment, and adaptation. The interface between self and the network of roles is important from an adult development perspective.

Levinson's concept of life structure is helpful here because it suggests that the importance of the individual roles a person plays, both social and gender related, is determined by their place in the larger structure or network of relationships between self and world. The life structure is one way of talking about the organization of various roles into a meaningful whole. For example, it is not just that mid-life women beome less family-oriented and more vocationally oriented but also that the life structure of their earlier years may have become oppressive, limiting, and unsuitable. Though one role may highlight change in the structures, it is the structural change that is basic.

Faith Development

Since there are many definitions of faith and this paper is concerned with faith development, a fundamental step in this section should be to ask of each concept of faith whether development is possible. So of Tillich's definition of faith we can ask, "What develops?" Commitment? Degree of concern? Or should we look for various types of objects of concern? This type of questioning helps to clarify what we mean by development of faith and to distinguish between concepts of faith that make sense in a developmental perspective and concepts that are incongruous with such a perspective.

The definition of faith given in the *Hypotheses Paper* is complex and should also be scrutinized as to what aspects of the definition fit a developmental perspective. This definition has the following aspects: 1) dynamic element, 2) of the individual's total being, 3) addresses issues of ultimate concern, 4) meaning of life and death, 5) nature of being, 6) existence and nature of Deity, 7) it is extremely personal and individual, 8) focusing less on creed and doctrine, 9) more on perceptions and values of an ultimate nature, 10) which are part of the individual's very being. How can we think developmentally, using his definition? Essentially, the definition says faith is a part of the person which deals with ultimate issues. Is that dynamic element a faculty of the person or is it a characteristic style of dealing with ultimate questions?

The definition of faith development provided by the *Hypotheses Paper* is also complex. It says faith development reflects: 1) the changing nature of 2) one's faith perception and understandings 3) through the developmental journey of life and that 4) through faith development maturing adults function in 5) increasingly complex and adequate responses 6) to life's ultimate questions and issues. In this definition faith development seems dependent on adult maturation and at the same time is responsible for the increasingly complex and adequate responses adults make to life's ultimate question. These definitions make it difficult to decide what faith actually is and what exactly would be the object to our investigation. If Faith Development is reflected in adult development, do we study adult development to get at faith?

Fowler's definition is also multifaceted. His concepts of importance for developmental study seem to be 1) "the process of knowing" 2) underlying the person's composition and maintenance of a comprehensive frame of meaning 3) generated from the person's attachments or commitments to centers of superordinate value, which 4) have power to unify his or her experiences of the world, thereby 5) endowing the relationships, contexts, and patterns of everyday life past, present, and future with significance.

Some important questions emerge from this definition. First is the comprehensive frame of reference first generated from attachments or constituted prior to the generation. What is the difference between the "process of constituitive knowing" and "composition and maintenance of a comprehensive frame of meaning?" If they are not the same thing, which has priority? Another question is, does the power to unify experience rest with the attachments and commitments, the composition of frames of meaning, or the constitutive knowing? In this definintion Faith Development seems to refer to the constitutive knowing process as it changes.

Fowler's faith stages, it seems to me, are of two qualitatively different types. The pre-adult Stages, 3 and below, seem to rest on cognitive maturation. The transition from stage to stage awaits the emergence of cognitive stages that Piaget and Kohlberg describe. The stages of adulthood, beyond Stage 3, are independent of cognitive changes, though based on prior cognitive development. While formal operations is a necessary though not sufficient factor in the transition from Stage 2 to Stage 3, there is no similar factor in transition to the later stages. These later transitions are based primarily on psychosocial experiences. This suggests that we may need to differentiate between the process of faith development in adulthood and pre-adulthood. While pre-adult forms of faith have the task of interpreting and maintaining meaning in psychosocial experience, they are closely tied to physical and cognitive maturation, and so we may be justified in thinking about development of those stages in the classical Piagetian way. With adulthood physical and cognitive maturation have peaked, and psychosocial experience becomes more determinative; the person, in addition, has the awesome responsibility of making serious life choices, investing in them, and being responsible for the results.

Erikson's work suggests that faith can only be partial prior to the emergence of an identity. It is only after the emergence of identity, which typically happens between late adolescence and early adulthood, that there is the capacity for deep commitment of self, intimacy, and fidelity. This view supports the idea of the need for different images of faith development in pre-adult and adult eras of life. A developmental view for the adult period would have to acknowledge greater conscious participation in formation of faith, increased capacity for accepting guilt, greater responsibility for what one does with one's life, and ongoing integration of the shadow (Jung) side of reality.

The criticisms, discussed in the *Hypotheses Paper,* of primarily cognitive definitions of faith make sense to me; yet, I think more can be said to help correct an overly cognitive view. It is not simply that affect and emotion may be excluded from this orientation but also that ideas of the unconscious, and that whole realm of being that depth psychology addresses, are not given significant treatment. Adult faith is not simply an issue of solving a moral dilemma. What seems at stake in adult faith is not simply the domain of right and wrong but rather maintaining the integrity of personal experience in the face of internal and external threats. Knowing that one's life is purposeful and good is not only a matter of reasoing; it is beyond reason, accepted without logical proof, yet maintained by commitment and action. To reason out the integrity of a life would perhaps lead to madness. The act of maintaining a sense of meaning is a passionate act that involves the gut as much as the head. There is something about Piaget's and Kohlberg's logico-mathematical model that seems inappropriate to be the language of the development of faith. There is something about faith that is not a rational movement nor simply a cognitive process. Faith moves in the realm of paradox, enigma, mystery, and encounters in the depths. Kierkegaard's sense of inwardness, subjectivity, and dread seems to invoke more appropriate images for our discussion. Concepts such as sin, metanoia, and irony speak of the soul's condition, and faith is a matter of the soul. The mythopoetic languages may be more revealing of the movements and stages of faith. "Inferno" and *The Pilgrim's Progess* may be more productive of insight in faith development than more scientific orientations.

Several significant omissions from the *Hypotheses Paper* should be noted. There is no discussion of faith and its relationship to madness or personal disintegration. The works of Allison, Boisen, MacNab, and Laing are instructive here. The importance of this area rests on the fact that if faith is a way of construing meaning, then its absence is despair, absurdity, meaning loss—precisely those issues one encounters in several forms of madness. Perhaps, the loss of faith can teach us much about faith itself. Lynch's work, *Images of Faith*, is also missing. Lynch views faith development as the education of the imagination through increasing encounter with the ironic such that the most mature faith will be able to integrate the negative side of existence. Fingarette's work, *Self in Transformation*, is also absent, again a perspective that views spiritual development as first the increased ability to accept one's guilt and in later stages the awareness and integration of various aspects of the self. These omitted perspectives provide an important corrective to the primarily rational cognitive approaches. Their value rests in their attempt to image faith as the active maintenance of a sense of meaning, worth, and integrity in the face of encounter with disorganizing experiences that emerge either from the eruption of unconscious inner forces, the pressure of external events, or encounters at life's limits. This "in spite of" (Tillich) quality and the imagery of struggle seem important to the life of faith.

Given the foregoing discussion, what concept of development can best give us a handle on this ongoing saga of the life of faith? How can we talk of Faith Development as a logical, orderly progression of irreversible stages and still make sense of ideas such as loss of faith, regression, and deep despair?

Faith Stages

The issue of the hierarchy of stages is problematic precisely because it sets up an ideal to be reached. If we view the faith development stages as getting better the higher we go, we make value judgments that may unconstructively categorize persons. An example may be helpful here. It would be precocious for a young man in his twenties to be overly concerned with issues of death and mortality. Such "morbid" concern may make it impossible for him to engage fully in the tasks of the period. He may refuse to marry, have children, and develop occupation because he feels death is his destiny: so why bother? The tasks of the twenties require investment in the exploration of life options; the faith of this stage requires a repressing of themes of death and an enhancing of youthful physical vigor. In his mid-forties, however, this same man's concern with mortality, death, destructiveness, and tentative withdrawal of investment from the world of young adulthood would be age-appropriate and definitely in the service of the tasks of that period. The twenty-year-old is not really at a lower stage of development. Rather, his faith may be appropriate for the tasks of his life at that given period of time. Similarly, a faith that integrates the ironic or becomes more universalizing is perhaps the level and quality of faith required to deal with a world of experience that is increasingly complex and difficult. Just as one would not push a teenager to have a mid-life experience or the insight those experiences bring, one would not necessarily want to push people from stage to stage, since the development occurs within the context of life experiences. Maturity is a relative concept, and one can be mature or immature at any age. One evaluates the maturity of a given period of life by the person's ability to manage the issues of that period, not by his/her ability to manage the issues of a period ahead of him or her.

A further note of caution is warranted here. We often speak of stages as if they are plateaus of happiness and feelings of peace. This, in my opinion, is not the case. Movement from stage to stage involves pain, struggle, despair, and perhaps finally new insight. Development is risky, and often change does not lead to better but to worse. Tillich's idea that courage is the capacity to take in nonbeing and Lynch's notion of the increasing irony of faith point in this direction. Faith seems to grow out of the dark nights of the soul in its confrontations at the limits of life. It is often easier and more comfortable not to confront nonbeing than to confront it and lose in the process. Our image of faith should not be a simply positive growth phenomenon.

Faith and the Unconscious

The maturing of the person does not simply mean moving from infancy through childhood to adulthood and developing skills to cope with external demands. The perspective of depth psychology indicates that maturing means learning to deal with impulses and instinctual desires that are often more powerful than the ego. In childhood, crude defenses protect the ego from a host of unconscious forces, yet these defenses need refining. The areas of the self that lie outside conscious awareness and ego control have important implications for faith.

Maturing implies becoming aware of the citizens of the unconscious and giving them expression in conscious life. Fingarette suggests, for example, that the transition from blame morality to guilt morality involves the awareness of one's own propensity to wrongdoing; only then does one give up the defensive strategy of projecting blame to avoid guilt.

Jung's view of individuation also includes the differentiation and full development of various areas of the self (e.g., shadow and persona) and the integration of them into the personality. Making the unconscious conscious is a process of insight that requires courage, risk, and a level of faith that has depth. Faith viewed from this perspective involves not only the commitments, loyalties, and trust of one's life but also the creative integration of a self that reduces its repressions and rigid defenses, that dialogues with its own underworld, that encounters and accepts the limits of life. The discussion again raises the question of faith's underside—despair, disorganization, and various forms of madness. We may ask what is the level or quality of faith expressed in madness. The diseases of the soul or self which madness implies seem connected to abnormal faith either in imagination or fantastic self–world relations or in the cessation of imagination. Developing a pathology of faith may throw light on pathology in general and help those who are concerned with faith to understand how they may be helpful to those in need of healing. Jesus seemed on so many occasions to link the dis-ease of a person to that person's faith. I am not referring so much to what is commonly called "faith-healing" but more to an understanding of how the problems of life may be bound up with the loss of trust and commitment or how on a deeper level the unconscious side of the psyche may go out of control and leave the person. From this perspective, the healings of faith may involve forgiveness, reconciliation, and reimaging, both in relation to self and others. Having raised this question of faith and healing, we must ask about a therapy that is educated by faith. How can we conceive or reconceive that relationship between two or more people that is supposed to bring healing? How can faith, in this case the trust in the helper or therapist and the entrusting of self to her/him, develop in a despairing soul? And how can it be tended, nourished, and strengthened?

Faith-work

I coined the phrase faith-work, realizing the uneasiness that many will feel in the presence of such a juxtaposition, to designate the process side of faith. The work meant here is not "good works" or any type of labor done in the world. What I mean is the psychospiritual work that is entailed in the shaping of one's life in accordance with one's value system and spiritual frame of reference and the interpretation of life events so as to fit them within one's meaning scheme. This type of work I designate as psychospiritual because it involves an inner process of cognition and emotion as well as imaging and interpretation. It is all done in the service of greater self-formation, self-definition, or relatedness to others and the overall scheme of things. The work of faith may occur in one's mediative and imaginative work in isolation, or it may go on in the dialogue of therapy or pastoral counseling or in communal rituals. It taps both conscious and unconscious aspects of the person.

Faith-work then refers to a process rather than to a structure or content. Structural development, insofar as I understand Fowler and others, refers to the style of composing meaning. Contents refer to specific dogmas, creeds, beliefs, objects, and persons in whom one has faith. The process dimension to which I refer as faith-work, in the broadest sense, refers to the continuous integrative shaping of one's life in accordance with the overarching framework of meaning one has chosen. This shaping and integrating become most crucial when the person confronts critical existential issues. Situations such as failure, loss, the need for important choices often threaten to disrupt the organization and meaning of life. The work of integrating these experiences into the self and broadening one's framework of understanding is faith-work.

Does this concept shed any light on the development of faith or the person's growth in faith? Three processes of growth emerge from my consideration of this concept. The first is increasing integration. This refers to the increasing inclusion of various aspects of the life and self within a broader self-identity. In Jungian language it means learning about the shadow side of the self, understanding the masks one wears, and being able to unrepress, so to speak, many hidden or feared areas of self and let them emerge into a broader sense of self. This process includes the "education through irony" mentioned by Lynch. This education of faith occurs as the person confronts death, illness, failure, and often crises and attempts to include them in his/her faith understanding.

The second process of development, closely tied to the first, is the process of shaping of one's life in accordance with the framework of meaning one has chosen. This process occurs as one tries "to live the life of faith." Here it is not just interpretation of experience that is at issue but also the decision to take a certain life direction and remain faithful to it. One's life can be shaped in accordance with a variety of factors, e.g., social pressure, the need for security, prestige, or the need to defend against certain instinctual forces. In a given life, any one of these factors may become the ultimate shaper of one's life, or they may all be subordinated to a spiritual vision that becomes ultimate. The shaping process is partial and ongoing.

The convergence of integration and shaping can lead to a third process of faith-work. One's life experiences may no longer be able to be shaped by the framework of meaning in which one lives, either because hitherto unexpressed urges require integration into one's life pattern, or one's life style becomes too contradictory of the meaning framework. The possibility emerges for a change in the framework of meaning. This change in the framework of meaning, because the framework is too limiting either to integrate aspects of the self or to shape the life satisfactorily, is a profound type of faith-work and I designate as a process of transformation. Faith-work then may be defined as a process that includes integration, shaping, and transformation. At present, and all this is purely theoretical, I would tie the phasic changes in these processes to the changes in the life cycle and suggest, as Levinson does, that there are periods of stability and periods of transition within these processes.

Faith-work may be understood within the context of Levinson's adult developmental tasks. We may ask what is the faith-work required during transitions as compared with structure building periods. Transitional periods seem to require the transformation and integration aspects of faith-work. The transitional processes require the type of faith-work that allows questioning, doubt, and destructioning without leading to total despair. The threat of disintegration requires a deep underlying trust that enables the person to negotiate the transition.

102

Faith-work, in stable periods, is typified by the shaping processes indicated earlier. Once new choices are made and one's meaning framework is clarified, the process of shaping one's ongoing life within that framework continues.

I indicated earlier that faith-work is a process that can benefit from pastoral counseling therapy, worship, and meditation. Outside help is most crucial during transitional periods; this is a time when mentors and guides may help an individual explore, question, modify, or integrate various aspects of experiences into a new configuration of life. Persons who understand or have gone through a mid-life crisis may be able to shepherd others experiencing a similar crisis by facilitating the doubting, disillusioning, and questioning. During this period, when the person feels lost or adrift, the guide may be a very stable and concrete reminder of firm ground, the other side, the light at the end of the tunnel. The guide, by being there, can enable the transitioner to face and work through these dark experiences and give comfort as well as insight.

The Interface

An important area of interface is the relationship between identity development and faith. Meissner, as well as Erikson, suggests that identity formation precedes the formation of a mature adult faith. Their reasoning is logical. Faith is the centered act of a person; it involves trust, commitment, and fidelity. An individual's identity develops out of commitments in the area of occupation, sex-role orientation, and ideology, as well as the integration of past identities, into a stable and meaningful present identity. Without an identity, then, there is no centered self with sufficient integrity and understanding to make mature faith commitments. The identity issue is pivotal because it illustrates two critical aspects of the issue of faith. The first issue is that of faith as the knowing, composing, integrating, imaginative aspect of the self (Fowler) and as such a precondition to identity formation. The second is faith as the act of commitment and fidelity of a centered person.

A real-life example may help illustrate these issues. Joy left home at 17 and married against the wishes of her parents. The marriage, to a man much older, was in part her way of leaving home and the world of childhood. She began constructing a new identity based on the role of wife and soon on the role of mother. The relationship to Jeff, her husband, was based in part on Joy's love of dance and her feeling that Jeff was a good dancer. In addition,

Jeff was sensitive and concerned, unlike many other young men she met. Joy's sense of valued-self was based on this image of herself and Jeff as fine dancers who had a good time as well as on her new roles of wife and mother.

The honeymoon did not last long. After their first child Joy became very unhappy because Jeff no longer took her dancing, and he often stayed out late or was away from home for extended periods of time. The negative turn of events threatened the fragile identity she had built. Joy left Jeff briefly and returned home. At home she had to face the guilt of going against parental wishes to getting married, as well as reenter the role of child in parental home. She returned to Jeff but was still very unhappy. At a very low point in the relationship, Joy decided she had to go to church and, in the midst of tears, took her three children to a storefront church. After several visits to the church, Joy, who was from a very religious family, decided to join the church and became intensely involved, going three nights weekly and on Sundays. This involvement in church eased her troubles, but she still felt an emptiness deep inside. At service one day she had a deeply moving experience and felt touched by the spirit. The emptiness began to fill up. Joy has since made religion and her relationship to the church and to God the center of her life.

The psychosocial and faith issues interlock in this example. On the psychosocial side there is the break with family and the attempt to establish an identity based on the marriage. The identity was threatened, and Joy felt guilty and depressed. Her move back home was not a solution; so she kept the marriage and tried to correct the relation with parent. Going back to church was, in part, a reacceptance of an important aspect of her past and the values of her family. The church provided a caring community that supported her physically and spiritually. The most important aspect of the situation was the breakthrough that the spiritual experience brought. Joy, in effect, while keeping the roles of mother and wife, transformed the negative experiences in the marriage by seeing herself as somewhat of a suffering saint. Instead of fighting or arguing with Jeff, as she used to, she tried to win him over and eventually got him to join the church. This is an excellent example of a situation where the contents of her life did not change but a new faith commitment enabled Joy to transform the meaning of her experience so as to support a new and positive identity.

The richest area of exploration of the interface, then, seems to be at points in life when the established patterns are challenged either by failure or by success and the individual must construe the contents of experience in new, more universal ways in order to integrate the threatening experience and maintain a life of wholeness and integrity.

Crisis and Faith

We may conceptualize crisis in relation to faith as a situation in which the organization, structure, and meaning of one's life are threatened or disrupted by given life events or experiences. One's self-concept and identity no longer are viable in light of what happens, so one must find a new way of envisioning one's life both past and present that will bring meaning out of the chaos of one's present experience. At points like these, one state of faith is at its limit, its form must be broken, and a new image must emerge; a new life motif must emerge to take its place. In the example used earlier, Joy was attempting to build an identity on roles of wife, mother, good dancer, independent young woman. The pain of the relationship made that identity seem negative and destructive rather than nourishing and positive. While she made little change in the elements of her life, Joy's breakthrough came when she reinterpreted the negative experience and saw herself as a suffering sevant type. The very source of threat, the pain, became a badge of distinction and proof of her worth and calling. Crisis is a central theme in the development of faith, and as faith encounters new crises and works through them, it may develop.

The Hypotheses
The central weakness of the hypothesis section is the lack of a clear theoretical position. As it stands, the hypotheses are not closely tied to any particular theory of Adult Development or Faith Development. The theoretical positions should be more fully developed so that the hypotheses may become less haphazard. Hypotheses ideally do not just test the relationship between two variables; they also attempt to support or disconfirm theoretical assumptions. A direct consequence of the theory issue is the lack of operational definitions of the major constructs that will make them amenable to the kind of testing proposed for Phase II. I suspect that developing instruments or questions that tap these areas of concern will be very difficult before basic decisions on theory and operational definitions are made.

Another problem is that the theories reviewed are broad frameworks that have interpretive rather than clearly predictive power. Their mode of study involves lengthy interviews that are then analyzed, using the theory as an interpretive framework to make sense of the material. To move from this style of research to a more quantitative, hypothesis-testing survey style would seem to require a tightening up of the theory that would make causal inferences possible. My review of the hypotheses will reflect concerns with the theory situation and other methodological problems.

1. *FAITH DEVELOPMENT occurs naturally as a part of the aging process.*
   This hypothesis suggests that basic developmental experiences in adulthood naturally lead to faith development. This is a difficult hypothesis to test because it is impossible to separate natural aging from cultural, psychological, and other factors—they are all given together. Even if we could separate them, how would we then measure faith as distinct from the cultural and psychological experience of an individual?

2. *Young adults are less concerned with FAITH DEVELOP-MENT than are those over 35.*
   The first question I must ask of this hypothesis is what would be measured. As stated, it seems as if degree of concern with faith development would be the target of our questions. The underlying question seems to be the differential concerns with life's ultimate values between younger adults and persons over 35. What aspect of our theoretical understanding suggests such a relationship? The work of Erikson, Kenniston, and others on late adolescence shows a blossoming of interest in ideology, philosophy, and world view. The establishment of identity often leads to profound questioning of the meaning and purpose of one's life. Levinson's work suggests that the late twenties and early thirties (age-thirty transition) can be a time of significant inner turmoil, while the thirties is a time of settling down. Fowler, in *Trajectories of Faith,* showed in several biographies—Malcolm X, Pascal, and Wittgenstein—that the late twenties and early thirties is often a time of significant faith change. Given this data, it does not seem likely that these hypotheses would be confirmed. Perhaps this hypothesis could be rephrased to ask in what way the young adult's concern about establishing vocation and family makes a difference to his/her faith commitment when compared to older adults who are not as concerned about establishing voca-

tion and family but have other concerns.

3. *The amount and nature of one's formal education is a positive factor in one's FAITH DEVELOPMENT.*

    The problem with confirming this hypothesis is that it would lead to the association between higher stages of faith and higher intelligence, academic achievement, and socioeconomic status. That is, in fact, a dangerous association. One could get into discussions such as what stage Jesus would have reached if he had had a Ph.D. from Harvard. Education in the school of life may be a more significant factor than formal education. Again, the theoretical assumptions are not clear. Are we saying that the stimulation of critical thinking enables the questioning and examination of faith? Critical thinking may stimulate the examination of one's religious background and childhood beliefs, but does that imply reexamining faith? A critical intellect, not restricted to the education, can analyze and conceptualize faith commitments but not engender these commitments. Experience in the school of life engenders faith commitments. Really to test the difference between the persons who have and those who have not had formal education is a rather difficult task because of all the other variables that have to be held constant.

4. *The extent of one's FAITH DEVELOPMENT in young adulthood has a significant impact on that person's vocational values durng young and middle adulthood.*

    The first question this hypothesis raises is the extent to which occupational choice is affected by faith development. Since occupation itself can be looked at from a developmental perspective, we may look at the critical points in the process, e.g., formation of early aspirations, training, and translation of dream into enterprise. For each phase in the process we may ask such questions as: Did the intital occupational choice reflect a vocational commitment based on some values related to the person's faith or level of faith development? Are periods of faith transition also periods of vocational questioning and reorientation? Martin Luther King, Jr., for instance, made a critical decision when he left the parish ministry and focused his work on the social ministry exemplified by his leadership of S.C.L.C. On order to test this hypothesis, however, we need a clearer definition of vocational values.

5. *The extent of one's FAITH DEVELOPMENT in young*

*adulthood has a significant effect on his/her values relat-
ed to family and close interpersonal relationships during
young and middle adulthood.*

A major problem with all these hypotheses, including this
particular one, is that the model and theory of faith development to be used is still unclear. In addition, this hypothesis requires a measure of sensitivity to family and close
friends in order to test the hypothesis. The theoretical questions here are, Why should a particular level of faith development make one more sensitive? What is the relation
between faith and personality such that it increases sensitivity? Do we include in sensitivity the critical perspective
that, say, a Fowler Stage 4 would bring to a relationship?
For example, a couple with two different levels of development, say, Stages 3 and 4, may have a different time communicating. Again, to decide that faith development is the
source of sensitivity in the relationship involves ruling out
a host of other variables that may be more germane to sensitivity in interpersonal relationship. A basic assumption
that this and other hypotheses suggest is that faith means
moral improvement. Is this what we expect?

6. *The dynamics of mid-life change affect the FAITH DEVEL-
    OPMENT of adults.*
    The first thing we need to do with this hypothesis is to nar-
    row down what is meant by "the dynamics of mid-life
    change." If mid-life change is different from faith develop-
    ment at mid-life, we must separate the two variables
    enough to be able to evaluate them independently. How do
    we evaluate or get at the "dynamics" if we use this word
    technically? Will we use age criterion, an experience criteri-
    on, or both to determine who has and who has not expe-
    rienced mid-life dynamics?

The various strands of the mid-life experience may have a
differential impact on one's faith. Deillusioning, Levinson's
term for the process of questioning the early adult dream
and coming to terms with the gap between aspiration and
achievement, may demand a faith stance that is critical,
destructuring, and disorganizing. On the other hand, the
experience of deillusioning may cripple faith and result in
developmental stagnation. Another mid-life theme, confronting one's mortality (Jacques), integrating the
young—old polarity (Levinson, Jung), is perhaps the most
painful and difficult aspect of the mid-life experience. Faith

could well be the factor that enables the person to work through these issues successfully. New experiences at mid-life may threaten the person's normal capacity for continued integration of meaning. For instance, the self-image based on young-vigorous-upcoming-successful business executive may be suddenly challenged by another image: aging-tired-demoted-indebted-divorced-middle-ager. The act of grasping a new positive sense-of-self requires a shift from the earlier way of making sense of who I am. Successful mid-life work seems to require a shift in the level of faith. This new level of faith, if achieved, must enable the building of a new life out of the ashes of the mid-life experience. One of the potentially important changes in faith understanding, at this time, is the awareness of the limitations of one's capacities and the freedom to appropriate and lean on powers outside oneself.

7. *Older adults are more concerned with FAITH DEVELOP-MENT than are those under 65.*
   It is appropriate for older adults to be more concerned with mortality, since, as Kübler-Ross and others suggest, death-work is an important task at the later phases of life. The older person may become more detached from the external world and more engaged in life review. Are we saying that these concerns reflect more concern with faith? I think a more important question is how the new concerns of older adults reflect faith. In what ways must faith change in order to come to grips with the issues of the older adult? We should avoid judgments that suggest that age-appropriate tasks of a period make one more concerned with faith. I suspect that the under-65 population is as concerned with life's meaning but this concern is expressed differently.

8. *There are developmental tasks of faith that occur throughout the ADULT LIFE CYCLE which, when dealt with responsibly, contribute to FAITH DEVELOPMENT.*
   How would the developmental tasks of faith differ from the stages of faith? Are stages in some way defined by the tasks to be done at a given time in the person's life? What distinctions are we making between "the developmental tasks of faith" and "faith development"? Perhaps if we conceptualize developmental tasks of faith as the tasks of faith in relationship to developmental issues, clearer questions for testing may emerge. We may coin a phrase such as "faith-work" similar to "dream-work" in psychoanalysis that

taps the faith dimension in various areas or periods of development. What are some of the critical tasks in which faith-work is required? The Early Adult Transition, for instance, is a time when identity is being formed, relation to parents and pre-adult world is being transformed, and choices are being made about occupation. What would "faith-work" involve in this time of life? This is a period of transition, turbulence, and often crisis. Faith in this period would involve making possible the uprooting, terminating, questioning acitivies inherent in this period. But it must also maintain and sustain a fundamental sense of wholeness. Even though relations to parents change, the sense of trust and care must be maintained. The "faith-work" at this point is to "hold together" the tension, the disruption and continuity, in order that the process may be completed with integrity. Does faith-work also transform faith itself? With the change of the early adult transition, the person views both self and world in a new way; new meanings emerge; new aspects of the self must be integrated with the self system. This may force faith out of the conventional (Fowler) mode into one that is more fitting to the life experiences of the twenties or early thirties.

9. *FAITH DEVELOPMENT in adults is increased as they can see its significance in their personal/professional lives* (learnable moment).

   The phrase "FAITH DEVELOPMENT . . . is increased" is not clear to me. Does it mean that development is accelerated, helped, prodded forward; or does it mean that faith increases, grows, develops? If it has the first meaning, then we need a way of measuring or finding out about the retardation of acceleration of development. If the second idea is meant, it seems circular to suggest that faith increases or develops as people see its significance in their lives. The suggestion that certain times or moments of experience have great potential for the transformation or growth of faith and that those moments are deeply tied to personal projects is reasonable. Learnable moments seem to be times of readiness for insight.

10. *There are significant differences in FAITH DEVELOPMENT patterns based on ethnic factors.*

   "FAITH DEVELOPMENT patterns" suggests a multiplicity of meanings. It could refer to the characteristic ways an ethnic group resolves crises or it could refer to a different array of stages or different movement through stages. In order really to test this hypothesis, we need to define explicitly what we mean by pattern.

The hypothesis raises an important theoretical issue, namely, what is the relationship between individual faith and the faith of one's ethnic community? Does the unique experience of a group of people enhance or inhibit the development of its members? How do the different historical experiences of ethnic groups lead to a difference in level of faith development?

This is a potentially important and rewarding hypothesis. It may indicate, for example, that members of more tradition-bound ethnic groups have a more difficult time breaking out of Fowler's Stage 3 into a more individuative faith. Another possibility is that the culture structures experience through rituals in such a way that particular developmental stages are less crisis-filled; hence, faith goes through less testing and trauma. At some level, the individual inherits and must transcend or transform the faith of his/her culture. More secular and less homogeneous cultures may leave an individual to his/her own resources, which perhaps increases problems and possibilities for faith development. Ethnic groups perhaps have their own central problems with which members must contend in faith. Blacks, for instance, must contend with the scars of slavery, racism, and segregation. Indians, perhaps, contend with dispossession, defeat, and reservations. Italian-Americans contend with yet other issues. How do the varied experiences stimulate or stifle faith? While these questions are vital, we must have a way of getting at possible differences in development. We may, for example, look at the initial events in the person's life that were tied to ethnic culture through particular ritual or religious practice to see how these events affected further movement in the life of faith. Or we may want to look at how certain changes in self or faith commitment impacted or were impacted by ethnic identity.

11. *There is a positive correlation between higher socioeconomic status and more advanced FAITH DEVELOPMENT.* When put with the hypothesis (#3) on educational status, this hypothesis suggests that the wealthy and well-educated, typically the same group, have the highest levels of Faith Development. Whatever happened to the Sermon on the Mount? If this hypothesis is confirmed, the study would

111

perhaps be interpreted as a study of white middle-class morality and ethics. What are the possible theoretical connections between Faith Development and wealth or socio-economic status? Certainly, the wealthy need little faith in relation to material survival and creature comforts—while the poor need much faith. Would a confirmation of this hypothesis mean that the poor or lower socioeconomic group had given up hope and given in to despair? If faith is developed through difficulty and struggle, should the hypothesis be disconfirmed?

This hypothesis is important to this study because it is a warning signal. First, the questions and measures should be sensitive to educational differences, and thus try to avoid or control for the kind of bias that will show persons with greater verbal facility as more developed. Second, we must not define faith in so intellectual a way that our study measures thinking alone. Blacks, for instance, display robust emotional expressions of faith even beyond intelligible words. Again, our index of faith development is of utmost importance.

12. *Women are more concerned with their FAITH DEVELOP-MENT than are men.*
I have raised critical questions about the use of the term FAITH DEVELOPMENT several times, and I must criticize it again. The term is used as if it refers to one's concern with home or family or job or health. What does concern with FAITH DEVELOPMENT mean? Does it mean that a person wants to grow in faith, wants to improve faith? If so, why not simply say concern with faith? Are we concerned with something called FAITH DEVELOPMENT? Or is this the study's label for variety of concerns?

This hypothesis proposes to measure quantity or degree of concern with faith development. I suggest that a more interesting issue may be how differing emphases or concerns of men and women reflect faith differently. At different points in the life cycle the sexes have different concerns. For example, in early adulthood women are typically concerned with the care of the young, which evokes concern with nurture, fertility, progeny, and the like, while men are more concerned with occupation, physical prowess, strength, heroics, and other matters. Religious institutions seem more geared to nurturance and caring than to heroics and strength, so men in early adulthood may find little support there for their typical concerns. Do the more feminine issues reflect greater concern with faith? Can faith be reflected differently in the two styles? It is recognized that men in early adulthood suppress issues of nurturance, tenderness, and weakness and, to a certain extent, allow the women to carry these concerns. Women often suppress issues of dominance and power in themselves while allowing men to live them out. It is further suggested that around mid-life these suppressed concerns emerge and demand resolution. Often, men become less dominated by heroics and more concerned with nurture and generativity, while women change in the reverse direction. Would these changes reflect faith concern reversals? I do not think so. What is important is to understand the adequacy of faith for the tasks at hand in a given period and how the differing orientations of men and women reflect faith in different ways.

13. *The variety and complexity of a person's social roles has a positive effect on his/her FAITH DEVELOPMENT.*
    The theoretical basis for this hypothesis seems to be that the more roles one plays, the more diverse experience one gets, and this broadening of perspective has a positive relationship to faith. Another theoretical conception may be that the more roles one plays, the greater the task of organizing these roles into a coherent, unified self-structure or life structure. If one is successful, then one has a stronger constitutive imagination, hence, stronger faith. Of course, the danger is also evident. With less capacity for integration, a diffusion of roles may result and lead to despair. The increased faith we see in those who play many social roles may not be attributable to the number of roles, because others who may have played or attempted to play many roles may have ended in confusion and thus not be represented in that subsample of those with many roles and high faith level. The real factor accounting for faith might then be capacity for role integration or something else.

15. *Adult FAITH DEVELOPMENT takes place more fully in the context of participation in a faith community.*
    Testing this hypothesis presupposes comparing the faith development of persons within faith community and those outside. The obvious problem here is that persons within faith groups may be those who are more concerned with issues of faith and so join groups in order to be strengthened. The higher level of faith among this group then could not be

attributed to group membership *per se*. At the same time, there will undoubtedly be people at all levels of faith within the same group, which means that nongroup variables also account for level of development. This last point may seem obvious; the real question it raises, though, is how, in fact, does group membership affect faith development and to what extent.

On a less methodological note, this hypothesis raises the issue of the relationship of individual and corporate faith. One issue here is that of form vs. content. The content of faith always seems to require communal ties, since one receives one's contents from the community. The act of commitment, an important aspect of faith, also seems to require relation to a community, but does the form or style of faith reflect the faith community to which one is attached?

17. *One's adult FAITH DEVELOPMENT is positively influenced by the faith development of one's significant others.*
    This hypothesis suggests that one's capacity to deal with the ultimate questions of life may be enhanced by relations to significant others who are developed in their faith. What theoretical relationship would account for such results? Perhaps the best theoretical connection is through a relationship of trust and support. A trusted figure can be an inspiration that makes a person try harder and even go beyond his/her limit. The understanding and guidance provided by important others can bolster courage and bring insight, thus strengthening faith.

    A methodological problem exists here, though. How will the study decide on the faith level of significant others? If the participant in the study is the source of this information, we have to assume that he/she is competent to tell the faith level of the significant other. Relations to significant others are themselves a construction that implies faith. Can the study rely on such reports to provide a true picture of significant others?

18. *A relationship with a mentor figure influences FAITH DEVELOPMENT positively.*
    This hypothesis shares much of the meaning of the previous one, but there are issues which make separate consideration important. The relational nature of that aspect of faith we call trust makes mentoring important to Faith Develop-

ment. The mentor guides, teaches, sponsors, listens to, and advises his or her protege. All these functions are not necessarily carried out in each relationship, but each of them implies trust and the building of trust. The core of the mentoring relationship is the mentor's belief in the protege's dream. This belief strengthens the resolve of the protege and increases for him or her the value of the dream. The dream is vision, imagined self-in-future, almost purely an act of faith. For the dream to emerge the young person must pull together strands of the valued self, skills, wishes, and desires and image out of them a future self to be fulfilled. Not only must this dream be imagined; it must also be passionately willed, a commitment must be made to it, and then it must be translated into a project or enterprise. The mentor, depending on the period of life and his/her connection to the dream, acts as a midwife, one who helps bring the dream to fulfillment. The mentor may also be a transitional figure standing in that no-man's-land of life's transitions helping to bridge the gap between periods or stages. The figure of the mentor has internal analogue or can be internalized as guide or spiritual father who walks with the young person through the most difficult of life's stages and supports, encourages, and beckons the individual.

The relationship to faith may not be purely positive, however; there comes a time when mentors must be given up, and often the termination of the relationship is either painful or destructive or both. A too disruptive break may undermine the faith of the protege; yet a break is necessary for his or her further development. There may be negative mentors, persons who elicit abiding trust and are transitional figures but lead the protege into doubt or wrongdoing. We may ask if such a person is a real mentor, but there are so many instances of persons being led down the wrong path in relationships of trust that I feel justified in suggesting that there are negative mentors.

20. *FAITH DEVELOPMENT occurs more during periods of crisis than during periods of stability.*
   The relationship between crisis and development is consistently suggested in the literature. The theory that development requires disruption and reorganization or reintegration spans many areas of development. The connection to faith, as stated in this hypothesis, seems to be that crisis

brings with it the experience of limits, anxiety, nonbeing, and other factors, thus forcing a consideration of the ultimate meaning of life. Another connection between faith and crisis comes from therapy. It suggests that greater insight, often the fruit of psychic upheaval, leads to higher levels of reintegration. On one level, then, we might say that faith develops in crisis because crises force the individual to confront issues of death and ultimacy. On another level, we might say that crises are resolved by deeper insights into the nature of life and the self. These new insights represent new integrations of meaning which are themselves more effective modes of faith.

But does crisis have to develop faith? I think not. Crisis sometimes destroys faith utterly and drives people mad. Often, the person ends in a stalemate, stuck at an earlier level of integration. We should not then be in too great a hurry to recommend crises as the pathway to growth.

While this hypothesis should definitely be tested, it would be useful to test several distinctions within it. One already alluded to is whether it is the awakening of issues of ultimacy or death that accounts for development in faith or the meaning, reorganization, which occurs. Another is to look at the differences between developmental crises, e.g., age-thirty transition or mid-life crisis or identity crisis, and crisis events not necessarily related to development, e.g., loss of job, death of loved one, and natural disasters. A third and important issue is the availability of support networks during the crisis.

A methodological difficulty in testing this hypothesis is that periods of crisis are more salient in memory than other periods. Persons may be more likely to forget those faith developing experiences not associated with crisis, so the report of development and crisis may be an artifact of memory. Another problem arises if we rely on participants to tell us if their faith improved. Such reports imply that the participant is competent to judge development from stage to stage. The participant's feeling that he/she has grown may really be an artifact of the relief felt because the crisis ended. Finally, development, growth, and other goals are socially desirable and are interpreted as indicating improvement, betterment, and the like. This implies that negative feelings may not be interpreted as development; yet one must concede that genuine faith development may lead to guilt, remorse, and sadness, at least for a while. All this suggests that how we get at development and faith requires much consideration.

21. *Persons in higher stages of FAITH DEVELOPMENT have greater faith resources for meeting the crises of adult life than those in more basic stages.*

This hypothesis is problematic for several reasons. First, it assumes that "higher stages" means graduation to an easier life. What else could having more resources mean than that one can meet challenges and overcome them without much hassle? This, if true, would perhaps reduce the chances for further development, since new crises would perhaps not be "real" crises. Another issue is that crises remain undefined. Are we talking about those unfortunate events such as death, loss, and the like, which affect us all or are we talking about developmental crises? If the first type of crisis is meant, the hypothesis may be true; however, positive results may be ambiguous, since ability and resource in dealing with such crises may be determined by factors other than stage of faith. If developmental crises are our concern, then it is important to point out that persons at higher stages are likely to be older and would have gone through more developmental crises than persons who are younger and more likely to be at lower stages. The only meaningful test of this hypothesis would be to compare persons going through the same developmental crisis who were at different stages of faith. To do this we would need a way of assessing faith resources.

Conclusion

A conclusion should tie up loose ends and bring discussion to a close; yet I find myself with new issues at the end of this response paper. By raising them now, I trust that they will bring together several strands of the ongoing discussion and facilitate, if not closure, a clearer understanding of this complex area. It is obvious, from all the foregoing discussion, that faith is a multifaceted concept that embodies structure, content, process, and function. A simple operational definition is difficult, not only because of the multifaceted nature of the concept but also because the concept functions as a lens: it helps us see, make sense of a set of experiences and behaviors. Thus, faith itself is a concept that makes intelligible a set of actions that would otherwise remain unintelligible. We see by means of faith. Attempting to see faith, as this research proposes to do, is to attempt to look at the lens through

117

which we view a variety of spiritual and psychological activity. If faith is in part a lens that enables us to bring into focus certain critical aspects of human experiences, can we approach it empirically the way we approach constructs such as self-esteem, locus of control, or other personality variables? In a sense, our task is to have faith disclosure itself as we look at particular configurations of personal experiences.

References

Allison, J. "Religious Conversion: Regression and Progression in an Adolescent Experience." *Journal for the Scientific Study of Religion.* Vol. 8, No. 1, 1969.

Anderson, J. E. "Dynamics of Development System in Process." *The Concept of Development.* Minneapolis: University of Minnesota Press, 1957.

Boisen, Anton T. *The Exploration of the Inner World.* A Study of Mental Disorder and Religious Experience. Philadelphia: University of Pennsylvania Press, 1936.

Ebert, J. D., and Sussex, I. M. *Interacting Systems in Development.* New York: Holt, Rinehart and Winston, 1970.

Erikson, E. H. *Childhood and Society.* New York: W. W. Norton, 1950.

Fingarette, H. *The Self in Transformation.* New York: Harper & Row, 1963.

Gould, R. L. "The Phases of Adult Life: A Study in Developmental Psychology." *The American Journal of Psychiatry. 129*:5, November 1972, 521-531.

Havighurst, R. J., and Feigenbaum, K. "Leisure and Life-Style." *Middle Age and Aging.* B. L. Neugarten (ed.). Chicago: University of Chicago Press, 1968.

Henry, W. E. "The Role of Work in Structuring the Life Cycle." *Human Development,* 1971, *14*: 125-131.

Jacques, E. "Death and the Midlife Crisis." *International Journal of Psychoanalysis,* 1965, *56*, 502-514.

Jung, C. G. *The Integration of Personality.* London: Routledge and Kegan Paul Ltd., 1940.

Kierkegaard, S. *The Concept of Dread.* Princeton, NJ: Princeton University Press, 1944.

Levinson, D. J., Darrow, C. N., Kein, E. B., Levinson, M., and McKee, B. *The Seasons of a Man's Life.* New York: Knopf, 1978.

Loevinger, J. *Ego Development*. San Francisco: Jossey-Bass Publishers, 1976.

Lowenthal, M. F., Thurnher, M., Chiriboga, D., and Associates. *Four Stages of Life: a Comparative Study of Women and Men Facing Transitions*. San Francisco: Jossey-Bass, 1975.

Neugarten, B. L. (ed.). *Middle Age and Aging: A Reader in Social Psychology*. Chicago: University of Chicago Press, 1968.

Vaillant, G. E. *Adaptation to Life*. Boston: Little Brown and Co., 1977.

Werner, H. "The Concept of Development from a Comparative and Organismic Point of View." In Harris, D. B. (ed.). *The Concept of Development*. Minneapolis: University of Minnesota Press, 1957.

White, R. W. *Lives in Progress*. New York: Holt, Rinehart and Winston, 1952.

Mary Wilcox

(MORAL DEVELOPMENT) is Director of Research at the Iliff School of Theology, Denver, Colorado. Her recent book, *Developmental Journey* (1979), has been accepted as a major extension of the research of Lawrence Kohlberg in Moral Development. Currently, Ms. Wilcox serves as the director of a research project at Iliff which is seeking to determine the relationship between biblical interpretation and moral development. She brought to the SYMPOSIUM the perspective of a related field out of which much of the Faith Development theory stems, and her probing sense of inquiry contributed significantly to the public dialogue.

6

Response to the Tentative Hypotheses Paper from the Moral Development Perspective

Introduction

This critique is written in response to the working draft of the *Hypotheses Paper* produced for the SYMPOSIUM on Faith Development in the Adult Life Cycle held August 10-14, 1981, at the College of St. Thomas in St. Paul, Minnesota. The critique is divided into three major parts:

Part I is a brief presentation of the relationship of the Moral Development model to Faith Development in the Adult Life Cycle.

Part II is a commentary on several issues raised in the *Hypotheses Paper*. A major emphasis in this section is on the need to be clearer about distinctions between "life stages" and "faith stages" and between "faith " and "faith development." such distinctions are critical for the formulation of a valid research design. This section also focuses on information and issues related to the Moral Development model.

Part III introduces new issues. First, it moves from the Moral Development model to the work of William G. Perry, Jr., in order to broaden the research base. Second, it describes research already in progress which relates the Perry model to the education of adults. It briefly describes some of the research at the Iliff School of Theology, Denver, Colorado, which is concerned with correlations between development and education and which introduces new data relating cognitive structural development to nonrational/imagistic/intuitive functions of the mind. Third, it introduces the concept of relationship between Faith Development and adult preferences in educational styles or methods. Fourth, it takes a look at some basic requirements for valid research in the realm of cognitive structural development theory, which includes Faith Development and then points out some potential problems.

Finally, it summarizes previous comments on the hypotheses and makes additional suggestions.

PART I

Relationship of Moral Development to Faith Development in the Adult Life Cycle

Moral Development is often perceived as something apart from Faith Development. Lawrence Kohlberg, the major researcher in Moral Development, saw it thus in an article published in 1974 (before the present refinements of Faith Development) and quoted in the *Hypotheses Paper,* page 33:

> We may expect parallel development of faith stages and moral stages. The critical question both psychologically and philosophically is whether moral development precedes (and causes) faith development or vice-versa.

My position is that this dichotomy distorts the relationship between the two, because in the actual life of an individual the two are inextricably welded together. Fortunately, for purposes of research, it is possible to separate and pull out different aspects of the person's thinking, or feelings, or behavior. But when one portion, for example, moral reasoning, has been analyzed, it functions like a rubber band attached to the center of the person and it snaps back into place as soon as it is released. We are then left with some valuable data, if our analysis has been done responsibly. But we must never forget that the actual moral reasoning of the individual is an integral part of that person.

This view of the relationship between Moral Development and Faith Development is supported by the Faith Development model itself. The model includes as one of its seven aspects the "Form of Moral Judgment." Descriptions of this aspect come directly from Kohlberg's research and have been incorporated by James W. Fowler into his Faith Development theory. One of Fowler's major thrusts is toward integrating the cognitive into a holistic image of the person. I will say more about this relationship in Part II of this critique.

More specifically, Moral Development is relevant to this project in at least four ways. First, Kohlberg's model of Moral Reasoning has been an important factor in the development of Fowler's Faith

Development model. Fowler writes in *Stages of Faith:*

> As a background for our conversations on faith and human development I want to communicate some of the immense richness I have found in the worlds of Jean Piaget, Lawrence Kohlberg and Erik Erikson. . . . as regards the timbers and foundations of my own work these three keep proving most fundamental.[1]

He goes on to describe five ways in which the structural developmentalists, Piaget and Kohlberg, have contributed to his research and theory. These five ways are:

1. the epistemological focus,
2. the focus on the "structuring of knowing as it gives form to the contents of knowledge,"
3. the rigorous concept of structural stages and the descriptions of these stages,
4. the perception of development as an interactional process and
5. the normative directions and implications of their work.[2]

I will expand on the second, third, and fourth points in other parts of this critique.

Second, ongoing research is confirming that there is a direct correlation between Moral Reasoning stages and other aspects of development related to the Faith Development model. The researcher can start with a determination of a subject's stage of Moral Reasoning and then closely predict how that person will interpret the Bible as symbol. Conversely, the research can begin with an analysis of a person's style of interpretation of the Bible and then predict within narrow limits the subject's stage of Moral Reasoning. This creates the possibilities for research designs that are less complex than those currently used in the field of structural development.

Third, the instruments used for scoring stages of Moral Reasoning have been in the process of development for over twenty years. Even with their limitations, they have been refined and in some cases simplified beyond most of the instruments used in related fields. Thus, they offer possible alternatives for the purpose of research in Faith Development. In Part III of this critique I will mention an objective test for the determination of Moral Reasoning stages.

And fourth, results from Moral Reasoning testing are correlating well with the "Intellectual and Ethical Development" model of William G. Perry. This model is currently used in research exploring relationships between structural development and the education of adults. Since part of the ultimate purpose of this project is to relate Faith Development to the concerns of those who teach adults, it seems that this connection might be of significance to the Faith Development in the Adult Life Cycle project.

Since I anticipate that the testing for Faith Development might be a problem area of the research design, I suggest that any insights that can be gained from the Moral Development model and its spin-offs may be of value in implementing Phase II of this project.

PART II

Comments on Issues Raised in the *Hypotheses Paper*

In this part I address several issues raised in the *Hypotheses Paper*. I have organized these into the following sections:

A. clarifying distinctions between "life stages" and "faith stages."
B. Clarifying distinctions between "faith" and "faith development" as it is based in structural developmental theory, referring specifically to the model developed by James W. Fowler. This might also be stated as clarifying the difference between looking at the *content* ("faith") and the *structure* of Faith Development.
C. Clarification of the Moral Development model and other material related to it and introduction of the concepts "cognitive conflict" and "interaction."

A. Clarifying Distinctions Between "Life Stage" and "Faith Stage"

As I have studied the *Hypotheses Paper*, I have found the use of the word "stage" unclear. For instance, in the summary section on "The Adult Life Cycle," page 28, Kohlberg's and Fowler's structural stages are introduced without explanation and without any distinction made between them and the life stages which are the focus of that section. Up to that point it had seemed clear that the meaning under discussion was "life stage," but throughout the rest of the *Paper* usage of the word "stage" is often unclear and inconsistent.

In the *Hypotheses Paper*, pages 42-43, the meaning of "life stages" is explained. However, on pages 47-48 "faith stages" is discussed at length but is never explained nor defined. I think this points to a basic problem with the *Hypotheses Paper*: the concept of structural developmental stages is never clarified, and this is reflected in a fuzziness at various places. Research into Faith Development, if it is to make use of Fowler's model, requires an understanding of structural stages. Admittedly, the concept is not one that is simple to define, and in the next section I expand on its meaning.

One way of clarifying the two types of stages for the purpose of this research project is to choose an already tested theoretical base for each type. For example, Levinson's model might form the context for research into "life stages," and Fowler's for the exploration of "faith stages." I question whether there is time to develop and test a new theoretical basis for this project, and I suggest that use be made of the most appropriate models now available.

B. Clarifying Distinctions Between "Faith" and "Faith Development"

Related to the confusion in usage of the term "stage" in the *Hypotheses Paper* are problems in distinguishing between "faith" and "faith development." In some parts of the *Paper*, including the hypotheses section, the two terms seem to be used interchangeably. This could make for serious deficiencies in the research design.

The two terms are defined on page 39 of the *Hypotheses Paper*. "Faith" is described as:

> . . .a dynamic element of the individual's total being which addresses issues of ultimate concern, such as the meaning of life and death, the nature of being, the existence and nature of Deity, and the like. . . .

"Faith development" is defined as:

> . . . reflect[ing] the changing nature of one's faith perceptions and understandings through the developmental journey of his or her life. It is through Faith Development that maturing adults function in increasingly complex and adequate responses to life's ultimate questions and issues.

125

The key phrase in the second definition that helps to distinguish it from the first is "increasingly complex." One's faith perceptions and understandings can change without the *structure* or *form* of the understandings becoming more complex. Let us look at the following example, in order to help in partially clarifying this distinction.

Gary and Jane both believe in God. Under the definition of "faith," they both address an issue of ultimate concern and they both subscribe to the existence of a Deity whom they call God. This is the *content* of their faith.

But Gary perceives God concretely, as an old man who lives in heaven, who wrote the Ten Commandments, and who punishes and rewards people, while Jane interprets God as an abstract benevolent force who is active in history and who is ultimate truth. Gary and Jane both read the same Bible and attend the same church, and in the adult class each is astounded at the ideas of the other!

These two views represent contrasting ways of understanding God and of structuring ultimate reality. Gary is concrete and literal and interprets all of his experiences in that way. Jane is very abstract in her thinking and has rejected the concrete ways which characterized her mode of interpretation in the past. She can remember that when she was in sixth grade she pictured God as Gary seems to do now and feels that she could no longer believe in such a God.

Gary and Jane represent two different stages of Faith Development. Each is looking at the same content of faith, "GOD," but each is structuring that content in quite different ways. Jane's style of interpretation can be described as much more complex than Gary's, or in the words of the *Hypotheses Paper,* as a more "complex . . . response to life's ultimate questions and issues." (I have intentionally omitted the word "adequate" from the quotation. This is a word requiring judgment based on stated criteria before it can be applied meaningfully to Faith Development.)

Gary and Jane might embrace quite different content. Gary could be an atheist, Jane a Buddhist. Yet they would structure their responses to "life's ultimate questions and issues" in the same style they used to structure their understanding of God.

I suggest that the structural dimension be made very clear in the definition of "faith stages" on page 47 of the *Hypotheses Paper.*

In looking at the proposed hypotheses in the last section of the

Hypotheses Paper, it appears to me that the following are concerned with exploring "faith" rather than "faith development".

#2. "concerned with matters related to life's ultimate values."
#7. "individuals focus more of their concern on issues of ultimate meaning."
#9. "seeing the significance [of Faith Development] in their personal/professional lives [cf. the 'learnable moment']."
#12. "sensitivity to faith issues."

In formulating the final hypotheses, I suggest that the intention for each be made clear and that this intention be represented by an accurate use of terms. Is a particular hypothesis exploring "faith" or "faith development," or is it intended to investigate the relationship between the two?

Research in the field of structural development needs to take these distinctions seriously.

C. Clarification of the Moral Development Model and Related Issues

In this section it is my intention to elaborate on the information related to the Moral Development model as it is presented in the *Hypotheses Paper* and then to add some new material derived from this model.

As I stated earlier, I take the position that the Moral Development model (also called "moral reasoning" or "moral judgment" model) is an intergral part of the Faith Development model. It constitutes one of Fowler's seven aspects and is separated from the whole only for purposes of analysis. Fowler's model attempts to look more seriously at "the whole person" than do other cognitive structural theories, but it still accomplishes this primarily through the device of looking through different "windows." Moral Development is one such window. Its major emphasis is on the cognitive, or thinking, functions of the person as he or she considers moral or ethical issues. It is highly useful to be able to isolate these different windows, but much of the value is lost if each window cannot be integrated into the whole. Much research tends to compartmentalize or polarize different fields of investigation rather than to push for reintegration after analysis. I prefer to view Moral Development as one window into the whole of Faith Development, with unique contributions to be made to the understanding of the whole.

127

To explore further this issue of integration of the models, I want to point again to the quotation from Kohlberg on page 33 of the *Hypotheses Paper*. In this excerpt, the separation between moral stages and faith stages is apparent. The question is raised as to "whether moral development precedes (and causes) faith development or vice-versa." Kohlberg then goes on to say:

> We hypothesize that development to a given moral stage precedes development to the parallel faith stages. . . . Moral principles, then, do not require faith for their formulation or for their justification. In some sense, to ultimately live up to moral principle requires faith.

This statement, published in 1974, probably reflects the embryonic state of the research in Faith Development, as well as what seems to be an unclear definition of "faith." If faith stages *include* moral stages, as in Fowler's model, then we cannot say that moral stage "precedes development to the parallel faith stage." What we can do is to hypothesize, and then test, whether the moral reasoning stage precedes or follows each of Fowler's others aspects. The present state of research seems to indicate that moral reasoning follows some of the other aspects, because it makes use of them. For instance, moral reasoning that requires the ability to "take the perspective of another individual as that person relates to a social system" cannot be accomplished until one is actually able to take that kind of perspective. This means that one must have an image of "social system," a characteristic of Stage 4 of Bounds of Social Awareness and Form of World Coherence from Fowler's model or of Community / Society from my model of Social Perspective. So Stage 4 of moral reasoning must be based in the achievement of Stage 4 of these other aspects, and therefore it must follow them in sequence of development. But all are bound together within the total context of Faith Development.

Another area of the *Hypotheses Paper* which calls for attention is that which relates Kohlberg's stages to ages, pages 27-28:

> From children and teenagers, the developmental literature suggests that the ability to structure beliefs is age related. Not until persons reach their teens are they capable of developing a referent-stage which includes a societal outlook, nor are they able to form "universal principles" (Kohlberg) or "universal faith" (Fowler).

There has been significant change in the data relating age to stage since Kohlberg's earlier publications. Much of this has come about through the development of greater clarity in distinguishing between content and structure (content being the subject about which one speaks, and structure the way in which that subject is understood and interpreted) and subsequent revisions of the scoring. One of the results has been that the relationships between age and stage have emerged in a new light. Kohlberg's research, as well as that of many others, confirms that most adolescents test within the range of Stages 2 and 3 of moral reasoning; a very few are beginning some Stage 4 reasoning. Most adults are found to use Stages 3 and 4, with some still at Stage 2, and a small percentage moving toward Stage 5. Some of the data coming from Harvard suggest that 5-10% of adults use Stage 5 reasoning; our research at Iliff has found that 6% of entering graduate students are beyond Stage 4.

The Hypotheses Paper, page 28, states that: "Adults, while they may not be in the more advanced stages of faith development, are not generally restricted by their cognitive ability." Since Faith Development is a cognitive model, the meaning here is unclear. Perhaps "cognitive" refers to "logical reasoning" or "form of logic," one of the aspects of Faith Development. It is believed that the development of this aspect must precede the other aspects of Faith Development, with the possible exception of "symbolic function." Recent research is showing that without doubt adults, when challenged under appropriate conditions, can and do develop in their cognitive complexity. But these conditions seem to be the exception rather than the rule.

It may be that for some persons logical reasoning "gets ahead" of the other aspects of Faith Development by a significant amount, but generally there does not seem to be much discrepancy. In other words, a person using Stage 3 of moral reasoning will be using logical reasoning that is consistent with Stage 3 structure and that is not sufficiently complex to permit Stage 4 moral reasoning. It seems that adults generally are restricted by their cognitive ability. This can be demonstrated through the following examples of data about, and characteristics of, the logical reasoning of adults.

First, one set of tests given to a group of college freshmen at a university in Oklahoma revealed that 50% of the subjects were concrete thinkers. (Concrete thinking alone does not permit moral reasoning higher than Stage 2). In another study, 43% of adults aged 45-50 were concrete thinkers.[3] Concrete thinking usually begins in children at ages 5 to 8 and is the major mode for most grade-school children. Apparently, it continues to be prominent in the thinking of many adults.

Second, one type of thinking categorized as logical reasoning is "compartmentalization." This means that the individual can come to contradictory conclusions without any recognition that the conclusions are in conflict. This type of logical reasoning is characteristic of both Kohlberg's and Fowler's models for Stage 3 reasoning. As an example, in the Iliff research we have an interview in which the student states firmly and repeatedly that it is wrong to steal in order to save a particular woman's life because this would be breaking God's commandment. Yet in almost the same breath the student says that one should steal to save hungry children, because he knows that God would approve of that. The student was completely unaware that there was any contradiction between his two reasons. Compartmentalization can put a serious limitation on the way in which persons make ethical decisions and the way in which they perceive God and all of life's experiences.

Third, another element of logical reasoning is that of "time." The young child has no sense of time. One can set out on an eight-hour trip with a six-year-old, explaining carefully how long it will take to "get there," and in five minutes the youngster will ask, "Are we there yet?" By middle grade school most children have a good sense of "time in the present." They can "tell time" and are generally aware of what this means in terms of schedules. But historical time has no real meaning. Grandma's childhood, the time of Jesus, and the age of the dinosaurs are all lumped together in some hazy distant past.

There is a similar progression, but at a more complex level, in the interpretation of time by adults. The *Hypotheses Paper,* page 25, says:

> Kimmel further states that in the first half of life a person 1) does allow for expansion, 2) is open to change and 3) is outward in viewpoint, while during the second half of one's life a person is concerned about 1) contraction, 2) inwardness, and 3) rigidity (33). Neugarten (54) commented that inner life becomes altered over the life span but that it is doubtful that people change internally at regular intervals since the present always has the elements of the past contained within it.

What is meant by "the past"? In the child we have found that it is separated into the immediate past, which has been experienced by the child, and all the rest of the past, which has been experienced by the child, and all the rest of the past, which had not been expected and which is undifferentiated. In our research at Iliff we have discovered that the meaning of the past for adults is largely determined by the structural stage of logical reasoning of the individual. In answer to questions about how the subject perceives tradition, we find:

1. At Stage 3, tradition is what one's family does at holidays (family customs) or what one's church does on Sunday morning. It is closely tied to personal experiences or the experiences of other persons one knows or has heard about. But for those individuals approaching Stage 4, tradition is perceived in greater depth, both in terms of history and in terms of the circle of human relationships. Subjects perceive themselves as part of the ongoing experience of the people of God, for instance, or of humankind in general, seeing their roots reaching back into the distant past and into all of humanity.

2. At both Stages 3 and 4, persons view themselves as shaped by their tradition. At Stage 3, this tradition is limited to a much narrower circle of relationships than at Stage 4 and to a much shorter meaningful time perception into the past. Here again it seems that cognitive ability does place limitations on the psychological reality in which each adult exists.

The next issue I want to address from the point of view of Moral Development is that which is mentioned on page 28 of the *Hypotheses Paper*. Here it is suggested that "all of the theories" recognize that individuals may "regress." It is unclear whether this refers only to life stages, or whether it includes faith stages, as analogies are drawn in what follows on page 28 "between these theories and the idea of faith development." Since the reference is blurred, I think it is important to clarify that the idea of regression is not a generally accepted part of structural stage theory. I do not know of any well-documented examples of significant regression in stages of Moral Reasoning. There may be reworking of encapsulated content, for instance, a concept of God that was appropriated concretely and carried along intact, in spite of a general structural change of thinking in other areas. Also, under conditions of emotional or physical trauma which deprive one of the energy to reason normally, the individual may be unable to tap the more complex processes of his or her reasoning structure. These phenomena may be important targets of research but are not the same thing as regression (change in structure).

Another important issue raised in the *Hypotheses Paper* on page 35 states baldly: "Piaget and Kohlberg . . . are biased in using the cognitive domain almost exclusively to explain moral behavior." This is a common misconception and, in part, probably arises from the label of the theory, "Moral Development." It is more accurate to talk about "development of moral reasoning" or "development of moral judgment." Whatever the title, the Moral Development model is explicitly and intentionally based in the cognitive domain. It is not intended to explain moral behavior, but rather it focuses on how persons think or reason about moral issues. Kohlberg has done some limited research exploring possible relationships between moral reasoning and moral behavior but does not suggest that moral reasoning is the only explanation for moral behavior. His research shows that there is some relationship between an individual's stage of moral reasoning and the *consistency* between behavior and reasoning.

> In a study of undergraduate students, reported in 1967, almost half of the conventional (Stages 3 and 4) subjects cheated while only 11 percent of those using postconventional reasoning did so.[4]

Thomas Lickona has written:

> . . . in fact, to be consistent with Stage 3 or 4 conventional moral principles, it is *necessary* to be "inconsistent"—to vary one's behavior to conform to the changing situational definition of the right thing to do. . . . At Stage 5, prediction of behavorial choice in a resistance-to-temptation situation is easier, since cheating is difficult to reconcile with postconventional considerations of honoring and maintaining equality with other test-takers.[5]

Paraphrasing Kohlberg:

> One's moral stage determines to a great extent how one perceives the issues in a situation, both in terms of which issues are recognized and how they are seen in terms of priority.[6]

This surely has some relationship to how one behaves, but it is only one factor.

One of the hypotheses, #4 on page 53 of the *Hypotheses Paper,* suggests exploration of relationships between Faith Development and behavior: "The extent of one's Faith Development in young adulthood has a significant impact on that person's vocational values during young and middle adulthood."

In the final paragraphs of this section, I will introduce two concepts which are essential to an understanding of cognitive structural developmental theory and which are basic to the Moral Development model. The first of these is "interaction." Interaction is the foundation to all understandings of how structural change takes place.

> Development in thinking comes as a result of . . . interactions between the innate (genetic) structure of the mind and the materials and activities of the environment.[7]

This tells us that there is an integral relationship between structure and content, between the content of faith and the structure of Faith Development. And the content includes the events and crises of the life-cycle. These contents are of tremendous importance in how one lives one's life in general and also in how one develops or fails to develop in the structural realm. I suggest that the term " interaction" be added to the list of concepts included in Faith Development, as it serves to clarify the linkage between adult life-cycle, faith, and Faith Development.

The second term I am proposing for inclusion in the list of concepts is "cognitive conflict." Cognitive conflict comes about through the awareness that there are inconsistencies and contradictions in one's thinking.[8] For instance, if the compartmentalizing student described earlier were to become aware of the contradictions in his perceptions of God, he might be thrown into cognitive conflict. Cognitive conflict can be resolved in two ways:

1. by changing the content to fit one's structure. ("God can contradict himself if he wants to.")
2. by changing one's structure in order to cope with an issue in a more complex manner ("Perhaps my way of understanding God needs to be re-examined.") The latter route *may* result in development toward a higher stage.

Cognitive conflict is another foundation stone of structural developmental theory. It seems to be the precipitating factor in structural (faith stage) change. It needs to be distinguished from the term "crisis" as it is used relative to the adult life-cycle. Crises may or may not precipitate cognitive conflict. If they do not, there will probably be no change in stage of Faith Development, but there can be significant growth in the content of faith and the acquisition of more adequate ways of coping within the same faith stage. Adding this term to the concepts related to Faith Development may again help to clarify distinctions between the different processes.

The Moral Development model adds a dimension to the concept of the "learnable moment" (page 44 of the *Hypotheses Paper*). In this definition, the "learnable moment" is related primarily to developmental tasks. I suggest that the structure of one's cognitive development is also critical to the ability to learn a specific body of knowledge. The adult at Stage 3 of Faith Development may have considerable difficulty finding any meaning in ancient history as something which helps to form his or her personhood. Or the adult at Stage 4 may be threatened by an objective critique of an ideological system which shapes his or her identity, thereby being unable to "learn" the presented information. The concept of "learnable moment" can be enriched and related more closely to Faith Development if it can include the structural dimension.

PART III

New Issues

In this part of the critique I suggest three new issues or major sources of information which appear worth exploring in terms of this research project. These are closely related to the Moral Development model. The three new areas are:

A. A look at the work of William G. Perry as a significant model for the purpose of research into Faith Development;

B. A look at research in progress relating structural development to other aspects of the person and to the field of education;

C. A look at some potential problems for a research design intended to explore the relationships between the Adult Life Cycle and Faith Development.

I will close the critique with:

D. Comments on the proposed hypotheses.

A. The Perry Model of Intellectual and Ethical Development

In the 1950's and 1960's William G. Perry directed a research project at Harvard University, the purpose of which was to explore the thinking of students. It was based on the principle that "if you want to study how people think, you must first get them to think"[9] Perry's book, published in 1970, describes the research process and its results. In the introduction to the book Perry writes:

> We describe in this monograph an evolution in students' interpretation of their lives evident in their accounts of their experience during four years in a liberal arts college. The evolution consists of a progression in certain forms in which the students construe their experience as they recount it in voluntary interviews at the end of each year. These "forms" characterize the structures which the students explicitly or implicitly impute to the world, especially those structures in which they construe the nature and origins of knowledge, of value, and of responsibility.[10]

Note that the term "value" is one which occurs often in the *Hypotheses Paper.*

As a result of his research, Perry identified nine positions which are structural in nature, the equivalent of stages in other models. In our research at Iliff we have been using Perry's model to assist in the interpretation of our interviews. We find it invaluable in the following ways:

1. It seems to form a bridge between logical reasoning and other factors and aspects of structural development;
2. Perry's factors seem to underlie much of what we have been describing in Moral Development and Faith Development;
3. It is relatively easy to identify some of the positions, particularly those that relate to the stage structure of the majority of adults;
4. It has given us handles with which we have been able to identify a major transition point between Stages 3 and 4;
5. It appears to correlate well with the stages of moral reasoning and with some of the aspects of Faith Development;
6. It is used as the basis for research exploring the relationships between structural development and the education of adults.

I will illustrate the essentials of Perry's scheme through examples from our research at Iliff. Two questions that form a part of one of our interviews of students at Iliff are:

1. Do you feel that your understanding of the Bible is true?

2. Are understandings of the Bible other than your own true?

In order to put these questions in context, I will quote from one of our reports:

> In our project, the initial interview of a student consists of

two parts: first, questions about three moral dilemmas based on the Standard Scoring Guide produced by Lawrence Kohlberg and associates of the Center of Moral Development at Harvard University; and second, a set of questions designed to elicit responses about social perspective, logical reasoning, and symbolism. The two questions quoted above are a part of this set. A subsequent interview, conducted later in the student's seminary program, consists of the same moral judgment interview plus a set of questions that probes for information about the student's educational experiences and professional self-understanding.[11]

Responses to the questions about truth have been very significant in enlarging our knowledge about the processes of Faith Development, especially through our use of Perry's model in interpreting the responses. For instance, Perry's first position is one of simple dualism. Authority and absolutes are "right." Authority gets its "rightness" from unquestioned absolutes. Here is a quote from one of our interviews which demonstrates this Position or style of interpretation.

> *Question:* Do you feel that your understanding of the Bible is true?

> *Answer:* Yes. That is an open-ended yes. I haven't learned everything about the Bible. But, I guess, primarily I believe what I believe up to this point because of many agonizing hours spent in meditating on different points and situations. I have accepted that peace that comes when you feel that you have reached what He wants you to know.

We see in this example a basic assumption that there is a truth ("what He wants you to know") which is the possession of a deity and which is absolute. Perry defines "absolute" as:

> The established order; The Truth, conceived to be the creation and possession of the Deity, or simply to exist, as in a Platonic world of its own; the Ultimate Criterion, in respect to which all propositions and acts are either right or wrong.[12]

We have found that this position correlates well with Kohlberg's Stage 3 of moral reasoning.

The next step in Perry's scheme involves the separation of areas of absolute truth claims from areas of recognized plurality. Subjects using this style are not able to give any criteria for evaluating conflicting claims other than that "everyone is entitled to his own opinion." Here is an example of this position from our research, in which the student is answering the same questions as above.

> "What I understand of it. I'm limited, but what I understand of it for me is good but I can't expect it to be good for anyone else. I'll never argue with a person . . . because that's what he feels, that's what he gets out of it, that's the meaning that he finds in it. I may not agree, it may not be what I believe, but I'll take his point of view, because I'm not the judge. I'm just kind of a player and it's not my job to tell someone else that's wrong or that's right.

Perry calls this "multiplicity," which he defines as:

> A plurality of answers, points of views, or evaluations, with reference to similar topics or problems. This plurality is perceived as an aggregate of discretes without internal structure or external relation, in the sense, "anyone has a right to his own opinion," with the implication that no judgments among opinions can be made.[13]

Another way of describing this position is to say that the subject cannot generate any criteria for making value judgments among competing truth claims. This position correlates with Kohlberg's Stages 3 to 3(4). Some subjects at the 3(4) stage begin to use what they call "logic" or "reasoning" as the criterion by which they evaluate competing truth claims.

A major shift occurs between Kohlberg Stage 3(4) and his Stage 4(3). This correlates with the shift from Perry's "multiplicity" positions to his "relativism." positions. At Stage 4(3) subjects question the meaning of the term "truth" and prefer other words such as "valid." Truth claims are evaluated according to multiple criteria. Here is an example:

> "I would say that my understanding in certain peak areas to a certain extent is true. . . . I know there are myriad ways of interpreting it. . . . Some people see reality [as] out somewhere there is a truth of interpreting the Bible, which is the proper way, which is the true way. *I* think reality is an incredibly complicated thing. I see that the Bible can be interpreted in a whole lot of different ways and that within certain brackets, within certain confines, they are all valid."

In this quotation, the subject describes the absolutistic position ("the proper way, the true way") and then goes on to contrast his own understanding with it. He considers different interpretations "valid" "within certain brackets, within certain confines." In other words, not every idea is just as good as every other idea; there are limits. Subjects often describe what they mean by these limits or criteria for valid biblical interpretation, such as the use of a responsible methodology, taking seriously the teachings of the church, respecting the insights to be derived from the people of God through the centuries.

The struggle with the concept of absolutes is resolved through a shift in the ground from absolutism to "relativism," defined by Perry as:

> A plurality of points of view, interpretations, frames of reference, value systems and contingencies in which the structural properties of contexts and forms allow of various sorts of analysis, comparison and evaluation in Multiplicity.[14]

Major values of this position stress rationality, analysis, and critical thinking. In our research at Iliff, we use the term "reflective" to describe this style of interpretation.

Much of the attention of our research project during the past year has been directed to the span from Stage 3 to Stage 4 of Kohlberg's stages and the equivalent shift from multiplicity to relativism (or reflection) of Perry's positions. In one experiment, the research team members focused on absolutes and authority in reading interviews and were able, without error, to identify those which had previously been scored at Stage 3(4) from those scored at 4(3).

We are not as clear about correlations between Kohlberg Stages 4-5 and Perry's higher positions. This lack of clarity derives in part from confusion between content and structure in the upper positions of Perry's model, and in part because we have not yet found time to focus on this area. At the higher end of this span— Stages 5(4) to 5—we find examples which we call "integrative."

> "The word that sticks out in that statement is 'true.' It is true for me at this time and place in my life . . . my understandings of how things are and all that. I think that this understanding is within tolerable limits of the understanding of the Christian community at large of what the Bible is and how it functions. But there is not any one true understanding. My life changes and the community's changes. But right now that is where it is and I have to act on it."

Characteristic of this stage is a sense of feeling comfortable with ambiguity and the ability to be committed within that frame of reference. Perry calls this position "Commitment" and defines it thus:

> An affirmation of personal values or choice in Relativism. A conscious act or realization of identity and responsibility. A process of orientation of self in a relative world. The word Commitment (capital C) is reserved for this integrative, affirmative function, as distinct from commitment to an unquestioned or unexamined belief, plan, or value.[15]

The *Hypotheses Paper*, page 29, includes the following statements in the summary section for the Adult Life Cycle:

> ... the human development literature is also biased in the direction of liberalism. It champions tolerance and flexibility over conservative adherence to absolutes. Again, recent discussions have challenged these assumptions, pointing out that the highest stages of development may involve an overlay of conviction and commitment that transcends simple libertarianism.

Perry's model gives us more objective terms for describing these various styles of interpretation, putting them in the context of Faith Development and, I hope, helping to remove the judgmental connotations. It also provides useful handles for relating Faith Development to the life stages of adults. His major categories are few in number and seem easier to grasp conceptually than do those of the other structural models. As an example of how we might use Perry's concepts in relationship to life stages, we can look at the tasks of adulthood, pages 22-23 of the *Hypotheses Paper*. For instance, what can we discover about the middle-age task of "assisting teen-age children to become responsible adults" when this task is interpreted in the light of Perry's model?

From a Stage 3 position of absolutism and dualism, this task may be understood within the context of certain tacitly accepted "right" ideas of what it means to be an adult. The "good" parent should be an example of these qualities so that the youth will also be "good." But when multiplicity enters into the situation, the complexity of a pluralistic society with its myriad "good" values can be overwhelming. There is no longer a clear image of what it means to be a "good" adult, and from the viewpoint of multiplicity there are no criteria for making choices among the competing images and values. In such a situation, the parent must either fall back upon absolutes or subscribe to whatever models of adulthood are "personally appealing" from among those that the culture has to offer.

But at Stage 4(3), the "reflective" position, the ability to analyze and to use criteria, becomes a major tool for decision-making. The idea of responsibility assumes its definitional meaning for the first time and is seen as involving societal and interpersonal obligations rather than focusing on the maintenance of good interpersonal relationships. Development is perceived for the first time as a process.

It becomes apparent that that particular task of adulthood can be perceived in quite different ways from the points of view of the different structural positions.

On page 48, of the *Hypotheses Paper* is this statement:

> Those persons for whom faith is an unchanging absolute often cannot understand Faith *Development*. Developmental faith is an anachronism for them. It is sacrilegious to speak of faith and change in the same breath.

Perry's model helps us to understand the dynamics of such a response. The concept of "character development," creates similar problems for the absolutistic position. Life is not seen in terms of development but rather as a collection of static values. Since many adults use this style of interpretation, research into its implications for life stages could be helpful for counseling, teaching, and preaching.

This brief look at Perry's model may suggest possibilities for use in Faith Development research. There is an accumulation of data supporting correlations among the theories, allowing the researcher to select those which are most suitable for a particular type of research.

B. Relationships Between Structural Development and Ways of Learning and Education

The relationship between Faith Development and education is raised as an issue in hypothesis #3, page 53, of the *Hypotheses Paper:* "The amount and nature of one's formal education is a positive factor in one's Faith Development."

There is research in progress, with preliminary data available, which informs this issue. Some of this is concerned with the relationship between structural development and the *amount* of education. The questions raised by the term "nature of one's formal education" are far more complex. This term might include the content or subject as well as the teaching/learning methods used. It will relate to the ways in which people learn and to the educational preferences of adults. In this section, I report on some of the research now going on and raise some issues for further consideration.

Research exploring the effects of the amount of education on structural development is currently carried out primarily from the context of Perry's model or variations of it. Since some correlation has been established between the Perry and Kohlberg models, these data are relevant to the hypotheses of the Faith Development project.

Of particular interest is the Reflective Judgment Interview developed by P. King and K. S. Kitchener at the University of Minnesota, used to explore the relationships between education and structural development.

> The research completed to date has consistently shown that levels of Reflective Judgment increase with age and level of education. . . . In other words, graduate students score higher on the RJI than do college students; college students, in turn, score higher than high school students.[16]

Efforts have been made to explore the relationship between the effect of educational level versus age or simple maturation. In one study, education appeared to be a more important factor than age. Another study suggests that "the difference between undergraduate and graduate students found in previous research is, in part, due to combined selection and maturation effects, rather than education alone."[17]

The Reflective Judgment scores of high school students are usually found to indicate the use of absolutism or beginning multiplicity. College students generally score in the middle range: higher multiplicity (beginning use of undifferentiated criteria). Graduate students typically obtain scores indicating higher multiplicity or relativism (reflection).[18] This correlates with the scores of entering Iliff students. Almost half of these students obtain scores of Kohlberg Stages 3-3(4), absolutism to higher multiplicity; 42% obtain scores of 4(3) to 4, reflective style; 6% score at Stage 4(5) or above.

This research relates structural development to the amount or quantity of formal education. Additional study is being done on the nature of education. One project has investigated the relationship between academic major and level of intellectual develop-

141

ment. In that sample, there was "no evidence that college major or academic program has a significant effect on level of Reflective Judgment."[19]

The longitudinal research project at the Iliff School of Theology is seeking to develop and test a theory of instruction. Results to date are suggesting clear relationships between higher faith development stage and certain areas of study. These areas of study seem to have in common similiarities in method rather than in subject matter. This is a fruitful direction for further research.

The Iliff study is also producing new data relating rational/nonrational learning (ways of learning). Of the students who scored at Kohlberg Stages 3-3/4, 16% perceived themselves as using rational and nonrational modes equally; for Stages 3/4-4 the figure was 10%; and for Stages 4-5 it was 61%. These results are based partially on subjective perceptions and require a change in research design for verification, but they suggest the importance of the nonrational to cognitive development.

The last data present some interesting insights into the concerns expressed on page 29 of the *Hypotheses Paper:*

> ... the literature on human development is heavily biased toward purely cognitive, rationalistic conceptions of growth. It tells how to become a philosopher but not how to become an artist. Literature produced since the late '60s and early '70s has begun to challenge these biases. The newer literature forces attention to be paid to growth in feelings, intuition, expressivity, and centeredness. It gives greater attention to growth from experiences, meditation, and reflection and less to growth from purely rational learning. The pedagogy of life has begun to reassert itself over that of the classroom.

It also speaks to the definition of maturity by Moran, page 19, of the *Hypotheses Paper:*

> The *ideal of maturity* definition, however, is primary because it provides the individual with the ability to integrate ... the rational and the non-rational. . . .

It seems quite possible that, in spite of all the efforts to analyze in research and to dichotomize in education, the human mind valiantly persists in its efforts toward integration!

"Educational preference" refers to the type of learning setting preferred by an individual. In broad terms, the distinction might be stated as "participatory" versus "nonparticipatory." The planning of adult education is usually done on the basis of subject matter and time schedule. Seldom taken seriously is the role of teaching/learning styles as an element in attracting adult learners.

Perry's model offers some clues for exploring learning styles. Does the person who is looking for absolutes and authority prefer a nonparticipatory transmissive style? Knowles describes the movement from dependence toward increasing self-directedness as part of the process of maturation, page 26 of the *Hypotheses Paper.* If one singles out dependence on absolutes and authority as part of this process, does this relate to faith development?

With the return of many mature adults to institutions of higher learning, efforts are being made to help the schools meet the special needs of these adults. Studies are being conducted to explore relationships between the adult life cycle, structural developmental theory, and the design of education. The Clearinghouse of Higher Education, at George Washington University, and the American Association for Higher Education have published a report[20] which might be of value to the Faith Development project. Here are some excerpts from it.

> Schemes of cognitive development, particularly Perry's work, have direct application to the design and sequencing of instruction. . . . Students at the lower stages need more structure, less diversity, more direct experience, and a personal atmosphere in the classroom. These same conditions can be experienced as constraints by students at higher stages.[21]

> Knowing the variations in development that shape students' responses is useful to instructors. It helps bring order out of a puzzling diversity of response, and relieves the instructor of the necessity of being all things to every student, while simultaneously enabling a better response to individual and group differences.[22]

A related issue is that of the Faith Development of persons in authority. "Early in his work, Perry analyzed examination questions and found that they related directly to positions on his scheme."[22] Does the instructor design examinations, and teach, out of an awareness of the structural development of the students, or unconsciously from the style of his or her own stage?

The research at Iliff suggests that certain courses are more helpful

143

to students developmentally who are at one stage than to students who are at a different stage. This raises the issue: Should teaching be done with the intention of stimulating Faith Development?

If education is a matter of concern for the research project on Faith Development and the Adult Life Cycle, it might be well to formulate some hypotheses that focus more specifically on the interface between education and Faith Development.

C. Research Design

The *Hypotheses Paper* does not give any clues about the research design for the project. Since many of the hypotheses are concerned with Faith Development, I think it is important to take a look at the bases for research in structural development.

The primary method for obtaining data has been the open-ended interview, used by Piaget, Kohlberg, Perry, Fowler, and in the research at Iliff. This method often comes under attack from those persons who consider only objective tests as valid. It is my position that the open-ended interview is the most effective way to bring in new data, to build a new theory, and to raise questions about previous conclusions. But it has a major drawback: it requires skill and experience on the part of the persons conducting and analyzing the interviews. It is also expensive, as it requires recording and transcribing of the interviews.

Attempts have been made to develop objective tests from the data derived from the open-ended interviews. The Defining Issues Test created by James D. Rest at the university of Minnesota is probably the most successful and most widely used of this type. It has a good correlation (.60s and .70s) with the Perry and Kohlberg tests.[23]

Since the purpose of this project is to look for the relationships between Adult Life Cycle and Faith Development, there is a need for accurate measurements of Faith Development. Without such careful testing, the validity and credibility of the results will be open to question.

D. Comments on the Hypotheses

Throughout this paper I have commented on the need to be more precise about definitions of terms. I believe that this same caution holds true for the statement of the hypotheses, not only in regard to terms but also pertaining to components to be tested.

The purpose of the research project, to increase understanding of the dynamics of the relationship between Adult Life Cycle and Faith Development, might be incorporated in an overarching hypothesis thus:

> *Progression through life stages can be correlated with progression through faith stages.*

This statement makes no assumptions about other causes such as education (hypothésis #3) or "changing value systems" (hypothesis #1). These variables probably need separate hypotheses, such as:

> *The changing values systems related to each life stage stimulate (or cause) development through the faith stages.*

> *The amount of one's formal education is directly related to one's stage of Faith Development.*

Terms such as "extent of one's Faith Development" or "increase in Faith Development" can be more precisely stated as "the stage of Faith Development," if that is what is meant. This will state precisely what it is that is being measured.

Hypotheses that are intended to relate *faith content* to *faith stage* or *life stage* should make clear what it is that is being related to what. For instance, hypothesis #7 states that "older adults are more concerned with Faith Development than are those under 65." The explanatory note, however, implies that what is meant is not Faith Development but faith issues. This might be restated:

> *Older adults are more concerned with faith issues than are those under 65.*

The same problem seems to be present in hypothesis #9, which states that "FAITH DEVELOPMENT in adults is increased as they can see its significance in their personal/professional lives (cf. the 'learnable moment')." This might be restated:

> *Development in faith stages occurs as adults can see the immediate significance of learning experiences in their personal/professional lives (cf. the "learnable moment").*

Some criteria that might be looked at in making the final determination of hypotheses are:

1. Does the hypothesis relate closely to the overall purpose of

145

the project?

2. Is appropriate testing available and is it usable for this project?
3. Is the sought information already available elsewhere?
4. Does the looked-for data require a longitudinal study? (Faith Development change is not instantaneous and longitudinal studies require intervals of several years between interviews.)
5. Is the information readily elicited by the research design?

Notes

1. James W. Fowler, *Stages of Faith: The Psychology of Human Development and the Quest for Meaning* (San Francisco: Harper and Row, 1981), pp. 38, 39.
2. *Ibid.*, pp. 98-101.
3. Mary M. Wilcox, *Developmental Journey* (Nashville: Abingdon, 1979), p. 97.
4. *Ibid.*, p. 172.
5. *Ibid.*, p. 174.
6. *Ibid.*
7. *Ibid.*, p. 19.
8. *Ibid.*, p. 80.
9. William G. Perry, Jr., *Forms of Intellectual and Ethical Development in the College Years* (New York: Holt, Rinehart and Winston, 1968, 1970), p. vi.
10. *Ibid.*, p. 1.
11. Mary M. Wilcox, H. Edward Everding, Jr., and Clarence H. Snelling, Jr., "Interpretation and Truth in Adult Development" (paper presented at the annual meeting of the Association of Professors and Researchers in Religious Education, November 1979), p. 1.
12. Perry, *Forms of Intellectual and Ethical Development*, glossary in foldout chart at back of book.
13. *Ibid.*
14. *Ibid.*
15. *Ibid.*
16. Janet A. Schmidt and Mark Davison, "Does College Matter? Reflective Judgment: How Students Tackle the Tough Questions," *Moral Education Forum*, 6 (Spring 1981), p. 9.
17. *Ibid.*, p. 10.
18. *Ibid.*, p. 11.
19. *Ibid.*
20. Rita Preszler Weathersby and Jill Mattuck Tarule, *Adult*

Development: Implications for Higher Education, AAHE-ERIC/Higher Education Research Report No. 4, (Washington, D.C.: American Association for Higher Education, 1980).

21. *Ibid.,* p. 48.
22. *Ibid.,* p. 49.
23. Lisa Kuhmerker, Marcia Mentkowski and V. Lois Erickson, Editors, *Evaluating Moral Development and Evaluating Educational Programs That Have A Value Dimension* (Schenectady, NY: Character Research Press, 1980), p. 116.

Gabriel Moran

(RELIGIOUS EDUCATION), Associate Professor of Religious Education, New York University, New York, is a prolific and widely respected educational scholar who writes and teaches out of his Roman Catholic heritage to a global community of all persuasions. His two recent books, *Education Toward Adulthood* (1979) and *Interplay: A Theory of Religion and Education* (1981) provide profound philosophical reflection upon adult religious growth. Dr. Moran's concern for clarity and precision of meaning in definition sparked many a meaningful discussion at the SYMPOSIUM.

7

Looking at the Images: The Perspective of Religious Education

My role in this SYMPOSIUM is to address the issue "Faith Development in the Adult Life Cycle" from the standpoint of religious education (section I). Then I will reflect on four topics (sections II, III, IV, V) drawn from the *Hypotheses Paper* (hereafter called the *Paper*). Finally, I will comment on the hypotheses themselves (section VI).

I. Religious Education

For over twenty years I have been writing about religious education. It might seem that I should be able to offer a quick definition and move on. Actually, I think after all this time I am sure of only one thing about the field and/or the profession of religious education: namely, it does not yet exist. The inclusion of the word "yet" in the last sentence saves the statement from sounding like one of despair. As a matter of fact I am quite optimistic about religious education coming to birth in the late 20th and the early 21st centuries.

Until recently there was no pressing need to have an entity called religious education. People passed on their tradition as best they could, mainly through the family, the community's or organizational ritual, and perhaps some schooling in the fine points of the tradition. With differing emphases Jewish, Catholic, Orthodox, Protestant, and Muslim could fit under that description. Although it is always dangerous to make the following claim, I do think that we face something genuinely novel in the later 20th century, namely, the religious ways meeting one another, often in conflict and sometimes in respect. The worldwide scope of this meeting is without precedent.

We are only at the beginning of this era, so that it is not surprising that religious education has not fully emerged. We have had departments of religious in the university for some years now. I applaud that development and consider it one aspect of a field of religious education (though few professors of religion would like to be called religious educators). A fully developed field would have to reach far more people than the often esoteric courses in the university do, and reach people by a variety of educational and religious means.

One can see some development to fill out the field coming from religious institutions such as churches and synagogues. Few of the people there call themselves religious educators, either. Catholics most frequently use religious education to refer to non-Catholic-school programs of church instruction. Protestants often use the term to refer to a liberal movement that has barely been alive since the 1940's. Jews find the term most handy in talking to Christians. Muslims, as far as I know, do not use the term. What each of these groups does educationally with its own people is integral to the total process of religious education. However, the illogical usage or the non-usage of the term "religious education" is significant.

What church/synagogue has done and continues to do is press home the particularities of the respective tradition upon the coming generation. No doubt, that effort succeeds to a degree. In some broader view of history, however, we may be concentrating too much of our effort on transmitting what has been. Paradoxically, the better way to transmit the past may be to stop making such a direct, concentrated effort. We might do better by creating a larger context of education that will preserve the best of the past while deepening our understanding of that past within a matrix of present relationships.

My advocated meaning of religious education (in contrast to currently operative meanings listed above) is that it should be a field in which I come to understand my own religious life in relation to other religious possibilities. Relgious education ought to have two distinct but related aims: 1) to change for the better my own religious practice and 2) to realize some degree of comprehension of other people's religion. The second aim is not tacked on as a useful addition, say, for those who might go on a tourist trip to India. The achieving of the first aim in the future will require a relation to people who are different. I was recently reading a book by a Muslim, and I thought that the experience must be similar to what Jews regularly experience in Christian speech and literature. "Christianity [or Judaism] was a very good religion with many sound elements that have been taken into Islam [or Christianity]." Although the book angered me and I fought it on every page, it did get me to think about the nature of Christianity more than most Christian books do.

The point is not that someone should do unto Christians as they have done unto Jews. What we need is a geniunc conversation eventually having many partners. Christians would have to know how Christian is related to Jewish and to Muslim, with Jews and Muslims speaking for themselves. If we had some understanding of how other people see themselves and how they see us, we might get a better perception of ourselves.

Undoubtedly, many people would consider such a circuitous journey too long and unnecessary. I do not have much hope of people getting convinced of this need by theoretical arguments. I do think that as religious movements tear up some countries and sweep over other countries, we may eventually recognize the need for religious education. In December 1979, the joke in Washington was that everybody in the government was speed-reading the Qur'an. The people no less than the government could use some basic education in religious matters, so as to understand what is happening between this nation and other parts of the world.

I should note that I am talking mainly about the United States of America. A brief excursion to England will be enlightening in trying to define religious education. British writers often use the term "religious education." For better or worse, the government-sponsored schools have tried to approach religion educationally. Writers are forced to some degree of ecumenicity if they use the term. I have a great deal of sympathy with the way British writers speak of religious education. My enthusiasm is tempered, however, by one assumption that most of these writers make. I quote from two books that are good studies—a fact that adds to my frustration:

> Religious education is concerned with enabling children to surrender themselves to any particular pattern of religious faith if they so wish, rather than directing to one pattern of self-integration.[1]

> The aim of religious education is to provide children with knowledge and skills which will enable them as they grow into maturity not only to see how varied are the manifestations of religious experience but also how their experience constrains them to consider the implications of a personal commitment.[2]

Both writers casually use the word "children" as the recipients of religious education. However, the ambitious aims that are formulated here surely require attention into adulthood. That is, there is consistency in making children the recipients if the aim is "to pass on our one true faith." In contrast, if the aim is to acheive understanding of diverse patterns and a commitment to what has been understood, then there is no consistency in excluding all but children.

I have quoted from British writers to dramatize how deep rooted is the assumption that religious education is exclusively for children. The record in this country is no better, and possibly worse. Despite the efforts of many people over recent decades, church education, synagogue education, and education in general retain their primary meanings as enterprises with children. The development of religious education at this moment of history requires a resistance to the assumption that it is exclusively for children. But the problem is with all education, so that the religious educator cannot simply assume that education is a perfected form that is waiting for application to religion. Instead, educational reductionism has to be resisted from the inside by a two-fold movement: the inclusion of religious matters as materials of education and the inclusion of nonchildren as the recipients of education.

This current project, FAITH DEVELOPMENT IN THE ADULT LIFE CYCLE, is therefore crucial to the very existence of religious education. What we are trying to study is not one of dozens of tasks that religious education might dabble in. I think that what is at stake is one of the prerequisites to the existence of a field deserving the name of religious education. The negative side of this claim is that the project becomes an extremely difficult one to formulate. As I proceed to criticize the concepts and assumptions in the *Paper*, I am not being negative about the project but merely insisting that we lack even a common language in which to formulate questions.

As an illustration, I advert here to the topic I will come back to in section IV, that is, faith. My interest as a religious educator is in *religious* development. (I leave aside for the moment the problems with the word "development.") Is the idea of "faith development" a part of religious development? Possibly, although I do not see that as the intention of people who write about faith development. On the contrary, the intention seems to be to create distance between the words "faith" and "religion," praising faith and then acknowledging that religion comes with the package. As a person interested in religious education, I am struck by the lack of reference to things religious in the *Paper*. By my count the adjective "religious" appears 20 times, while the word "faith" is used 284 times. That may not be surprising in an essay on faith development; nonetheless, as the word "faith" edges the adjective "religious" out of sight I am less sure of what is being talked about and I am unsure whether the category of faith development is helpful to developing a field of religious education.

My final comment in this introductory section is something I will come back to repeatedly. Although religious education may be in a nascent stage, there ought to be enough of the field to challenge the assumptions and the concepts being used in studies of adult development. Two forms of resistance are possible. One is to stand solidly within the language of one's religious tradition and issue negations to much of what the culture offers. At times that may be the best one can do. The more common approach of religious education should be to resist the culture's simply taking over all the good words and deciding what they will mean. One religious group, or several in coalition, should remind the culture of the religious roots of the language it speaks and force a recognition that its cherished terms are highly ambiguous.

II. Adult

This section is an analysis of one of those terms that connotes, the contemporary world assumes, a very simple idea, namely, adult. A discussion of what the word "adult" means would usually be dismissed as silly hairsplitting. I presume that in the present context a discussion of the meaning of "adult" would be allowed as possibly significant. In this regard I do not see the *Paper* as a whole to be sufficiently aware of the ambiguity of the word "adult."

In this section I cannot avoid commenting on the summary of me in a paragraph, pages 18-19 of the *Paper*. It is always a little dispiriting to see one's ideas summarized in a paragraph. However, I sympathize with the people who had to collate all this material in a short space. Put another way, I will try to be as nondefensive as I can in restating what I wrote in the second chapter of *Education Toward Adulthood*.

First, what I am interested in is the meanings of the word "adult." If someone thinks that this approach will not yield much fruit, she/ he may be right. But if what I have written and am saying is to be understood and judged, one has to know what I am trying to do.

As far as I can tell, no one else who is summarized in this section of the *Paper* is asking the same question that I am. I am unsure why I am tucked in between Erikson on one side and Bromley, Boelen, Levinson, et. al, on the other side. They seem to be engaged in dividing up adulthood into its appropriate periods, while I have nothing to say on that topic in Chapter Two of my book. Actually, I am stuck back on the opening sentence (p. 18) of this section, which reads: "Adulthood is the latter period of the life span, following adolescence and childhood." Is this assumption true? I think not, or at least it is only partially true, and the partiality obscures the questions of adulthood and adult development.

What gives me the right to say that the statement is not (adequately) true? Because I can point to innumerable examples of a different meaning for the word "adult"/"adulthood," some of those examples contradicting the opening assumption. I repeat that my method is *not* to say, "I think the proper definition of adult is . . ." but rather, "The meanings of adult as demonstrated by the way people use the word "adult" are. . . ." At some point later I advocate that one meaning of adult should be brought to center stage while we try to move another meaning toward the wings. Before I make such advocacy I need to know what are in fact the meanings of adult. Obviously, someone can debate my findings, but the evidence for debate has to be in reference to the question asked.

To illustrate my problem with the statement, "Adulthood is the latter period of the life span, following adolescence and childhood," one need only look at the summaries of the two authors following me. In Bromley's seven stages the third is called late adulthood, followed by four stages after late adulthood. All of adulthood (20-60 years) appears to be an intermediary stage between adolescence and the four stages of life that follow.

In the summary of Boelen we are told, "The entire categorization is included so that the context in which 'adult' fits can be noted." Then we are given ten stages which end at 45. Is that really the whole context in which adult can be understood? There is nothing very unusual about these two summaries. It is very common practice to use adult/adulthood in such a way that adulthood is *not* "the latter period of the life span." Anyone who cares to study the usage in the Unites States today will find that adulthood is something that comes and goes. A few writers seem to know exactly what they are doing by this usage. More often we are affected by cultural assumptions concerning connotations of the word "adult." The cultural pressure leads us to a confusing and inconsistent use of the words "adult"/"adulthood."

A second main point I wish to make in this section is to note that the word "adult" functions as both adjective and noun. It is more complex and confusing than the word "child." When I use the word "child," everyone knows I am referring to persons of a certain age. If I wish to refer to the qualities the child supposedly has, I have two adjectives at hand, namely, "childlike" and "childish." We can discuss the ambiguities of childhood by using one adjective that is strongly positive and one that is strongly negative.

I think we are often trying to do something parallel or analagous with the word "adult." Studies of adult development are attempts to get at not only what it is like to be an adult but what it is like to be adult. Lacking the adjectives "adultish" and "adultlike," we use one word to cover the ground of one noun and two adjectives. We have a severe conflict over the desirable way to be adult, but we lack the words even to state the question.

My third point in this section is that the distinction of nominal meaning and adjectival meanings of adult led me into sorting out the two differing ideals of being adult. The point of *Education Toward Adulthood* (which the *Paper* does not indicate) is to show that these conflicting ideals are embedded in imagery, language, and institutions. I trace the conflict of two consistent patterns in educational, religious, social, developmental, and service spheres (Chapters 3 to 7).

The first sentence about me (page 18) says that "[he] attempted to define 'adult' and holds that the best operative meaning of adult is the *ideal of maturity.*" That does not convey very well what I attempted. My interest, as I have said, was not to define adult but to locate its meanings. I group these meanings in four categories, admitting that one could divide further but that four are accurate enough for my purposes. Of the four meanings the third and the fourth hold out an ideal, a set of qualities (e.g., economic independence) which people will find or should find desirable. If I then restrict discussion to these two ideals of adulthood, I do think one of them is preferable. In fact, I think every person in this culture thinks that one or the other is preferable. I advocate making clear what the choice is and then getting consistent means to enhance the possibilities of the more desirable ideal.

I do not hold that "the best operative meaning of adult is the *ideal of maturity.*" No one of the four meanings is "best"; when referring to simple matters of chronology, then the chronological meaning is the best, or at least it is the appropriate meaning. Between the two meanings that refer to an ideal or to qualities of human life, I said I think one meaning is "better," in the sense that I would advocate changing our institutions to make that ideal possible for more of us in more effective ways. To say that I want to make that ideal the ideal of maturity is not a false statement in the *Paper,* but it is nearly tautological. Maturity just as much as adulthood demands a filling out of meaning. The *Paper* does try to do that in the next sentence with a set of my phrases.

My fourth and final point here is to suggest what is at stake in the conflict over ideals of adulthood. The first ideal is the one I describe as dominating modern Western thought. The influence of the mathematical and experimental sciences is evident. Perhaps even more significant, though not usually obvious, is the form of our economic life. The adult as descriptive of desirable qualities is stated in psychological terms with emphasis on what the modern world has decided is rationality (the ability to think abstractly and thereby distance one's thinking from the physical world). In economic terms (again what the world since the 18th century chooses to call economics) there is emphasis upon being a productive, jobholding, useful member of society. Small wonder that old people tend to disappear off the scale of adulthood.

Most people are caught within this dominant ideal of adulthood because they have not the desire or the means to escape from it. In fact, I am not sure that anyone can fight his/her way out of this framework so long as the existing ideal is so strong. Nonetheless, one can open some zones of freedom and get a sense that one is taking some small steps in the right direction. With my preceding comments I have given away my conviction that this modern ideal of adulthood is bad—in the long run, bad for us all. I did say that some people have no desire to escape the confinement of this ideal. Obviously, they do not think that it is so bad, and—in the short run, at least, before they cease to be adult—they see it as a good thing. I would say that if you are born white, male, healthy, to rich, white, United States parents, this ideal may look tailor-made for you.

I will cite one author who clearly and thoughtfully puts forward this position. In *Personal Destinies* David Norton has a chapter entitled "Stages of Life: Childhood, Adolescence, Maturation, Old Age."[3] In the text adulthood is used interchangeably with maturation. The author tries to find an ideal form for each of the four stages, but there can be no doubt that life moves upward to Stage 3 and then suffers a sharp decline in Stage 4. Human life matures until adulthood, to be followed by something after adulthood when human life is not going anywhere. An immediate question one would have to ask is whether suicide would not be appropriate whenever one is sure that maturity has disappeared. Norton, like many other philosophers, would prefer to see a dignity in accepting the fact that one's life has been lived. Up to now our culture has been willing to let people die at their own pace (though it is not only the present administration that is impatient with the growing number of Social Security recipients). We may be lucky that all the consequences of this ideal of adulthood have not been drawn or that we still live off the residue of a religious way of looking at life.

I am suggesting that this ideal is nonreligious and possibly anti-religious. It may have a place for religion of some kind because it is capable of taking any human concern and turning it into a product or a commodity. Religion then becomes a good thing if you find it useful to get you through the night or the next stage. However, the most mature do not need it. Children have it, and the old may need it, and women seem to take to it. The healthy, adult, white males who are running things do not need that commodity. I would suggest that much of the literature on adult education, adult learning, and Piagetian epistemology assumes this ideal of adulthood. To its credit, much of the literature today under the aegis of "adult development" is struggling to find a different ideal. Put differently, researchers are finding that some of the aged, some women, some minority groups *have* a different ideal.

That alternative ideal I have tried to describe from several angles. I would say that its chief characteristic is an unresolvable tension between contrasting qualities or concepts (e.g., dependence and independence). The word "unresolvable" does not preclude reaching greater stages of integration, harmony, and peaceful co-existence. Adulthood in this meaning is something I move toward until death. To be consistent, I have to say also that it is what I am moving toward (and partially realizing) at age 6 or 16. This usage does not prevent me from using adult to refer to specific ages. However, "adult development in adult years" can be two different meanings of adult. One could also study "adult development" in preadolescents. As an adult can be childlike, so a child can be adultlike. I think it is legitmate to study people 20 to 45 years old, or 16 to 80, or any other age span. But adult development that would hold out an adequate adult ideal toward which to develop cannot exclude old people and children. The old have to be at least implicitly there as "the very adult," the most dramatic reminder of what we are all developing toward. The children have to be there not as the opposite of adult but as representatives of some facets of life that get obscured by people in certain age periods.

I do not take issue with the summary definition on page 29 of the

Paper that identifies "Adult Life Cycle" with the age period from adolescence to death (in contast to writers who explicitly or implicitly make it adolescence to old age). My concern would be that the major issue then seems to be dividing up those years into "stages of adulthood." What I have tried to indicate in this section is that shapes, forms, or stages of adulthood can be an almost entirely different question than dividing up the years from adolescence to death. This second question would eventually rejoin the first, but I think it must be asked separately. If it is not asked, then most of the forces of our culture will conspire to keep the dominant ideal just where it has been. We will all be developing, maybe more than people once did, in the "adult life cycle," but it will be down a track trying to join that elite who know what adult really means and have the linguistic and institutional powers to enforce their ideal.

III. Imagery

This section is a further illustration of how I would approach the question of maturity and adulthood. I claim one must fight for the words and especially one must notice the imagery presupposed by the words. Notice that the question is not usually the imagery advocated but the imagery assumed. If there are two conflicting meanings of adulthood, then there are likely to be two differing images always hovering in the background. How does one imagine the journey (if that is an appropriate image) of human life?

I would suggest that the first ideal is almost perfectly captured in the image of a straight line going up and forward. The second ideal is more difficult to imagine, but the closest one can come is a sphere. A religious way of thinking resists the closure of all human images, but the point is to work toward the least inadequate image before finally acknowledging that it, too, eventually fails. Note that the choice is not straight line versus circle. That choice is found in books which wish to prove that Christianity saved humankind from the despair of a closed circle and provided the only imaginable alternative, namely, an arrow. The choice I am describing is between an image that reduces to two dimensions (straight line and circle being minor variations) and a three-dimensional image which allows for an enormous range of variations.

The question, as usual, is not which is the right image or the true image. Obviously, both images describe something about human life, or else they would not be functioning in people's lives. My argument is that the image of an arrow is less adequate than that of a sphere to comprehend all of life's twists and turns. Not accidentally, the image of sphere cuts across Eastern and Western religions, primitive and contemporary forms of religion.

We can test the significance of this choice of imagery against the *Paper's* discussion of development and related terms like growth and progress. What image of development is asumed by writers on development? Or the question is: What has been the development of development? Who developed developmental theories? Do those people have sexual, economic, and other kinds of bias toward arrows? I know from conversation over the years with James Fowler that he has been acutely conscious of this question, and *Stages of Faith* (see Note 4) shows his struggle with the problem.

Today almost all writers on development show some trace of embarasment or nervousness about their theories. They feel caught in a bind. Why be interested in development unless one believes that the latter development is better than the earlier stage? Saying that aloud, however, seems to go against our democratic ethos and to claim that the writer/speaker is one of the better class of people.

Researchers can avoid some of the difficulty if they restrict the claim of what they are measuring. Thus, if Piaget's work is on the development of abstract thinking, I see no problem in claiming that the advanced stage is better than an earlier one. Does anyone deny that a twelve-year-old is better off *in this respect* than a five-year-old? Kohlberg's scheme would be less problematic if it were admitted to be a measuring of people's capacity for abstract thinking about moral dilemmas. One could hardly doubt that Stage 6 people are better than Stage 3 people in that respect. But Kohlberg gets himself into trouble, and his followers worsen the problem by talking of Kohlberg's scheme of "moral development." Then we are caught in what might be called the Kohlberg dilemma: Should we deny that Stage 6 is better than Stage 3 when everyone knows that the point of the system is to move up the scale, or should one make the arrogant claim to be among the most morally developed part of the race and capable of rendering moral judgments on everyone else?

Why do not Kohlberg and followers talk instead about measuring people's capacity for abstract thinking about moral dilemmas? Two reasons, I think. The first is that hardly anyone would be interested. Kohlberg had seemed to be providing the answer to part of the problem of the public school in the United States. That problem, which goes back to the origin of the public school, is the desire to provide morality without the "divisiveness of religion." I think that the desire is misguided and that Kohlberg's scheme cannot do the job. Whether or not anyone likes it, religion and morality are so mixed together that the premature and complete disjunction of the two realms obscures the questions of personal development.

The second reason for talking of "moral development" has more legitimacy. People who are teachers, clergy, or counselors really do need some guidance. To be a parent or even to understand oneself, one looks for some standards of moral excellence. Is it not appropriate to ask whether some ways of living are better than others, recognizing that this question unavoidably involves us in moral and religious judgments? I think that the desire is understandable and perhaps unavoidable. If we assume some ideal of maturity or adulthood (as I claim we all do), then we constantly render judgments on ourselves and others in relation to that standard. What modern scientific techniques might do is eliminate some of our worst biases, provide us with a wider range of data, and remind us that individually and collectively we are all fallible.

The *Paper* says that the stages are not hierarchical (pp.42, 47). I would agree that that is desirable if by hierarchical one assumes an image of an arrow going up and forward. (One might try to recover other religious meaning from the word "hierarchy" but I am assuming it is stuck in the image of higher and lower.) Avoiding a hierarchy can be attempted by flattening all choices to a supposed equality. The other possibility is that one can undertake a larger revision to an image that does not ask: top or bottom. The image of a sphere and the movement toward its center provide a better basis than an arrow on which to render our fallible human judgments. Theories of development that try to be "nonjudgmental" about religion and morality come down hard on the side of maturity meaning cool and calculative objectivity. What then governs life are a polite etiquette for those who can make the grade and varying degrees of coercion for those who cannot.

Although growth and progress are heavily invested with the imagery of the arrow, we probably cannot speak today without such words. The task is to bring resistance to some of what governs their imagery. The metaphor of growth seems to come from the biological world. John Dewey popularized the image in education, but he spent his latter years trying to distinguish the kinds of growth that educate and the kinds that miseducate. After all, in an organism growth occurs rapidly at the beginning, and then a kind of steady state is reached. Presumably that is the reason why the adult was neglected by developmentalists, that is, because of the uncritical application of a biological image to the whole human realm.

The fight today for a share of developmental turf by students of the adult might simply toss them into the other main source of the growth image: economics. Our modern economies (and individual economic lives) are strongly bent toward the principle that growth means expansion and increase. Whereas in the organismic world unlimited growth can mean cancer, economics comes down on the side of the expansion of wealth. I know of no arguments whether a 12% CD (Certificate of Deposit) is better than a 5% passbook account. No one has trouble imagining the growth of money. We presume that biology is the source of our meaning for growth, but when that fails we unconsciously turn to economics. Do we have any other way to imagine growth? In Neugarten's study of middle age and aging, the years after midlife are described as "regressive growth." I presume she is playfully stating a near contradiction in terms. Can we find sources that might make sense of such growth? Perhaps there cannot be a science of human development, including "adult growth," without drawing upon art, morality, and religion. We render judgments on the growth of an artist using standards other than biology and economics. For many centuries people have sensed that there is moral, spiritual, and religious growth.

A traditional language that spoke of spiritual progress or spiritual growth cannot be easily integrated into contemporary language. Perhaps much of that tradition should be left to rest. However, there is one point about the tradition I would like to stress here. A person could grow in the virtues, and other people could recognize such development. Since a person had to integrate the virtues, it was more difficult but not impossible to judge who was a "virtuous person." What was not forgotten, however, was that a person was capable of backsliding and that a person of great moral/religious development could perpetrate terrible crimes. No maxim in medieval philosophy is more important than "the corruption of the best is the worst."

I do not think that the Middle Ages reflected a great deal on the imagery needed to express this conviction. They did not have to contend with the widespread counterassumption that moral development goes forward and upward through invariant stages. My image of life being ordered around the center of a sphere allows for some long-term circling, some shortcuts, and the permanent possibility until death that one can become morally/religious eccentric.

In religious terms the center of the sphere is God, who is always near but never under our control. I think religions claim to offer help in reducing the eccentricity of our lives in relation to the One

161

"who is closer than the great vein in your neck." Of course, the help consists in strange sayings that tell us to stop worrying about how to help ourselves and instead to receive the help we need. In Jewish and Christian religions the paradox is unavoidable of doing everything both as if all depended on us and as if all depended on God. We are therefore called to meticulous concern with moral/religious matters, while at the same time warned that we are not final judge of anyone including ourselves. Is that an unintelligible or impossibly complicated way of thinking? I think not, and I think there are women in Gilligan's study and Fowler's work who clearly illustrate this kind of thinking.[4]

I said "women" in the previous sentence because I am thinking of the Gilligan subjects, all of whom are women, and two of Fowler's interviews in *Life Maps* and *Stages of Faith*. Whether it must always be so or not, the image of a centered sphere is more likely to come from women than men. The *Paper* adverts to the discrimination against women in studies of adults (pages 26-27), though the question may be a larger one than stereotyped sexual roles. The corrective may require more than some additional data on women. If women were admitted as full-fledged members of the human race by researchers on development (and as researchers on development), it might change the very meaning of development.

The studies which assume what I call the first ideal of adulthood are relentlessly sexist in language and imagery. Norton's *Personal Destinies* that I earlier cited fits the bill. Another striking example is Roger Gould's *Transformations* (Simon & Schuster, 1978). He constantly opposes bad childhood and good (that is, rational) adulthood, the latter not seeming to include anyone over 50. Consistent with those assumptions is Gould's strongly sexist language. Ironically, the writer of the *Paper* uses he/she in summarizing Gould's point of view. Introducing "he/she" to someone's writing where it does not fit is not feminist progress. On the contrary, that tactic further obscures how sexist language is expressive of assumptions about political, social, and institutional life. Of the 76 entires in the bibliography I count 23 as authored or coauthored by women. That is extraordinary progress over surely what would have been the case ten years or even five years ago. Nevertheless, there are many new studies by women and/or about women that will need incorporation into this project.

IV. Faith, Belief, Religion

In responding to the third part of the *Paper* on faith development, I will discuss its treatment of faith, and then I will make some comments on Fowler's work. Since Kohlberg is treated in this part I will include an addendum on Kohlberg.

My discussion of faith will mainly be a wrestling with the work of W. Cantwell Smith. His influence is very strong in the *Paper,* and although he is mentioned on page 46, his name does not appear in the bibliography.[5] Following the lead of Smith, I will look at the relations of faith and belief, of faith and religion.

When I finished reading Smith's *Faith and Belief* a couple of years ago, I wrote a letter of appreciation to the author. I said that his exhaustive study of the historical roots of the word "faith" had taught me a great deal, including much I had not known about my own Roman Catholic history. I also said with great regret that I have what is perhaps an insurmountable difference with him over the use of the word "faith" in contemporary English. My difference with many Christian theologians is that they are trying to make the word "faith" bear a burden it cannot bear. In the most exalted meaning of faith that theologians praise, faith is nothing less and nothing more than a single subjective pole within a matrix of relationships. I think it is very dangerous either to neglect development or to speak in disparagement of words like belief, religion, doctrine, and revelation.

The *Paper* begins this section by listing quotations about faith (pages 30-32). None of these quotations is particularly clarifying. The summary on page 38 goes through a similar exercise, ending with the sentence: "These are but illustrative; the list could be endless." A list of quotations could perhaps be endless, but I dare say that the number of difficult choices about how to use the word "faith" is probably less than half a dozen. The quotations, at least for me, do not sharpen the issue of why and how thoughtful people disagree about the meaning of faith.

The thesis of Smith's book begins with the title *Faith and Belief,* and that is also where I begin my disagreement with him. What Smith is against is clear, namely, the reduction of the word "faith" to the meaning of the word "belief" in modern times. I am with him 100% on that stand. How does one then proceed to state an alternative? Smith's answer is that faith and belief mean two different things. I think that is an overreaction which results in a new kind of narrowness and dichotomy. Smith continually restates his position that Jewish, Christian, Hindu, and Muslim documents are all about faith and not at all about belief. The accuracy of that claim depends not only on what is in ancient documents but also on how one chooses to advocate a use of faith and belief in relation to contemporary meanings. Smith can write (page 38) sentences like: "That religious people are expected to believe something is a modern aberration." The statement is no doubt intended to shock, but it is neither very clear nor very effective in opening new doors. I would rephrase the claim to read: "That only religious people are expected to believe something and that religious people are expected only to believe something is a two-fold modern aberration." What I am suggesting is that instead of faith and belief being two discrete meanings, the meanings overlap. Faith is by far the richer term within which several meanings of belief can be found. Sometimes when people use faith they mean something equivalent to one of two verbs: to believe (in), followed usually by a person or something like a cause; to believe (that), followed by a direct object, often in the form of a sentence one accepts as true. Sometimes faith is equivalent to belief when the latter word is (perhaps intentionally) ambiguous; grammatically it is a noun, but the word refers to an attitude of mind, an active outlook on the world. Finally, faith in its most reduced meaning simply means belief(s)—the plural indicating this usage for sure—when the reference is to those objects of the verb "to believe that." I have not introduced any complexity into the relation of faith and belief that is not already present wherever ordinary Americanized English is spoken.

To sharpen the issue, I'll use the *Paper's* paragraph that starts on page 47: "Beliefs are ways by which faith expresses itself." I might have been able to accept this statement as a slightly peculiar way of expressing the relation, but the sentences that follow create the kind of dichotomy I cannot accept. Faith does not express itself; people express themselves. Those people (perhaps all people) who "have faith," that is, have an attitude toward creation of believing (in), express themselves in part with and in beliefs. Although "beliefs express faith," we need to be clear about what that phrase means, and specifically whether the meaning of belief is extrinsic or intrinsic to faith.

Let me use an analogy for this crucial distinction. A demeaning way of speaking of people who labor is to call them "hands." After a while managers can forget that the laborers are people not (exclusively) hands. I would be on the side of a reformer who insists that the laborers not be called hands. However, the reformer should not forget that the hands are the expression of the laborer, the means of livelihood for a farmworker or automobile worker and the reason why management ever developed the language of hands in the first place. I can put the issue dialectically by saying: My hand is me in that it expresses me; my hand is not me in that it does not fully express me. My hand is mine insofar as it has no existence separated from me; my hand is not mine insofar as the relation is not owner to owned possession. My hand is not inside me; my hand is not outside me. Notice that one can speak of a loaf of bread, a painting, or an automobile as human expressions; there is a range of meaning for the word "expression" when referring to these different objects, but those distinctions are not necessary for my analogy. My question is: Are beliefs to faith as either the Fords or the hands of Ford workers are to the laborers in Ford plants?

I think that the answer to my question is reflected in the rest of the paragraph on page 47: "[Beliefs] are the expression of the human's need to communicate and to translate experiences into concepts or propositions." I think not. Whatever verb might mediate between experience and proposition, it is not the verb "translate" because that verb presupposes propositions. The verb "translate" gives away the fact that human experience is unavoidably propositional. We translate from one propositional experience to another propositional experience. Faith exists only when part of its intrinsic meaning is belief. One cannot have faith and then secondarily and external to faith have beliefs.

The paragraph continues: "Beliefs . . . become something outside the individual to which the person can only intellectually affirm, deny or question." I do not agree. Why say that an expression, a formulation in words, is outside the person? My words are not outside me. Presumably the relation to a group or organization is referred to here. When a group to which I belong talks about *our* beliefs, some of those things may not be *my* beliefs. Discrepancies between individual and group should probably be expected, but many religious groups cannot face that fact. If there is extreme discrepancy I would have to consider severing my relation to the group or more exactly, consider whether the severance has not already occurred. When statements no longer expressing faith are recorded and left on shelves, they may be outside faith, but why call these things beliefs? They may have been someone's beliefs in the past, but there are no beliefs *outside all* human beings. If the *Paper's* phrase "only intellectually" is intended to exclude passionate involvement, I disagree again. People get very passionate about their own beliefs and other people's beliefs. I would wish to claim that anything deserving the name belief engages us in nothing less than an intellectual way, that is, with reason and emotion together.

My concern with the relation of faith and belief is part of my concern with the relation of faith and religious expression. The *Paper's* opening sentence under the heading "Religion" says: "A logical extension of the concept of faith is the meaning of religion." I do not understand that sentence, but note that the first two books cited, Belgum and Westerhoff/Neville, both seem to define religion as *including* faith. That subsuming of faith does not seem to be what the *Paper* intends, but the above authors who are cited may be closer to ordinary English.

In Christian writing, Catholic as well as Protestant now, the word "religion" is a poor stepchild to the word "faith." (It is noteworthy that Jewish writing does not go that route). I might be able to accept the disparagement of the noun religion if the line were drawn between it and the adjective religious, as in religious experience, religious symbol, religious education, and so forth. I do not see that distinction often made, so that the religious is also disparaged. As a result, the spectrum of bodily, social, institutional objectifications of the inner, personal activity of "believing in" and "believing that" is not what gets studied as important.

Any author who keeps telling me I should have faith instead of religion isn't addressing my problem at all. Obviously, if by faith is meant the gift by which God saves us, who is not going to praise that? If religion means some collection of dead things from another era being packaged by ad men today, few of us will praise religion. My problem is somewhere in between those two categories with a lesser meaning of faith and a greater meaning of religion/religious. I am involved in thinking, choosing, acting in ordinary and therefore ambiguous ways. I am involved in trying to be responsile, trusting and trustworthy, caring and careful. That means being loyal to people, to convictions, to some overall image of personal integrity. That is what I call my religious life. I hope it has developed over the years, though I imagine if someone studied it, he/she could criticize the development.

If someone were to ask me whether my faith has developed, I am not sure the question would register at all. At least I could only answer by distinguishing several meanings of faith. At the most profound level of its meaning, faith (as Smith found in Jewish, Christian, Muslim, and other history) means simply have you accepted rather than rejected God. Here faith is undifferentiated, and one cannot put an adjective before it. Are you believer or infidel? To this question about my faith I can only say: I have it, or I don't have it. I hope I have it, but only God knows. We, of course, can look for signs of whether faith is really there by studying a person's attitude to all of creation (and thereby God). Even in the contemporary world, where the religious meaning is seldom more than implicit, this usage of faith appears in politics, psychology, economics, or baseball. One is either a believer or not. The opposite of faith is nihilism. Some individual nihilism might be thought fashionable, but our contemporary world knows (far more clearly than the 18th and 19th centuries knew) that the world cannot exist without faith. In Alexander Bickel's saying: "No one wants everyone not to believe in anything."[6]

Another possible meaning to someone's asking about the development of my faith would be an inquiry into my beliefs. I think that question is a legitimate one though not a particularly profound one. My beliefs are important but perhaps not so important as many other activities of my life. In the PBS television series *The Long Search* the narrator asked almost every group: What do you people believe? Invariably, they looked puzzled and said: Why ask that question? Why don't you come see and perhaps even participate in the way we live?

My comments on Fowler will be brief. I have the highest admiration for his work, and I think he has an invaluable collection of data on which to base our reflections. I have expressed to him many times my reservations about his use of the word "faith." I do not so much have a personal disagreement with him as a difference with how contemporary Christian theology is trying to right itself with its own past and with the contemporary world. Fowler relies heavily on Smith, with whom I have expressed disagreement. He is also rooted in H. Richard Niebuhr, for whom I also have great respect. I just wish Niebuhr were here to rewrite his fine book of forty years ago, *The Meaning of Revelation*. I will simply raise some questions that might help to start conversation with Fowler.

1. Following his use of Smith, Fowler writes in *Stages of Faith* (page 14): "The failure to probe beneath this shallowing of faith, equating it with the modern understanding of belief, means to perpetuate and widen the modern divorce of belief and faith." I cannot understand that sentence. I agree that faith to a large degree has been shallowed so as to be equated with belief. But that image is incompatible with talking about a modern *divorce* of faith and belief. In fact, it is Smith who is advocating if not divorce then estrangement. The modern world to its own good has not divorced faith and belief. Smith and Fowler are the ones proposing a separation.

2. I think that Fowler with the word "faith" and sometimes despite the word "faith" is describing the complexity, ambigui-

ty, and movement in people's lives. As a result his language and imagery do include some circling back. The movement has at least some similarity to a sphere and to moving around a center. Fowler sometimes uses a diagram of two cones, one inverted inside the other.[7] The earliest stage of an undifferentiated faith makes possible a circular movement later.

3. I think one could read Fowler's early stages as parallels with Kohlberg's. The real test, however, is where the scheme goes when it gets to stages 4, 5, 6. I am impressed with the complexity that arises in Stage 4 and then the crucial move beyond that point. The interviews which he puts in Stage 5 speak to me the most. In *Stages of Faith* (page 194) he writes: "as is characteristic of Stage 5 it was a new beginning that had to reclaim and reintegrate elements of strength from her childhood faith." I would only have the concern again that the word "faith" may not be able to carry the whole burden of this circling back and of reintegration in the present.

I am somewhat troubled by Fowler's comment (page 211) that when he talks about stages of faith "it is always Stage 6 that people are most interested in. The more 'secular' the audience, the greater the interest." Is that because people—especially "secular" people—are waiting for the answer at the top when the ambiguity is left behind, the knot is untied, and we enlightened ones can see how it all fits together? Is there a false expectation suggested by all such theories of development, and, if so, does that expectation need to be explicitly disallowed? Maybe it is my own underdevelopment, but I am not expecting anything further or greater in this world than what Fowler characterizes as Stage 5. In *Life Maps* he has an excerpt of an interview with a monk who is classified as Stage 6. The man may be well developed in faith but the printed words left me unpersuaded that down that path is progress. In *Stages of Faith* there is no interview for Stage 6. Instead there are a number of names (e.g., Gandhi, King, Bonhoeffer, Mother Teresa). I simply do not see how those people form a structural group.

Addendum: Kohlberg

My remarks here are mainly to relate Kohlberg to Fowler. The *Paper* (page 32) begins by saying: "Fundamental to any study of

Faith Development is the pioneering research of Lawrence Kohlberg in Moral Development." I do not know why that is the case except that Kohlberg seems to have influenced the kind of classification system which Fowler developed. At this point in the development of development, we should note the discontinuities as much as the influence.

From what I can piece together in Kohlberg, he has supposed the exploration of faith stages as an interesting project that might parallel his own scheme. On occasion, however, he argues the question of whether faith stages precede or follow his moral stages. I doubt that this question at all acknowledges the ambitious project which Fowler and others intend by faith stages.

Kohlberg as a product of our Western rationalistic culture is able to put faith next to reason and even to dabble in the posibility that faith is *above* reason. What he does not acknowledge is the question: Does modern reason make sense at all without the originating attitude of "believing in" and without reason itself being a form of belief? I think Fowler and James Loder are looking for a different way of knowing that subsumes modern technical reason.[8] The most developed knowing would then be rooted in community, conviction, and commitment. In other words, I wonder what Kohlberg would think of his scheme being a somewhat minor variation within Fowler's.

At times Kohlberg almost seems to admit something of that kind. His formulations, however, are a standard brand of rationalism, as in the early Wittgenstein: "Whatever can be said, can be said clearly; beyond that is the mystical." Kohlberg takes us up the scale (in Wittgenstein it was a ladder) to the one principle which governs all below. Having made each stage depend on the one above, he comes to disappointment at Stage 6. At this point the question is very simply, "Why be moral?" And Kohlberg's six stages have no answer. But then appears a superstage: "The faith orientation rquired by universal moral principles I call stage 7 through at this point the term is only a metaphor."[9] Indeed, the term is (nothing less than) a metaphor as is the whole developmental scheme. The question is, how good a metaphor is it? My impression is that the whole metaphor of stages needs reexamination on the basis of Fowler's alternative and other major criticisms of the last decade.

In summary, I do not think that we can take what reason has come to mean since the 18th century and simply add faith to it. Part of my skepticism about the term "faith development" is that it may not force us to confront the centuries-old split of faith (for those who like that kind of thing) and reason (for those who just want the hard facts). I know that Fowler is struggling against the modern dichotomy, and maybe his use of the word faith can do it. But faith is one of the two categories caught in the dichotomy. One cannot reconstruct reason without bringing outside help to the word (e.g., intelligence, experience, symbol). Modern reason cannot reason its way out of its predicament. Faith needs help, too, from words that have been relatives through the centuries (e.g., trust, virtue, revelation). Even if faith is claimed to be the most important category, might it be viewed at times through other lenses?

V. Interface

My response to this all too brief section of the *Paper* will try to make connections to what I have already written and to what are needed concepts for the study.

My first and main point is that I think the word "interface" is thoroughly inappropriate. I admit to having a general prejudice against the term. In this case I think I know why I do not like it. The metaphor of interface comes today from the computer world (which borrowed it from either the seamstress or the geologist) and connotes two things or two columns of numbers juxtaposed. This project is investigating the possibility that seemingly disparate issues may at some level interact, interplay, interrelate. The ideal relation might be a mutuality in which each element corrects, enriches and transforms the other. In actual practice, before there can be mutuality, there may have to be a stage of simply resisting the powerful partner's tendency to swallow the opposition. The term "interface" captures neither of these activities.

The religious in life has as much right to be heard in public as the language of technical rationality (including such words as interface). However, we do not start from a position of equal partners but from a world in which one kind of knowing is most valued and one image of development is so dominant that we can hardly imagine other meanings for the word. Those of us interested in religiousness and faith may have to spend the coming decades just reminding scientific researchers that they have altogether neglected or badly distorted the faith/religious question.

In some ways it is fortunate that studies of adult development are at such a primitive stage. They might still be susceptible to change of language and imagery. A protest in the name of faith/religiousness might actually get a hearing. Gail Sheehy, who did a respectable job in summarizing studies of adult development, also made some protest in the name of women. The same cannot be said of religion. In her original manuscript Sheehy had a section on religious experience that her editor cut out. I would have liked to have seen what she had there because the published book *Passages* (Bantam, 1977) does not show much feel for religious questions. What Sheehy identifies as religious, the confinement of beliefs imposed in childhood, is an obstacle to maturity or adulthood. Sheehy says she is interested in religious matters, but I think it is a foreign country to her. Or, more sadly, she may be in a country where the language is spoken and she does not recognize it.

One of Sheehy's key words is crisis. I agree with the *Paper* that this idea might be a bond between what are assumed to be ordinary secular concepts and faith/religious ideas. I think, however, I would try to push the question back one step from crisis to limit. The word "crisis" suggests that one has reached some kind of limit and that previous ways of acting are no longer appropriate. Crises concern whether a limit can be passed and, if so, how a limit can be surpassed. Limit is a metaphor which needs more exploring than it usually gets. I have looked with little success for someone who could explain how the image of limit case in mathematics is or is not being assumed when developmentalists use the word "limit." If an important metaphor is not examined, then I suspect we assume a literal and reduced meaning. In this case we might assume a person walks up to a line and then steps over it. How does one imagine limit in a spherical image?

Limit, with all its possible meanings, is intimately tied to religious history: the story of finitude in relation to infinitude. Everything that is created and visible to us is finite (has limits) according to Jewish, Christian, and Muslim traditions. Yet the human animal has infinite pretensions or in any case is not satisfied with anything finite. We need to bring some of religion's sophisticated dialectic to bear on our little crises in life. Religious people have always known quite well that birth and death are two crises of grand proportions. As researchers fill out the description of intermediary crises, the religious meaning of crisis ought to be insisted upon. When a 35-year-old business executive wakes up some morning and says he does not care about getting out of bed anymore, he may be having besides a job crisis a faith/religious crisis.

It would be intriguing though too glib to say that secular developmentalists should study the stages and the faith/religious researchers could study the transitions. The word "conversion" is a fine, old term that should be worked into this framework. Fowler is

171

very cautious about identifying religious conversion with a change of stages. He uses conversion for significant change in the contents of faith and distinguishes that from structural stage change (*Paper*, p. 49). I think I understand his point. However, it is possible there are several kinds of conversion? Would there be an advantage in using conversion for stage change, too? Could that better bring together structure and content? A use of conversion as a central image could be a way to resist the secular developmentalist tendency to imagine lines forward and upward, and at the same time to resist religious groups who use conversion to refer to God crashing in from above. Neither group respects the meaning of the word "conversion"; the two groups are closer to each other than either supposses.

VI. Hypotheses: Some Comments

I wish to make an extended comment on hypotheses #10 and #15 and then go back over the others to question the formulations.

What struck me in #10 and #15 is the use of the word "community." I was surprised to see that word in the hypotheses because it is so much in absence from the *Paper* as a whole. The word "community" (as well as communal and communion) appears about a half dozen times in the *Paper*. I had begun to think that someone had systematically excised the word. I could understand that the word "community" has been so overused, misused, and abused that someone might feel it should be abandoned. I do not share that view, and in any case a simple abandonment would not face up to the issue.

The uses of the word on page 32 and page 50 are in connection with Westerhoff/Neville talking about religious ritual. However, on page 50 and then again in hypothesis #15 the phrase used is "faith community." I know I am out of the mainstream here, but I simply have no idea what is meant by faith community. The phrase has become common in recent years. Previously one heard more about a religious community, a term that does mean something to me. A person's attitude of believing in (God/creation) finds expression, support, development in the language, art, ceremony, architecture, and so forth of a religious community.

While I do not know what "faith community" means and therefore cannot comment on the disagreement referred to in #15, I have no doubt whatever that faith develops (in those aspects which can be said to develop) in a religious community. For me that is hardly more than a definition of terms. The real problem is to identify what deserves to be called one's (religious) community. A church, or a subdivision of church, may love to call itself a community, but that does not make it so. Hypothesis #10 (as well as #17) is part of this question. For some people their ethnic group may supply part of the meaning of community, though I would resist the inclination to think of community as an ethnic question. My suspicion is that very few of us today have "a community." Cultural diversity and personal mobility have radically changed but by no means eliminated the need for and the existence of community. If we are fortunate, we have several levels of community today. We have a small circle of family/friends who give us affection and identity. Then most of us have overlapping circles of groups we influence and are influenced by. The meaning of community can shift around considerably, can widen or narrow on different occasions. For that reason I like to talk of the communal relations in our lives that are partial embodiments of a greater community still to be realized.

As the last sentence indicates, my concentration on the word "community" and my concern with its near absence have to do with our image of where development moves. I cannot imagine writers like Stanley Hauerwas or Alisdair McIntyre writing about development without community being the central issue.[10] The growing uniqueness of the person is either toward greater exclusivity or toward greater and greater communion. My understanding of Judaism and Christianity is that they are religious of communion and community: the union of humans which differentiates as it integrates. Development in such an image means loving the one who is close and in need as a sign one is willing to love the neighbor who is farthest away. In principle, no creature can be excluded from an attitude of respect, care, and thanksgiving. Death is entrance to a more embracing communion with the whole world.

Hypothesis #2. The issue is important, but it contains a paradox: If adults in their 20's are not generally very conscious of "life's ultimate values," then does that become their appropriate stage of faith development? That is, they are concerned with faith development precisely by not being much concerned with faith development. To repeat myself on this point, I think the category of religious development would much better state the case. Young adults continue to develop religiously whether or not they give much thought to faith development. Their faith has become embodied in images, symbols, institutions, and ceremonies. These things continue to develop, even if almost imperceptibly, until young adults experience a crisis in their settled lives.

Hypothesis #3. I would plead for a replacement of the words "formal education" by schooling. The phrase "formal education" was invented by school people to obscure the fact that there are a number of forms of education. I would also like to see the words "traditional religious relationships" explained. I suspect that what is meant here is that the individual's behavior no longer agrees in full with the larger religious organization to which she/he belongs. For example, it might be a Catholic who seldom goes to Sunday Mass or a Jew who does not obey the dietary laws. What may have happened is that the person has redefined what "in and out" of the organization means. I do think it is important what increased schooling has an effect on this issue.

Hypothesis #7. The concern with people over 65 in some ways parallels #2. While young adults may not think much about faith development the old may not be explicitly thinking about either faith development or death. Even more than with the young, the attitudes of the old have become embodied in their persons. I think it has been shown in other studies that the old do not wish especially to talk about death. Their focus is on a way of accepting life and doing the best they can with the time given to them. How the concepts of life and death are integrated seems to me the issue. Studies of the old that concentrated on such things as frequency of church attendance distort the question of faith/religiousness in old age.

Hypothesis #8. The question of developmental tasks is an intriguing one. I would like to see some examples of what might qualify as a task. Robert Havighurst's attempt to list tasks (pages 22-23) seems to me to go well beyond any knowledge we have of what every human being has to learn to do. On these same pages, however, it is stated that some of Havighurst's 21 tasks are "somewhat dated," and need updating. I would agree, and I hope the implication is not that we should find 21 tasks that are up to date with "contemporary life-style." What is revealed by the datedness of his list of 21 is that we do not know 21 things that every human being is supposed to learn to do. What Havighurst listed in the 1940's is not surprisingly male biased. It was a rather well kept secret in modern history that the important tasks—the essential tasks— were mostly done by women. If I were to try listing the tasks, I am sure every adult must learn, I do not think I could go past 6 or 8. (They might show some correlation with what were called the corporal and spiritual works of mercy.) Barbara Myerhoff in her study of an old people's center describes the women as contented "perhaps because they did what has to be done, did it as well as it could be done, and knew that without what they did there would be nothing and no one."[11]

Hypothesis #9. I think the statement of the hypothesis is good. I disagree with the first sentence of the explanation. I grant that adult education literature does use as an axiom that adults must see immediate results, but I think this axiom is an obstacle to exploring the full range of educational possibilities with adults. Adults and children do have to see significance in what they are learning. The significance can be a broad philosophical and religious kind, not necessarily reducible to some immediate practical application. That statement is more true of adults than children. If anything, adult education literature has it backwards. We ought to be concerned with giving children immediate results as a symbolic embodiment of the greater results they cannot have while they are children in our society.

Hypothesis #11. I suppose that this thesis should be asked, though I would certainly hope the answer is negative. Kohlberg's scheme does suggest a positive correlation with socioeconomic status, a phenomenon that means to me the scheme is class-biased as well as sex-biased. A correlation between socioeconomic status and "moral development" reveals how misleading the phrase "moral development" is here. That the rich and well-schooled are superior in handling abstract reasoning about someone else's moral dilemmas is no mystery. To conclude that the rich and well-schooled are better developed morally flies in the face of much of human experience including religious history. If people who are rich and well-schooled come out better at faith development, that would indicate a need to reexamine what is being studied and with what instrument.

Hypothesis #12. An hypothesis like this one belongs here. However, I wonder if there are two or three different questions being asked. Is the interest in whether women are more concerned with faith development or whether women are more concerned with *their* faith development? Or, possibly, are women more developed when it comes to faith? From reading the hypothesis' explanation, I gather that a negative finding is expected (especially if one is a feminist). But proving that women are *not* more concerned with faith/religiousness would not take us far. Why should it not be a more neutral statement about the ways men and women are probably the same and the ways we suspect men and women are different? Perhaps this one has to become two or three hypotheses.

175

Hypothesis #16. I have doubts that this one is more than a definition of terms. If one decides to apply the word "faith" universally, then one can perhaps make that stick. Here is one of those few times that the word "religious" shows up in the *Paper* and the usage is to create distance between the words "faith" and "religious." Why attempt to sever the link between faith and religious reality? (The words "persuasion," "affiliation," "relationship" do not clarify the issue here.) My preference is to define religious in a somewhat arbitrary way (just as one can somewhat arbitrarily define faith) as intrinsic to the human animal. Obviously, some people will not accept the word "religious" as applicable to them, nor will they accept the word "faith." Of itself that fact does not mean the usage is incorrect. We should never forget, however, that some people are extremely suspicious of extending faith/religious language to them. In any case, that something can be called faith/religious development in people not "formally affiliated" with a church, synagogue, or other institutions seems to be true by definition rather than be an hypothesis.

Hypothesis #18. The presence of a mentor figure is an interesting hypothesis to explore. It is related to but probably should be distinguished from the communal circles I referred to above. In contrast to most of the points the relationship of faith and adult research might be reversed here. Why ask if the mentor relation also functions in religion? Is not the mentor relation a reduced version of the guru/disciple relation found in so many religions? People in adult research might have more quickly recognized the mentor relationship in its good and bad aspects if they had known more bout religion. I think the hypothesis should be phrased to investigate the positive and negative sides of having a mentor or a religious leader.

Hypothesis #21. The final hypothesis restates my uneasiness about the entire conception of development. The assumption is that one moves to *higher* stages. Why higher? Perhaps so long as stages are numbered 1, 2, 3 . . . the pressure is irresistible to imagine that the movement is up (instead of integration around a center). I have little doubt that Kohlberg's 5 is higher than 4 and that his 6 is higher than 5. I would hope that Fowler's 5 is not higher than 4. I do not think the religiously developed find themselves higher. How they view themselves and what resources they draw upon in meeting big problems would be interesting to test.

Notes

1. Raymond Holley, *Religious Education and the Religious Understanding* (Boston: Routledge and Kegan Paul, 1978), page 38.

2. Edward Hulmes, *Commitment and Neutrality in Religious Education* (New York: Macmillan, 1979), page 11.

3. David Norton, *Personal Destinies: A Philosophy of Ethical Individualism* (Princeton: Princeton University, 1976).

4. See Carol Gilligan, "In a Different Voice: Women's Conception of the Self and Morality," in *Harvard Educational Review*, 47 (November 1977), pages 481-517; James W. Fowler, *Stages of Faith*, (New York: Harper & Row, 1981); in Lawrence Kohlberg's collection of articles, *The Philosophy of Moral Development*, (New York: Harper & Row, 1981), he dismisses Gilligan with one refrence in the whole book (page 354) despite the fact that Gilligan's work is a devastating critique of Kohlberg's assumptions.

5. W. Cantwell Smith, *Faith and Belief*, (Princeton: Princeton University Press, 1979).

6. Alexander Bickel, *The Morality of Consent*, (New Haven: Yale University, 1975), page 25.

7. James W. Fowler, "Faith Development Theory and the Aims of Religious Socialization," *Emerging Issues in Religious Education*, ed. Gloria Durka and Joanmarie Smith (New York: Paulist Press, 1976), page 20.

8. *See* James Loder, *The Transforming Moment*, (New York: Harper & Row, 1981).

9. Lawrence Kohlberg, "Education, Moral Development and Faith," *Journal of Moral Education*, 4 (1974), page 14; for his most extensive treatment of the issue, see "Moral Development, Religious Thinking and the Question of a Seventh Stage," in *The Philosophy of Moral Development*, (New YOrk: Harper & Row, 1981), pages 311-72.

10. *See* Stanley Hauerwas, *A Community of Character* (Notre Dame: University of Notre Dame, 1981); Alasdair McIntyre, *After Virtue: A Study in Moral Theory* (Notre Dame: University of Notre Dame, 1981).

11. Barbara Myerhoff, *Number Our Days.* (New York: E. P. Dutton, 1978, page 268.

James Fowler

(THEOLOGY), is Professor of Theology and Human Development, and Director of the Center for Faith Development at Candler School of Theology, Emory University, in Atlanta. He has emerged as an international leader in Faith Development during the past ten years with his pioneering research in the field, including his development of a stage theory of Faith Development. Dr. Fowler approaches the topic from a theological perspective, but his findings are grounded in extensive interviews with hundreds of persons. His major work in this area, *Stages of Faith: The Psychology of Human Development and the Quest for Meaning,* was published in 1981. In addition to his formal paper, his contribution to the SYMPOSIUM was particularly helpful in the clarification of the theological and developmental issues that arose in general discussion.

8

Stages of Faith and Adults' Life Cycles

Introduction

For most of my teaching career, issues of faith and human development have been central in my attention. Since 1972 my associates and I have interviewed nearly 400 persons, ranging in age from $3\frac{1}{2}$ to 90, in the effort to deepen our understanding of faith across the life-cycle. In various writings I have set forth an evolving theory on faith and human development.[1] As I speak and interact at this conference, therefore, and as I work through the compilations and proposals of the *Hypotheses Paper*,my contributions will necessarily be shaped by my own previous work in this area. For this reason it seems that the most helpful way I might begin is by setting forth, as economically as I can, an outline of the relevant parts of what I have come to call faith development theory. In presenting this brief overview I will indicate points at which either my previous work or the *Hypotheses Paper*–or both–call for correction or clarification. These preliminary indications will then receive more extensive treatments at later points in this study.

Faith

The term "faith" denotes a rich, multilayered phenomenon. My own effort conceptually to grasp and unify these many dimensions owes a great deal to theologians Paul Tillich, H. Richard Niebuhr, and Fr. William Lynch, and to historian of religion, Wilfred Cantwell Smith. From these various sources and others, and from personal observation and reflection, I have come to see faith as a complex phenomenon integrating at least the following characteristics:

1. A dynamic disposition of the total self giving character to a person's way of moving in life . . .

2. Arising from and correlated with a comprehensive image (or images) of the conditions of existence taken as a whole . . .

3. With both (1) and (2) being shaped by the person's commitments of trust in and loyalty to a center or centers of value, an image or images of power, and a "master narrative" or narratives, which orient her/him to patterns of order, coherence, and meaning characterizing the ultimate conditions of existence.

4. Like selfhood, faith takes form and is sustained in community; it is inherently relational. Our relations in faith are *triadic* and *covenantal* in form. Our investments of trust in and loyalty to other persons, and of theirs with us, are deepened and ratified by our *shared* commitments to centers of value, images of power, and master stories that transcend and include us and them, conferring value, significance, and truth on our lives.

5. Faith shapes its initiatives and responses in our lives on the bases of modes of knowing which combine imagination, valuing, or affections and reasoning in a complex "logic of conviction." The symbols, rituals, stories, and teachings of religious traditions as well as other ideological systems can become the mundane causes of faith's awakening and growth.

6. Faith, with the characteristics represented in (1) through (5), undergoes formation and transformation in the interaction of persons with the changing events and circumstances that constitute the force-field of their lives. As an ongoing process faith includes times of doubt, darkness, loss of orientation and meaninglessness, as well as times of disclosure, ecstasy, and profound intuitional participation in the character of ultimate reality. A person's self-awareness, intentionality, and conscious grasp of the elements or dynamics of his/her faith vary in accordance with the person's developmental level.

When viewed in these ways faith is not to be equated with *religion* or *belief*. Faith, so described, is a generic or universal feature of the human struggle for identity, community, and meaning. Religious traditions are the living, cumulative representations of the faiths of persons and groups in the past and present. Elements of a religious tradition can become gifts to faith's imagination, awakening, shaping, and forming new communities of faith. *Belief* or beliefs constitute an important mode for expressing and communicating faith, and are one of the vital constituents of a religious tradition (especially of western Christianity). But belief is not to be equated with faith. For contrasting religion and belief with faith, a statement by Wilfred Cantwell Smith is particularly helpful:

> Faith is deeper, richer, more personal. It is engendered by a religious tradition, in some cases and to some degree by its doctrines; but it is a quality of the person, not of the system. It is an orientation of the personality, to oneself, to one's neighbors, to the universe; a total response; a way of seeing whatever one sees, and of handling whatever one handles; a capacity to live at more than a mundane level; to see, to feel, to act in terms of a transcendent dimension.[2]

Human Development

To study faith as a central dynamic on human development, I have found it necessary to draw on two distinct but related families of life-span developmental theory. The first includes psychosocial theories of the life cycle; the second we will call constructive developmental theories. One of the pervasive ambiguities in the otherwise rich survey of literature included in this conference's *Hypotheses Paper* results from the failure to distinguish between these two bodies of developmental theory. To draw these distinctions at this point may serve the double purpose, therefore, of helping to set forth my own way of relating faith to human development, and of calling the conference and subsequent research efforts to take note of these important differences.

When we use the term "life-cycle" we are usually referring to ways of looking at the course of human life, taken as a whole, in terms of a succession of phases related to maturation, physiological changes, and the correlated alterations of self-image and social role which they bring. Daniel Levinson makes this point in some helpful ways:

> The term "life cycle" . . . suggests that the life course has a particular character and follows a basic sequence. According to the *American Heritage Dictionary*, the words "cycle" and "development" have the same root source: *kwel*. The Latin form of *kwel* is *colere*, the Greek *Telos*. They are sources for contemporary English words such as circle, evolve, completion, wheel, inhabit, culture, cultivate. The term "life cycle" contains the basic meanings of such words, but they are rarely made explicit. I would like to articulate two of the key meanings.

181

First there is the idea of a *process* or *journey* from a start-ing point (birth, origin) to a termination point (death, con-clusion). To speak of a general, human life cycle is to propose that the journey from birth to old age follows an underlying, universal pattern on which there are endless cultural individual variations. Many influences along the way shape the nature of the journey. . . .

Second, there is the idea of *seasons*: a series of periods or stages within the life cycle. The process is not a simple, con-tinuous, unchanging flow. There are qualitatively different seasons, each having its own distinctive character. Every season is different from those that precede and follow it, though it has much in common with them. The imagery of seasons takes many forms. There are seasons in the year: spring is a time of blossoming, winter a time of death but also of rebirth and the start of a new cycle. There are sea-sons, too, within a single day—daybreak, noon, dusk, the quiet dark of night—each having its diurnal, atmospheric and psychological character. There are seasons in a love re-lationship, in war, politics, artistic creation and illness. . . .

To speak of seasons is to say that the life course has a cer-tain shape, that it evolves through a series of definable forms. A season is a relatively stable segment of the total cycle. . . . To say that a season is relatively stable, however, does not mean that it is stationary or static. Change goes on within each, and a transition is required for the shift from one season to the next. Every season has its own time; it is important in its own right and needs to be understood in its own terms. No season is better or more important than any other. Each has its necessary place and contributes its spe-cial character to the whole. It is an organic part of the total cycle, linking past and future and containing both within itself.[3]

The metaphor of season fits well with that family of theories which Erik Erikson, with his broadening of the Freudian psychosexual perspective, has taught us to call *psychosocial* the-ories of human development. From the dawning of language and storytelling members of our species have used image, myth, and metaphor to characterize and distinguish different eras of the life cycle and to characterize the strengths, contributions, and limits appropriate to each. Homer's *Iliad* and *Odyssey* can be inter-preted as, among other things, depictions of the first and second halves of Odysseus's life, with the contrasting virtues, self-images, and strategies appropriate to each.[4] Plato built his educational theory on a groundwork of observations and accepted wisdom about the capacities and development needs of persons in the different ages and phases of life. Confucius had a clear and picturesque sense of the appropriate skills, attainments, and modes of self-investment in each era of one's life. St. Paul drew on a common store of wisdom in reflecting on modes of faith and knowledge possible in childhood and in full adulthood. Traditional Hindu wisdom saw the male life cycle in terms of four distinct eras, each with its distinctive tasks and directions of energy and care. Shakespeare grasped the different ages of life in vivid, humorous images as he depicted the movement from the infant ("Mewling and puking in the nurse's arms") to the old man lisping and whistling into second childhood.[5]

In our century since Freud, there have been Charlotte Buehler, Carl Jung, and Robert Havighurst, in addition to Erikson, and more recently, Sheehy, Gould, Levinson, Vaillant, Bridges, and a host of others, who have been given us more elaborate and detailed theories of "development tasks" and "predictable crises" in the course of life-span development.

Psychosocial theories of the life cycle appeal because they resonate with and extend our experiences and observations. They map the course or journeys of our lives. They help us identify the turnings and the dangers, the challenges and the satisfactions of each life period. They give us a sense of overall direction and meaning, provide names for our experiences, and afford a sense of solidarity with others who have preceded us or who will follow us in the journey. As reflective narratives constituting rich "everypersons' stories," they constitute the elements of a philosophy of life, helping us to anticipate and assent to the invincible movement of time and change which we experience.

Theories of the life cycle must be distinguished from and contrasted with the other major family of development perspectives. These we call *constructive* development theories. Constructive development theories have emerged more recently and have appealed to more specialized audiences than the psychosocial approaches. They have their rootage in the seventeenth and eighteenth centuries' philosophical concerns with epistemology. With the work of Descartes, Locke, Wolff, and especially Kant, modernity became preoccupied with understanding the bases for attaining rationally certain knowledge. This involved investigation of the *a priori* categories of thought which underlie critical reflection upon experience. With Kant and since, we have recognized that "reali-

183

ty'' is a construction or composition. He sought to illumine the operations of mind, not given in experience, which make reliable knowledge possible.

As an extension of Kant's critical philosophy, the idealists Hegel, Schelling, and Fichte gave phiolosophical accounts of the rise of critical self-awareness and of the evolution of human consciousness underlying it.[6] These ideas, joined with later nineteenth century offshoots of the theory of biological evolution, underlie the work of the twentieth century constructive developments J. Mark Baldwin, John Dewey, Jean Piaget, and Lawrence Kohlberg.

Constructive developmentalists (genetic epistemologists, as Baldwin called them) have taken Kant's account of the *a priori* categories of mind and investigated their orderly emergence in the process of cognitive development.

In my recent book I have dealt in detail with how faith development theory finds it necessary to expand the rather narrow understanding of cognition which characterizes the foci of Piaget's and Kohlberg's theoretical constructs and research. While referring you to that source for further reading, let us draw now in a systematic way some principal contrasts between life cycle and psychosocial perspectives on the one hand, and constructive development approaches on the other. This can be done most economically by way of the following chart:

	Psychosocial, Life Cycle Perspectives	Constructivist Developmental Perspectives
Focus of Theory	Changes in psychosocial relations and roles, including self-image, due to chronological aging, biological maturation, stabilization, and decline. Appeal to reader's personal experiences and observations of others in communicating the predictable developmental challenges or tasks of the healthy person.	The integrated operations of knowing, valuing, and interpreting which constitute a person's style of understanding and maintaining meaning. Concern with *how* (how (the structuring) person construes experience as well as with the *what* (the *content*) of the interpretations constructed.
Methods of Research	Clinical interviews providing life histories geared toward reconstructing the lifecourse as well as illumining the challenges and issues of the present. The most adequate research results from longitudinal data. Analysis yields theories of "eras," "ages" or "seasons" as well as understandings of transitional phenomena.	Semiclinical interviews involving the posing of problems or dilemmas (hypothetical or real) which elicit respondents' ways of constructing, interpreting, and formulating a position in relation to them. (In faith development interviews [Fowler] a life history is also taken.) Analysis yields both the themes of the *content* of moral-reasoning or meaning-making and the structuring operations of knowing and valuing underlying them.

View of Development	Epigenetic perspective: Schedule for the emergence and maturation of new capacities (physical, cognitive, emotional) across the life cycle, coordinated with correlated changes of social role, status, relationships, and images of self.	Genetically endowed potentials for operations of knowing and valuing which constitute successive "styles" of meaning-making. Operational structures do not emerge automatically as a function of chronological age and biological-social maturation. Structuring potentials are actualized under impact of environmental challenge, stimulation, and support. The stage-like patterns of operations emerge in a predictable sequence exhibiting greater adequacy resulting from increasing complexity, comprehensiveness, flexibility, and augmented capacities of self-transcendence and reflection.
Concept of "Stage"	A "Time," "phase," "Season," or Passage" of one's life characterized by an age-related set of existential issues or challenges, and by the inner growth and outer changes required to meet them. Closely tied to biological aging and to bio-culturally established "life-tasks," psychosocial stages come more or less on schedule and cannot be avoided.	The integrated set of operations of knowing and valuing which shape and interpret a person's constructions of experience. A stage is constructed not by the particular "contents" of a person's system of meaning, but by the "laws" or patterns of knowing and valuing which organize them. The operations constituting stages can be described in formal models. Structural stages emerge in a predictable sequence, invariant in order. Each includes and carries forward the operation of previous stages. Chronological age and maturation are necessary but not sufficient for stage transition; healthy persons may arrest or stabilize at any structural stage, becoming resistant to further structural transition.

Constructivist Stages of Faith and Adult Development

Of the seven stage-like positions we have described in constructivist theory of faith development, four have particular interest for students of faith development and the adult life cycle. I provide here two kinds of brief characterizations of these structural stages: the first will be prose summaries taken from the chapters on each stage in *Stages of Faith* (page numbers at the end of each section refer to that book). Following these prose summaries in each case will be a synoptic display of structural aspects of the stages as models of styles of knowing and valuing and of composing one's relatedness to self, neighbors, and the transcendent. These come from the chart on pages 244 and 245 of *Stages of Faith*. For detailed descriptions of these aspects see Fowler and Keen, *Life Maps*, pp. 60–95.

Stage 3. Synthetic-Conventional Faith

In Stage 3 Synthetic-Conventional faith, a person's experience of the world now extends beyond the family. A number of spheres demand attention: family, school or work, peers, street society and media, and perhaps religion. Faith must provide a coherent orientation in the midst of that more complex and diverse range of involvements. Faith must synthesize values and information; it must provide a basis for identity and outlook.

Stage 3 typically has its rise and ascendancy in adolescence, but for many adults it becomes a permanent place of equilibrium. It structures the ultimate environment in interpersonal terms. Its images of unifying value and power derive from the extension of qualities experienced in personal relationships. It is a "conformist" stage in the sense that it is acutely atuned to the expectations and judgments of significant others and as yet does not have a sure enough grasp on its own identity and autonomous judgment to construct and maintain an independent perspective. While beliefs and values are deeply felt, they typically are tacitly held—the person "dwells" in them and in the meaning world they mediate. But there has not been occasion to step outside them to reflect on or examine them explicitly or systematically. At Stage 3 a person has an "ideology," a more or less consistent clustering of values and beliefs, but he or she has not objectified it for examination and in a sense is unaware of having it. Differences of outlook with others are experienced as differences in "kind" of person. Authority is located in the incumbents of traditional authority roles (if perceived as personally worthy) or in the consensus of a valued, face-to-face group.

The emergent capacity of this stage is the forming of a personal myth—the myth of one's own becoming in identity and faith, incorporating one's past and anticipated future in an image of the ultimate environment unified by characteristics of personality.

The dangers of deficiencies in this stage are twofold. The expectations and evaluations of others can be so compellingly internalized (and sacralized) that later autonomy of judgment and action can be jeopardized; or interpersonal betrayals can give rise either to nihilistic despair about a personal principle of ultimate being or to a compensatory intimacy with God unrelated to mundane relations.

Factors contributing to the breakdown of Stage 3 and to readiness for transition may include: serious clashes or contradictions between valued authority sources; ; marked changes, by officially sanctioned leaders, or policies or practices previously deemed sacred and unbreachable (for example, in the Catholic church changing the mass from Latin to the vernacular, or no longer requiring abstinence from meat on Friday); the encounter with experiences or perspectives that lead to critical reflection on how one's beliefs and values have formed and changed, and on how "relative" they are to one's particular group or background. Frequently the experience of "leaving home"—emotionally or physicially, or both—precipitates the kind of examination of self, background, and lifeguiding values that gives rise to stage transition at this point.

Aspect:	Stage III
A. Form of Logic (Piaget)	Early Formal Operations
B. Perspective Taking (Selman)	Mutual interpersonal
C. Form of Moral Judgment (Kohlberg)	Interpersonal expectations and concordance
D. Bounds of Social Awareness	Composite of groups in which one has interpersonal relationships

E. Locus of Authority	Consensus of valued groups and in personally worthy representatives of belief-value traditions
F. Form of World Coherence	Tacit system, felt meanings symbolically mediated, globally held
G. Symbolic Function	Symbols multi-dimensional; evocative power inheres in symbol

Stage 4. Individuative-Reflective Faith

The movement from Stage 3 to Stage 4 Individuative-Reflective faith is particularly critical for it is in this transition that the late adolescent or adult must begin to take seriously the burden of responsibility for his or her own commitments, lifestyle, beliefs and attitudes. Where genuine movement toward Stage 4 is underway the person must face certain unavoidable tensions: individuality versus being defined by a group or group membership; subjectivity and the power of one's strongly felt but unexamined feelings versus objectivity and the requirement of critical reflection; self-fulfillment or self-actualization as a primary concern versus service to and being for others; the question of being committed to the relative versus struggle with the possibility of an absolute.

Stage 4 most appropriately takes form in young adulthood (but let us remember that many adults do not construct it and that for a significant group it emerges only in the mid-thirties or forties). This stage is marked by a double development. The self, previously sustained in its identity and faith compositions by an interpersonal circle of significant others, now claims an identity no longer defined by the composite of one's roles or meanings to others. To sustain that new identity, it composes a meaning frame conscious of its own boundaries and inner connections and aware of itself as a "world view." Self (identity) and outlook (world view) are differentiated from those of others and become acknowledged factors in the reactions, interpretations, and judgments one makes on the actions of the self and others. It expreses its intuitions of coherence in an ultimate environment in terms of an explicit system of meanings. Stage 4 translates symbols into conceptual meanings. This is a "demythologizing" stage. It is likely to attend minimally to unconscious factors influencing its judgments and behavior.

189

Stage 4's ascendant strength has to do with its capacity for critical reflection on identity (self) and outlook (ideology). Its dangers inhere in its strengths: an excessive confidence in the conscious mind and in critical thought and a kind of second narcissism in which the now clearly bounded, reflective self overassimilates "reality" and the perspectives of others into its own world view.

Restless with the self-images and outlook maintained by Stage 4, the person ready for transition finds him- or herself attending to what may feel like anarchic and disturbing inner voices. Elements from a childish past, images and energies from a deeper self, a gnawing sense of the sterility and flatness of the meanings one serves—any or all of these may signal readiness for something new. Stories, symbols, myths, and paradoxes from one's own or other traditions may insist on breaking in upon the neatness of the previous faith. Disillusionment with one's compromises and recognition that life is more complex than Stage 4's logic of clear distinctions and abstract concepts can comprehend, press one toward a more dialectical and multileveled approach to life truth.

Aspect:	**Stage IV**
A. Form of Logic (Piaget)	Formal Operations (Dichotomizing)
B. Perspective Taking (Selman)	Mutual, with self-selected group or class—societal
C. Form of Moral Judgment (Kohlberg)	Societal perspective, Reflective relativism or class-biased universalism
D. Bounds of Social Awareness	Ideologically compatible communities with congruence to self-chosen norms and insights
E. Locus of Authority	One's own judgment as informed by a self-ratified ideological perspective. Authorities and norms must be congruent with this
F. Form of World Coherence	Explicit system, conceptually mediated clarity about boundaries and inner connections of system

G. Symbolic Function	Symbols separated from symbolized. Translated (reduced) to ideations. Evocative power inheres in *meaning* convcyed in symbols

Stage 5. Conjunctive Faith

Stage 5 Conjunctive faith involves the integration into self and outlook of much that was suppressed or unrecognized in the interest of Stage 4's self-certainty and conscious cognitive and affective adaptation to reality. This stage develops a "second naïvete" (Ricoeur) in which symbolic power is reunited with conceptual meanings. Here there must also be a new reclaiming and reworking of one's past. There must be an opening to the voices of one's "deeper self." Importantly, this involves a critical recognition of one's social unconscious—the myths, ideal images, and prejudices built deeply into the self-system by virtue of one's nurture within a particular social class, religious tradition, ethnic group, or the like.

Unusual before mid-life, Stage 5 knows the sacrament of defeat and the reality of irrevocable commitments and acts. What the previous stage struggled to clarify, in terms of the boundaries of self and outlook, this stage now makes porous and permeable. Alive to paradox and the truth in apparent contradictions, this stage strives to unify opposites in mind and experience. It generates and maintains vulnerability to the strange truths of those who are "other." Ready for closeness to that which is different and threatening to self and outlook (including new depths of experience in spirituality and religious revelation), this stage's commitment to justice is freed from the confines of tribe, class, religious community, or nation. And with the seriousness that can arise when life is more than half over, this stage is ready to spend and be spent for the cause of conserving and cultivating the possibility of others' generating identity and meaning.

The new strength of this stage comes in the rise of the ironic imagination—a capacity to see and be in one's or one's group's most powerful meanings, while simultaneously recognizing that they are relative, partial, and inevitably distorting apprehensions of transcendent reality. Its danger lies in the direction of a paralyzing passivity or inaction, giving rise to complacency or cynical withdrawal, due to its paradoxical understanding of truth.

Stage 5 can appreciate symbols, myths and rituals (its own and others') because it has been grasped, in some measure, by the depth of reality to which they refer. It also sees the divisions of the human family vividly because it has been apprehended by the possibility (and imperative) of an inclusive community of being. But this stage remains divided. It lives and acts between an untransformed world and a transforming vision and loyalties. In some few cases this division yields to the call of the radical actualization that we call Stage 6.

Aspect:	**Stage V**
A. Form of Logic (Piaget)	Formal Operations (Dialectical)
B. Perspective Taking (Selman)	Mutual with groups, classes, and traditions "other" than one's own
C. Form of Moral Judgment (Kohlberg)	Prior to society, principled higher law (universal and critical)
D. Bounds of Social Awareness	Extends beyond normal class norms interests. Disciplined ideological vulnerability to "truths" and "claims" of outgroups and other traditions
E. Locus of Authority	Dialectical joining of judgment-experience processes with reflective claims of others and of – various expressions of cumulative human wisdom
F. Form of World Coherence	Multisystemic symbolic and conceptual mediation
G. Symbolic Function	Postcritical rejoining of irreducible symbolic power and ideational meaning. Evocative power inherent in the reality in and beyond symbol *and* in the power of the unconscious processes in the self.

Stage 6. Universalizing Faith

Stage 6 is exceedingly rare. The persons best described by it have generated faith compositions in which their felt sense of an ultimate environment is inclusive of all being. They have become incarnators and actualizers of the spirit of an inclusive and fulfilled human community.

Their readiness to relinquish themselves for the sake of love and justice at the moral and religious levels involves a significant shift in the standpoint from which they see the world and themselves in it. These persons, who have a profound indentification with and participation in an inclusive commonwealth of being, largely transcend a centration in the "I." For them, it seems, because the self has found its ground *in* and identity *with* being, their way of composing and moving in the world avoids much of the self-centration that limits and distorts most "normal" perception. In their vision there is a union of opposites that is not longer experienced as paradoxical.

Persons of universalizing faith are "contagious" in the sense that they create zones of liberation from the social, political, economic, and ideological shackles we place and endure on human futurity. Living with felt participation in a power that unifies and transforms the world, they are often experienced as subversive of the structures (including religious structures) by which we sustain our individual and corporate survival, security, and significance. They are often more honored and revered after death than during their lives. The persons who may be described by this stage have a special grace that makes them seem more lucid, more simple, and yet somehow more fully human than the rest of us. Their community is universal in extent. Such persons are ready for fellowship with persons at any of the other stages and from any other faith or cultural tradition.

Aspect:	Stage VI
A. Form of Logic (Piaget)	Formal Operations (Synthetic)
B. Perspective Taking (Selman)	Mutual, with the commonwealth of being
C. Form of Moral Judgment (Kohlberg)	Loyalty to being

D. Bounds of Social Awareness	Identification with the species. Transnarcissistic love of being
E. Locus of Authority	In a personal judgment informed by the experiences and truths of previous stages, purified of egoic striving, and linked by disciplined intuition to the principle of being
F. Form of World Coherence	Unitive actuality felt and participated unity of "One beyond the many"
G. Symbolic Function	Evocative power of symbols actualized through unification of reality mediated by symbols and the self

Earlier in this paper I took pains to draw distinctions between life cycle, psychosocial theories and constructivist developmental perspectives. With our brief overview of constructivist stages of faith completed, it remains in this section for us to ask how these constructivist faith developmental stages relate to the phases or eras identified in various of the psychosocial elaborations of the life cycle.

Daniel Levinson's account of the major adult eras (the twenty-year—more or less—division of the life cycle into four roughly equal phases or seasons) parallels nicely Erikson's older account of focal crises and developmental challenges. Though the particulars of both men's accounts are subject to ongoing revision as research continues, it is my judgment that the rhythm of the changing eras of adulthood which they have discerned will prove to be an enduring contribution. Assuming that this prediction proves correct, it makes sense to ask whether our research into stages of faith has yielded any insight regarding the ideal or optimal times of change for faith development stages and how such times might be related to the changes of eras Levinson and Erikson have described. The following chart shows the parallelism of transitions between these two types of perspective which seems on the basis of preliminary research to be optimal or ideal. The paragraphs following the chart provide a brief explanation.

Table 3.3 Psychosocial and Faith Stages: Optimal Parallels

Levinson's Eras and Erikson's Psychosocial Stages	Fowler's Faith Stages
Era of Infancy, Childhood and Adolescence	
Trust vs. Mistrust	Undifferentiated Faith (Infancy)
Autonomy vs. Shame & Doubt	1. Intuitive-Projective Faith
Initiative vs. Guilt	(Early Childhood)
Industry vs. Inferiority	2. Mythic-Literal Faith (School Years)
Identity vs. Role Confusion	3. Synthetic-Conventional Faith (Adolescence)
First Adult Era	
Intimacy vs. Isolation	4. Individuative-Reflective Faith (Young Adulthood)
Middle Adult Era	
Generativity vs. Stagnation	5. Conjunctive Faith (Mid-life and beyond)
Late Adult Era	
Integrity vs. Despair	6. Universalizing Faith

From *Stages of Faith* by James W. Fowler © by James W. Fowler, 1981.

A reflective examination of these parallels suggests that during the rapid revolutions in cognitive, psychosocial, and physical growth that occur during the years from birth to twenty-two (Levinson's first era), we recognize four different structural stages of faith. Not all children experience these faith stage transitions on this time schedule; some arrest or proceed more slowly, and it is not too unusual to find an adult whose faith outlook is best described by the structures of Stage 2. Ordinarily, however, Synthetic-Conventional faith does take form during adolescence and represents the culminating form of faith for the first era of the life cycle.

The period from seventeen to twenty-two, the time Levinson sees as marking the transition to the early adult era, corresponds with what appears to be the optimal time for beginning a transition from the Synthetic-Conventional toward the Individuative-Reflective stage of faith. For a variety of reasons many persons make the physical and psychosocial transition into adulthood without undergoing the reconstructive work of a faith stage change. As they encounter the various predictable and unpredictable crises of their twenties and thirties, many of this number will make belated and usually more difficult transitions in faith stage. Some never do. Only with extended longitudinal studies will we gain reliable knowledge on these matters. Our preliminary research suggests, however, that if the transition from Stage 3 to Stage 4 does not occur before or during the mid-life transition, it chances of occurring at all decrease markedly.

In sum, for some adults Synthetic-Conventional faith becomes a stable, equilibrated, lifelong structural style. For others it gives way, in the early adult era, to an Individuative-Reflective style. The structuring of this latter stage is ideally suited to the tasks and challenges of the first adult era.

Again, we find that for a fair number of adults this stage (4), formed in the twenties or thirties, becomes a permanently equilibrated style of orientation. Although it may suffer buffeting in the middle adult transition, it can persist and sustain persons through the middle adult years. Our knowledge of these matters is based on observation and conjecture rather than on solid longitudinal studies. My hypothesis is, however, that the work of the mid-life transition is better done if it includes or corresponds to a transition in faith stage as well.

It appears that at each of the major era transitions the shaping of the new era's life structure is enhanced if we bring new and enriched ways of being in faith to them. Put negatively, to approach a new era in the adult life cycle while clinging too tightly to the structural style of faith employed during the culminating phase of the previous era is to risk anachronism. It means attacking a new agenda of life tasks and a potential new richness in one's life meanings limited with the pattern of knowing, valuing, and interpreting experiences that served the previous era. Such anachronism virtually assures that one will settle for a narrower and shallower faith than one needs.[7]

Toward a Model for Theory and Research on the Stages of Faith and Adults' Life Cycles

In the previous section, I sketched the leads from my research regarding the optimal or ideal correlations between adult transitions in structural stages of faith and the movements between the *eras* of adult life cycles proposed by Erikson and Levinson. My discussion intended to make it clear that the pilgrimages in faith of many adults differ from what I called "optimal." Some adults arrest their structural development in the Mythic-Literal stage; others equilibrate for decades in the Synthetic-Conventional form of meaning making. For a significant number of a transition to an Individuative-Reflective style of faith occurs only in the late thirties or forties, resulting in a much more disruptive reworking of their way of being in faith than if the transition had occurred in their twenties. As this exampel suggests, a structural transition in one's faith stage may, in fact, be the precipitating factor in an otherwise unanticipated psychosocial crisis of substantial significance. When an adult man or woman in her or his mid-thirties begins to construe self, others, and life meanings with new depth of questioning, with a new inclusiveness of issues, and with a radical insistence on pressing to the bottom of things, those closest around him or her may react with dismay, withdrawal, anger, or a sense of baffled betrayal. For the person undergoing this reconstruction of faith, these responses—as well as the feeling of being at sea and confused—can lead to a sense that one is coming apart, or losing one's grip. Bob Kegan is fond of saying about the experience of structural stage change, "No, you're not going grazy; but you may be out of your mind!" Poignance and reality are added to this quip to recognize that a structural stage change in faith means a change of faith communities. That is to say, one finds it difficult to relate to the members of one's previous network of sustaining relations in faith, without modification, due to one's new ways of seeing and being.

Another significant dimension of this effort to see the relations between constructivist stages of faith and psychosocial changes in the life cycles of adults come into focus through the work of Richard Shulik on aging and faith development.[8] In his study of forty persons over age 60, Shulik administered Fowler and Kohlberg interviews, but also used interviews and projective tests to measure the quality of persons' awareness of aspects of the aging process. Developing a scale which he called "age-sense," Shulik could rate the range, subtlety, and impact of the cues—internal and external—that one is aging. He found significant distinctions between persons at faith Stages 3, 4, and 5 as regards the aware ness of aging. It does not go too far to say that the experience of aging as construed by a person best described by structural faith Stage 3 is, in important ways, not the same experience as that reported by the same-aged person best described by faith Stage 5. Shulik's research opens up very promising avenues for further inquiry: do persons best described by Stage 3 *have* mid-life transitions? If so, how do they construe nd make sense of them? How are their construals alike, and how are they qualitatively different from, the experience of mid-life transition as reported by a 4-5 structural stage transitional? We can see research of this kind focusing on the construal and ways of coping with *each* of the several predictable psychosocial "passages," as well as with unanticipated changes, disruptions, or losses to which all adults are subject. To address this range of issues, arising from the interfacing of structural developmental stages of faith with psychosocial crises or transitions, complicates and enriches both the theory of adult faith pilgrimages and the corresponding research direction that will be required to study them.

I will try in the latter part of this section of my paper to pull together in a unifying model the elements for a theory of the varieties of adult faith pilgrimages. But before an effort at unifying these elements will be very fruitful, I am afraid we must complexify things a bit further.

Bernice Neugarten has a very helpful way of sorting out conceptual confusions in the effort to model processes of human growth and change. In a recent article she warned of the dangers of too quickly linking the notions of adulthood and development:

> Because the term "development" has been used with such a wide variety of philosophical as well as scientific meanings, it will be strategic for purposes of the present discussion to avoid the awkward juxtaposition of the terms "adult" and "development," and to speak of the need for a psychology of adulthood in which investigators are concerned with the orderly and sequential changes that occur with the passage of time as individuals move from adolescence through adulthood and old age, with issues of consistency and change in personality over relatively long intervals of time, and with issues of antecedent-consequent relationship.[9] (*Underlining was added.*)

This warning points to the need to distinguish those factors in the faith pilgrimages of adults which may properly be identified as exhibiting "orderly and sequential changes that occur with the passage of time" from those that do not. And given our previous analysis, we can enrich her question further. We need to clarify which dimensions of change in adult faith pilgrimages link order and sequence with *time* in a necessary conjunction. These need to be contrasted with those changes which focus on qualitative, developmental restructurings, arising out of the interplay of life's dissonances and a person's readiness to reconstruct, but without being intrinsically tied to the controlling imperatives of time.

From Neugarten's own work we get a helpful characterization of the kinds of dimensions of personality which fall in this latter category—dimensions which show "orderly and sequential" qualitative developmental changes, but which do not emerge automatically with the passage of time. These, she says,

> . . .are issues which relate to the individual's use of experience; his structuring of the social world in which he lives; his perspectives of time; the ways in which he deals with the major themes of work, love, time and death; the changes in the self-concept and changes in identity as he faces the successive contingencies of marriage, parenthood, career advancement and decline, retirement, widowhood, illness and personal death.[10]

One can readily see the kinship between this kind of focus in developmental studies and that of the structural developmental stages of faith. In both, time (maturation) and psychosocial challenges are *necessary* factors in development, but they are not by themselves *sufficient* to bring about structural developmental change. Implied in Neugarten's approach is what Shulik makes explicit: adults deal with and construe their psychosocial crises and challenges differently in accordance with their general ways of structuring experience. If constructivist stages of faith continue to prove powerful and true, as regards their characterization of developmentally related (orderly and sequential) styles of making meaning, they will provide an important component in the more comprehensive, multidimensional theory we need for modeling the richness of faith pilgrimages in adult life cycles.

In concluding this section of my paper, I want to sketch briefly the interrelated components I am coming to see as necessary in any theory of adult faith development that will really help us. In what follows I ask you to think of these dimensions as denoting interpenetrating variables in the faith movement of adults through time. Some of these components may be more susceptible to survey research than others. Any thoughts we have about empirical testing and verification of the aspects of these components, or of the model as a whole, can be considered only after we have sketched the parts.

On the accompanying chart I have labeled the six components which I will try to interrelate in this model with the letters A through F.

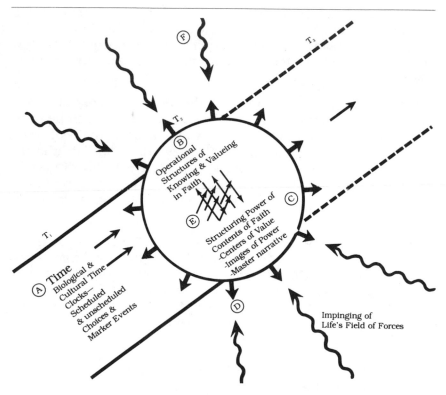

Toward a Model of the Dynamics of Adult Faith

By James W. Fowler, PH.D. For "Stages of Faith & Adults Life-Cycles" Symposium on Faith Development on the Adult Life Cycle

As you examine the chart, imagine that you are looking down from above at a dynamic model. The central ellipse is moving from left to right. It is three-dimensional, with E being a depth dimension interacting from below with the interchanges of B and C above. D means to include all of the arrows radiating from the central ellipse. These radiating arrows, taken with the ellipse, represent the dynamic shape of the adult's life structure (Levinson) at a given time (T_2). At other times (T_1 or T_3) the life structure will have had, or will take on, a new shape and pattern of relationships, involvements, and investments of the self. Let us consider now in more detail the components elements of the model.

The letter A points to the dimension of *time* and to the critical importance of time in adult faith pilgrimages. Psychosocial theories of the adult life cycle are providing, with varying degrees of complexity, a theory of the interrelation of what Neugarten has called the biological and sociocultural "time clocks." These internal and external clues pace the periodicity of predictable phases of building, appraising, modifying, and culminating the life structure of an era. In the effort to understand the character and dynamism of faith in an adult's life, it is of critical importance to know *what time it is in his or her life* and to have reliable knowledge of what existential issues and challenges predictably come with the time-fullness of this period of his or her life.

The moving ellipse in the chart represents the dynamic center of being, knowing, and acting which, in *interaction* with the impinging *Bio-Socio-Econo-Politico-Religio-Cultural field of forces,* constructs and alters a person's life structure. Within the ellipse I have tried to represent the intuiting, orienting, choosing, interpreting, committing, initiating, responding, persisting *activity of faith* as it exerts structuring power in the forming and maintaining of an adult's life structure—in time and in interaction with life force-field.

Within the central ellipse three sources for the structuring of meaning interplay in faith's structuring activity: the letter B represents the operational structures of knowing and valuing which underlie a person's appropriation and organization of the contents of her or his faith. The level of these operations determines the quality of a person's self-reflection, and her or his taking the perspectives of others. These operations, at any given stage, constitute the person's capacity for awareness of his or her values and commitments and affect the degree to which intentional self-responsibility for the direction of development in faith can be taken. These formally describable operations of knowing and valuing determine how a person will interpret and appropriate the meanings of symbols, stories, and concepts. This component of the model represents the dimension of faith development best accounted for in the structural developmental stage model with which I have most consistently worked. Depending on the structural stage of faith that best describes a person, he or she will have greater or lesser awareness of and responsibility for the structuring power of components C and E, to which I now turn.

The letter C in our central ellipse stands for the structuring power exerted by what I have, too glibly, called the "contents" of the person's faith. Referring back to our opening discussion of faith, I mean by *contents* of faith, three principal factors: first, the dominant center or centers of value, in relation to which the person's own living derives values, and by which he or she prioritizes the other "goods" in the life structure. Second, the letter C includes the image or images of power which elicit one's dependence and reliance for sustenance in a dangerous world of power. Though we rarely talk openly about our fears and anxieties, including centrally our fear of death for ourselves and our loved ones, how we align ourselves with power or powers promising us "more being" exerts a significant structuring influence in the choices and relations that constitute a life structure. And third, the letter C includes what I have called the "master narrative" by which we discern the patterns of power and value in action which give character to the conditions of our existence taken as a whole. Our "master stories" are the interpretive paradigms, conscious or unconscious, by which we make order or coherence of the force-fields of our life. They help us discern a *Tendenz* or overarching meaning into which we seek to fit—or to oppose—our lives.

In *Stages of Faith* I begin to tackle the issue—often neglected by structural developmental theorists—of the structuring power of the *contents* of faith.[11] But for the most adequate treatment of this component of our emerging theoretical model, we need to give careful attention to the school of religious ethics concerned with the "ethics of character."[12]

Now a word about the depth dimension in the central ellipse, represented by the letter E. There is neither time nor space here to do justice to this component. But no theory or model of adult faith pilgrimages can afford to neglect the powerful role of the dynamic unconscious in the shaping of faith, and in faith's contribution to building and sustaining a life structure. Only gradually in childhood do we separate and wall off the interaction of what will become the conscious and unconscious dimensions of mental and emotional life. From deep within the psyche, personal, social, and, perhaps, species memories give form, energy, and direction to our interests and attention. The capacity of certain stories or symbols to address us in moving and transforming ways results from their resonance with primal processes in the depths of our psyches that are largely inaccessible to conscious awareness and reflection. Yet they exert immense structuring power in our choices and affinities, and in our repugnances and aversions, as we form and change out adult life structures.

The patterns of interplay between the components we have labeled B, C, and E have their own developmental history, which, though very complex, are essential to understanding for any adequate model of development in faith.

I have not mentioned explicitly until now a sixth component of our model, that represented by the letter F. Earlier I referred to the impinging force-field of our lives, including among the influences that of religiocultural factors. Religion has a special function as *the* cultural entity concerned with the formation of faith. As we suggested at the beginning of this paper, religious traditions are the cumulative expressions of the faith of communities of persons from the past. As the bearers of religious symbols, of normative images of the human vocation, stories, ethical teachings, and so on, religious communities of faith can and do play a special role in the interaction by which faith contributes to the forming and re-forming of adults' life structures. Religious communities themselves are structured by the power of the *contents* of their shared faith visions. In their interactive invitations to adults—when they "catch"—they do so because of their resonance or interest uniting the persons' quest for a viable content and stance in life with the elements from the tradition's richness.

Other communities of meaning than religious ones (political parties, voluntary associations working for causes, and the like) can also be bearers of ideological and symbolic contents which can serve and attract faith constructions.

Such communities of interpretation, whether specifically religious or not, usually also have what I have called a modal/developmental level.[13] In the structural developmental perspective, such groups may be said to have an "average expectable level" of adult development. Persons are attracted to groups around their modal levels. An adult whose faith is structurally less developed than a group's mode will find himself feeling deviant in such a community. Equally important, an adult whose faith is structurally more developed than the group's will find herself experiencing alienation and perhaps being labeled as deviant as well. This issue of the modal developmental structural stage of groups may have great significance for understanding why persons are attracted and feel "at home" in certain groups. It may also explain why continuing membership in a religious group may stifle or retard further structural development in faith.

Finally, there should be a letter X on our chart. This would be to represent the initiatives of the divine toward us in our lives of faith. The questions of revelation, providence, and the work of God's spirit are matters of theological concern and discussion. We stand in several different communities of interpretation as regards these issues. Yet, we dare not omit acknowledgement that, prior to our being and awakening to faith, we are given life, we are acted upon, we are approached and drawn toward relationship with that One in whom we live and move and have our being. If this paper and this model have focused almost exclusively on the dynamics of *human* responsiveness to this transcendent Other, it behooves us to close by acknowledging that a conviction of the sovereign initiative, power, and priority in being of the Holy underlies all that has been offered here for our understanding of the human side of faith.

Some Concluding Remarks and Research Directions

If the model presented in the previous section proves to be a helpful pulling together of important components of development and change in adult faith, it should contribute to our elevation and reworking of key hypotheses for further research. In my reflection upon the hypotheses in the last section of the consultation research paper, I have been impressed with how essential it is to clarify and pin down the crucial terms. In the body of the paper, with its helpful review of pertinent literature, we are given many definitions of such key terms as faith, adult life cycle, life tasks, and so on. The summary definitions, however, with their commendable effort at simplicity, lack any unifying theory or model in relation to which they could take on consistent, integrated, and therefore useful meanings. Oliver Wendell Holmes once said, memorably, "For the simplicity on this side of complexity, I would not give a fig. But for the simplicity on the *other* side of complexity, for that I would give anything I have." Our task is to work toward a simplicity, an elegance, on the other side of complexity.

Given the effort I have made here to sketch a model of dynamics in the faith of adulthood, as well as to address and clarify certain key concepts, I think I can be most helpful by closing with some proposals of several directions for research which promise to bear valuable fruit if we pursue them properly.

A theory or model which coordinates what can be studied empirically in each of the component dimensions should enable us—in the study of individual lives, at least—to construct and follow longitudinally the richness of growth, change, and development in faith. Some of the dimensions of this model are susceptible of survey research—especially those having to do with the meaning of time to persons, according to biological and sociocultural time clocks. Other dimensions will require careful in-depth interviewing, not only of the persons being studied, but also of those who are part of the interviewee's life structure. Life structure research (Levinson's biographical approach) coupled with faith development interviews, which give access both to the formal structuring and the contents of faith, will be mutually enhanced in value, giving us rich and reliable data on the relation between faith espoused and articulated, and the life structure as shaped and lived. Linked with longitudinal studies of time perception and the actual timing and impact of predictable and unpredictable crises, such research would yield extraordinarily valuable insights into the dynamics of adult faith pilgrimages.

In conclusion, I want to focus five related but more limited areas for research.
1. Varieties of experience of predictable and unpredictable crises of adult life cycle, depending on structural stages of faith. Research and describe the differences in persons' reported experiences and ways of coping with the predictable and unpredictable challenges or crises of adult life, resulting from their structural stage of faith development.
2. The issue of modal developmental levels of faith in groups and their attractive power as well as their blocking or restraining power.
3. The kinds of educational, liturgical, evangelical, and aesthetic approaches in religion preferred by persons at different structural *and* life cycle stages or phases.

4. A comparison and contrast of the patterns of growth in faith (including psycho-social change and structural stages) in persons of a variety of secular faith outlooks with those whose content of faith is explicitly religious and who are intrinsically involved in communities of faith. This would mean looking at the impact of conversion, justification, and sanctification in relation to the model offered here and in contrast to those whose ideals and ideologies are nonreligious. Are there secular equivalents and parallels for adults to religious conversion, justification, and sanctification?

5. Careful and extensive research on normative images of adult man/womanhood in our respective religious traditions. Even when they claim to be merely descriptive, theories of adult development (physosocial and constructivist) have their overt and covert normative commitments to determinate models of adult maturity. These need to be critically assessed in light of the cumulative wisdom about the human vocation represented by our religious heritages at their best.

Notes

1. Fowler, *Stages of Faith.* San Francisco: Harper & Row, 1981; and Fowler and Keen, *Life-Maps.* Waco, Texas: Word Books, 1978.
2. Wilfred Cantwell Smith, *Faith and Belief.* Princeton, New Jersey, Princeton University Press, 1979, p. 12.
3. Daniel J. Levinson, *et. al., The Seasons of a Man's Life.* New York: Alfred A. Knopf, 1978, pp. 6–7.
4. William Bridges, *The Seasons of Our Lives.* Rolling Hills Estates, California: The Wayfarer Press, 1977, Ch. II.
5. *As You Like It,* Act II, Scene VII.
6. Josaiah Royce, *Lectures on Modern Idealism.* New Haven: Yale University Press, 1919.
7. *Stages of Faith,* pp. 112–114.
8. Richard Norman Shulik, "Faith Development, Moral Development, and Old Age: An Assessment of Fowler's Faith Development Paradigm" (Ph.D. diss., Committee on Human Development, Department of Behavioral Science, University of Chicago, 1979).
9. Bernice Neugarten, "Adult Personality: Toward a Psychology of the Life Cycle" in William Sze, Editor, *The Human Life Cycle,* New York: Jason Aronson, Inc., 1975, p. 379.
10. *Ibid.,* p. 382.
11. *Stages of Faith,* Section 23. "Form and Content: Stages of Faith and Conversion."
12. Stanley Hauerwas, "Character, Narrative, and Growth in the Christian Life" in *Toward Moral and Religious Maturity,* James W. Fowler and Antoine Vergote, eds., N.J.: Silver Burdett Company, 1980.
13. *Stages of Faith,* p. 294.

Robert Wuthnow

teaches sociology at Princeton University with special emphasis in the sociology of religion. As a consultant to the Lutheran Church in America and the National Council of Churches, and in his participation in the SYMPOSIUM, Dr. Wuthnow brings the reflection of the sociological community to matters of religious concern. He has a continuing relationship with the Project as a consultant for the Gallup Organization in its development of the Phase II research design.

9

A Sociological Perspective on Faith Development

The task of these remarks is to cast the discussion of Faith Development within the framework of sociology. The literature on Faith Development has to date occurred largely in the context of developmental psychology with some input from religious education and has been shaped by the terminology and assumptions of these disciplines. My intention here is not to propose additional jargon from yet another academic discipline, but to use the perspective afforded by sociology to question some of the assumptions that have thus far gone unchallenged.

I shall argue that the Faith Development model, as presently formulated, is fundamentally biased by the secular, technical-rational cultural context in which it has been nurtured and, as such, represents a serious departure from the concepts of faith that have been inspired by most of the world's great religious traditions. While the architects of this model have occasionally sought to reckon with its more obvious limitations, they have offered more in the way of *ad hoc* denials and qualifications than anything resembling major modifications of the basic system. Practitioners seeking simple guidelines from the model rather than academic complexities are, therefore, likely to be led seriously astray in their uses and applications of the model. It is imperative, both for practitioners and for theorists, that the assumptions on which the Faith Development edifice has been erected be clearly understood.

In offering these critical remarks I wish to acknowledge at the outset that there is much to be learned from the Faith Development literature. Chiefly, it represents a serious effort to demonstrate that the structures of cognitive reasoning which have been the focus of a vast body of psychological research have implications for the manner in which individuals process religious information and symbolism about basic values and life concerns. If this were all the Faith Development literature claimed to have accomplished, there would be no reason to complain. In its major formulations, however, the Faith Development model has been described in broadly inclusive terms suggesting that it not only enjoys the status of an empirically grounded theory reflecting genetic human capacities, but that it somehow captures the essence of religious faith as well. It is these grandiose claims to generality that must be relativized in the light of sociological criticism.

A Sociological Perspective

Sociology is the study of collective life—groups, communities, institutions, whole societies, and cultures. It emphasizes the effect of social events, of subcultures and social strata, of community differences on attitudes and life styles. It is the discipline within the social sciences which has paid special attention to the vast differences existing among ethnic and racial groups, among strata of different occupational and educational composition, within local and regional communities, and across the various religious subcultures. Like any academic discipline, however, sociologists approach their subject matter from different perspectives. It is important, therefore, to begin with a clear understanding of the perspective being employed.

While sociologists have not paid particular attention to the concept of Faith Development, or even faith for that matter, they have given much consideration to the closely related issue of religion. And much of this work has been conducted from a perspective that has been openly critical of religion or at least has not taken religion very seriously as a basic human concern. The tradition of inquiry and criticism inspired by Karl Marx is one example. Others in the pantheon of sociological giants—Max Weber and Emile Durkheim, for example—also worked from a perspective of personal unbelief and public mistrust of religion. Theirs was a quest for invariant laws which would explain away the existence of religion rather than contribute to its understanding.

It would be possible to engage in, say, a Marxist analysis of Faith Development, producing arguments quite different from those currently available in the literature. To do so, however, would probably not contribute a great deal to the discussion nor make best use of contemporary sociological thought on religion.

A second sociological perspective that may come readily to mind among those with some knowledge of the discipline, particularly in light of the proposal that a large-scale survey be conducted to examine Faith Development, is the perspective of quantitative statistical sociology. There is much to be learned from this perspective. Sociologists working in the quantitative statistical tradition have not only amassed great quantities of information on relevant factors concerned with the Adult Life Cycle and other demographic and cultural variables, but have also devised methodologies for operationalizing and testing concepts of equal subtlety and complexity to the concept of Faith Development. I do not wish to make this the principal focus of these reflections, since there are significant problems with the concept of Faith Development itself which are more urgent to consider.[1]

The perspective to be employed here is called "critical theory." The critical tradition in sociology stems from work initiated in Europe prior to World War II and carried on with increasing intensity under a variety of rubrics on an international basis since that time.[2] The central concern of this perspective is to raise to consciousness the underlying assumptions which shape both action and discourse in social life and through critical reflections on these assumptions to enhance the capacity of human beings to make informed choices about their lives. The critical perspective is rooted in hermeneutics, from which it recognizes the interpretive quality of "knowledge," and in phenomenology, from which it borrows the assumptions that all "facts" are constructed realities influenced by the social and cultural contexts in which they are created. In various ways the critical perspective has already been employed in works on modern religion by Robert Bellah, Peter L. Berger, Clifford Geertz, and Paul Ricoeur. This perspective offers a framework from which to examine the assumptions inherent in the Faith Development schema.

A Critical View of Faith Development

Approaching the subject of Faith Development from the vantage point of identifying cultural assumptions that have shaped it, one is immediately struck by the cultural particularity of the concept of faith itself. To Westerners at least, faith is rooted firmly in the Judeo-Christian tradition. Abraham stands as the great biblical example of faith—a man called by God for a special purpose, a man who exhibited a minimal level of trust in the leading of God, but whose faith ultimately was itself a gift from God and was sustained and nourished by God. While the world's other great religions have employed terms to express similar concepts, as Wilfred Cantwell Smith has shown in his book *Faith and Belief,* the concept itself is peculiar to the Hebrew tradition and the world religions that descended from it.[3]

Within the Judeo-Christian tradition the idea of faith has also

211

been decisively influenced by the historic figures and movements which sought to make it an element of conviction in the lives of ordinary peopel: Martin Luther, John Calvin, Jonathan Edwards, the Wesleys, to name a few, and by the theological communities they inspired. The meaning of faith varies from denomination to denomination as does the manner in which faith development is perceived and prescribed. In some traditions faith is viewed as an active search on the part of the individual, while in others it is regarded as a passive acceptance of divine love. In traditions adhering closely to Reformation doctrine, faith is associated with the initial or foundational experience of God's grace as a provision of salvation, while in others faith is understood to be an ongoing or recurring expression of the person's desire to walk more closely or "faithfully" with God.

The effects of secularization have seriously affected the manner in which modern faith is understood. Writers of the Enlightenment era scorned the notion of faith in divine revelation as a kind of emotional or mystical attitude and sought either to replace it entirely with a purely empirical form of reason, a view for which Voltaire might be taken as an example, or to establish it on a firmer cognitive footing subject to rational verification, as in the case of Locke. Seeking to place the nature of faith in a more secular environment, social scientists and many theologians who were inspired by the Enlightenment gradually abandoned the concept of faith entirely, preferring instead to speak of "religion." Faith came to be the exclusive property of the individual, a subjective component of religion, distinguished chiefly by trust, emotion, or intuitive commitment grounded neither in empirical evidence nor in cognitively sophisticated religious understandings.

In the past few decades, philosophical and social scientific treatments of religion have come increasingly to associate religion and faith with the idea of meaning and purpose. Tillich's conception of ultimate concern, Wittgenstein's distinction between the world of facts and the meaning of the world, Clifford Geertz's idea of sacred symbols mediating between ethos and world view, and Peter L. Berger's notion of symbolic universes—all represent this new orientation. While faith itself has received little explicit treatment in this literature, the quest for meaning has been conceived of as the essential element which inspired both traditional religious faith and its contemporary alternatives. Meaning is taken as a cognitive, emotive, and volitional orientation toward the nature and purpose of life as a whole.[4]

This survey of scholarship shows that the concept of faith has been subject to significant cultural variations. Recent discussions of Faith Development, however, purport to have gotten around these cultural influences and to have discovered a set of invariant structures describing the development of personal faith. These structures are said to conform to universal principles which describe faith itself, not simply some psychological aspect of religion. Moreover, they are claimed to be rooted in the character of human physiology in such a way as to make them operative despite different cultural traditions or theological contents.

These are powerful claims indeed. And like all scientific models advanced in the name of universal truth, the Faith Development perspective has been put forth with the usual qualifications required to protect it against its more obvious points of criticism. James Fowler presents his theory of faith stages in a disarmingly personalistic style, embedding his scientific generalizations in a rich web of personal anecdote, folk wisdom, and autobiographical detail. He mixes in terminology from his own training in theology which gives the theory a dimension of mytho-poetic richness beyond its harsh empirical abstractions. He also calls for a holistic, humane, practical application of his theory rather than a detached, reductionistic understanding of faith. And finally, he notes briefly at the conclusion of his considerations the possibility that at least in some milieus divine grace may break through the human dimension and on occasion upset his generalizations.

These disclaimers and stylistic appeals notwithstanding, there is nevertheless a determinative set of assumptions which constitute the major thrust of the theory. Some of these assumptions are explicitly acknowledged, others run through the theory without overt treatment, while still others are flatly disavowed at specific points in the discussion even though they clearly inform its underlying structure. While the qualifications that have been added to the basic theory make it difficult to present any definitive sketch of its basic elements, the following are assumptions which clearly inform the fundamental structure of the theory.

1. The theory is basically concerned with *cognitive* processes. That which "develops" is not the individual's spirituality, holiness, level of trust, closeness to God, ability to accept others, depth of religious experience, or any of the myriad of other relations or terms or attributes frequently associated with faith and discussed in the Faith Development literature, but the individual's capacity to conceptualize imagery about ultimate values and to process ideas about that im-

agery. Development, so conceived, consists of an increasing capacity to make ever more complex distinctions about the relation of self to one's imagery of the ultimate environment—between natural rules and those ascribed by family and peers, between general principles and specific applications, between factual statements and alternative sources of authority, between literal and metaphoric statements, and between egocentric and transcendent conceptions of reality. Although faith has often been described in theological contexts an an act of emotion and will involving the total person in active behavior as well as cognition, these aspects do not constitute the principal dimensions along which stages of faith are identified. The essentially cognitive orientation of the Faith Development schema is also evident in its dual assumptions that people are capable of verbalizing faith in research investigations and that faith development is appropriately the subject matter of educational programs. Indeed, the desire of religious educators to develop such programs and to create instructional materials for them constitutes a major share of the contemporary interest in faith development.

2. The theory is essentially *humanistic*. That faith is strictly a property of the human realm rather than a gift from the supernatural is a basic assumption of much of the faith development literature. Moreover, the quest for universality in this literature prevents much of it from even addressing faith in traditionally religious terms. One might turn to the index of Fowler's book *Stages of Faith*, for example, expecting to find detailed references to the biblical story of Abraham. Not one. After making this discovery myself, I turned next to "Jesus" and "Christ," thinking the author might have been more Christocentric than I had expected. Not a reference. Quickly, I searched for other biblical figures and finally, under the heading "Scripture," found one. One. A brief footnote to Hebrews 11 in reference to a comment about it in an excerpt from a verbatim interview. Nor was the index any more replete with references to modern religious figures. Martin Luther received no attention at all. Only the great writers in the mystical tradition received more than passing comment. Within the framework of Fowler's theory, of course, this is not surprising. His view of faith is entirely humanistic. Faith is the human search for God. Although God apparently comes out of the clouds on occasion to reveal divine purposes, these revelations are

what Fowler refers to as grace, not faith. Reared in the Wesleyan rather than in the Reformation tradition, Fowler conceives of faith as "man's part" in the bargain with God; faith is a way of manifesting "good faith," rather than something itself bestowed by God or something impossible to conceive of without God's assistance. For the individual to pursue a relation with the divine or the transcendent, he or she must first think up a name for the transcendent, give cognitive expression to this dimension of reality. Consequently, it becomes possible to examine the Faith Development process entirely within the observable human realm. Nor is this assumption uniquely Fowler's. Although the SYMPOSIUM was attended predominately by religious educators and clergy, both the *Hypotheses Paper* guiding the SYMPOSIUM and the SYMPOSIUM itself could easily have been mistaken for the work of humanistic psychologists, so infrequent and with such embarrassment were the uses of religious language.

3.   The theory is meant to be *empirically verifiable,* if not already empirically verified. The schema is grounded, not in philosophical or theological reflection, but in evidence obtained or obtainable from in-depth interviews and social scientific polls. In the early 1970s, when Eastern religions were gaining prominence in the United States, it became popular for jokes and anecdotes to be structured around the story of a religious seeker climbing to some remote section of the Himalayas to secure advice from a wise guru, only to receive some blunt instruction he or she had never imagined. We have now arrived at a similar situation in the field of faith development, it appears. One can imagine a story about a group of religious educators seeking out a wise oracle in some strange land and asking, "What is faith, and how does it develop?" Whereupon the wise oracle replies, "Do a survey!" The irony of such a story is that the religious educators may not have considered consulting the wise oracle in the first place. Even those with deep reservations about the validity of survey research have not suggested assembling a panel of renowned theologians or philosophers to make pronouncements about the nature of faith or even calling on those few esteemed individuals presumed to have arrived at the highest stage of faith development to reveal their wisdom about the processes of faith. Rather, they have called simply for a different means of collecting empirical data.

4. The theory is *reductionistic*. This is not surprising, since the purpose of theory is always to provide a simplified model of reality. It is worth stressing this fact in the present context, however, because much lip service has been given in the Faith Development literature to the importance of viewing faith holistically. Faith, the argument goes, is more than religion, more than moral reasoning, more than a view of meaning and purpose; it is a total approach to life that varies from individual to individual and from situation to situation. Yet the leading theory divides all of this complexity into *six* categories which any psychologist or pastor can learn to identify with a brief updating. These categories, moreover, turn out to be essentially three rather than six, if Fowler's arguments are believed, since stages one and two are presumed to apply primarily to children rather than adults and in nearly 400 interviews only one example of stage six was obtained. In short, the entire adult world is alleged to be understandable, as far as faith is concerned, in terms of a distinction between stage three and stage four and a second distinction between stage four and stage five. This fact is all the more perplexing, since the proponents of this model frequently cite as one of their reservations about survey research its tendency toward simplification! A more appropriate expression of this concern, it would seem, would be an effort to construct a more complex model of Faith Development, a task that could actually be facilitated by the multiciplicity of data obtainable from research and by modern computing and statistical techniques to manipulate models far more complex than those currently provided by clinical observations alone.

5. The theory presents a *reification* of faith. In many religious traditions, particularly those mystical and contemplative traditions from which many of the examples of persons representing higher stages of faith development have been drawn, the essence of faith is regarded as a daily journey which must be lived and experienced, and if insights about it can be derived at all, they are intuitive insights which consist of what Herbert Richardson has called a "felt-whole" rather than an object of rational reflection.[5] The emerging literature on Faith Development, by comparison, makes faith an object, like a laboratory fetus, which can be removed daily from its jar on the shelf, monitored for development, inspected for signs of incipient disease, and compared with its peers in neighboring jars. All this, of course,

is vehemently denied by those who have fomented the current discussion of Faith Development. Yet the very act of making something into a concept for discussion, by virtue of the clarity it provides about that particular aspect of reality, necessarily restricts the richness and diversity of reality that might otherwise be experienced. For those who are inclined already to view their faith as a developmental sequence, the objectification of this sequence may prove valuable indeed. But for others whose experience of faith stems from the richness of life itself or from the fullness of God, great damage may be done.

6. The theory is *normative*. Although virtually everything that has been mentioned thus far could be said about any scientific theory and would matter little if the focus of inquiry were simply scientific description, the literature on Faith Development contains a normative dimension which differentiates it sharply from purely descriptive investigation. At the most specific level, the normative implications inherent in the hierarchical model proposed by Fowler have been recognized and repeatedly criticized. Although Fowler has boldly denied any such normative intentions, his recurrent references to "higher" stages, "more advanced" stages, the pictorial usage of spiralling imagery in his publications, and his linkage of stage six with the "kingdom of God" in his most recent work give these denials a hollow ring. At a more general level, the underlying thrust of the Faith Development discussion is itself normative in that the goal of this discussion is explicitly to create *practical* applications. For something to be "practical," of course, is generally regarded as a great virtue in our society. If we substitute the terms "technical" or "technological," however, we escape some of the unquestioned connotations of the term "practical" and begin to see some of the negative potential implicit in the Faith Development schema. What is being said is not only that faith is an object but also that this object can be manipulated. Technologies can be devised to further it along—books, conferences, educational packages, training courses, workshops. And professionals—the technicians—must be trained to implement and supervise these technologies. No longer can the faith of little children, which Jesus admonished his followers to emulate, be considered sufficient. Instead, people will have to learn how to improve their faith, to advance to new stages, and to develop fully the potential inherent in the stage they are presently in. Re-

ligious educators will clearly have work to do, for technology, once created, seldom lies idle. Faith will become an object amenable to the process of technical manipulation. The sad struggle expressed in the John Lennon song may be an accurate description of the faithful: "I really want to know you, lord, but it takes so *long,* my lord."

7.   The theory, finally, is *individualistic.* Significantly, it is not the relation between faith and social justice, or between faith and the religious community, that has captured the imagination of scholars and practitioners, but the manner in which faith develops as individuals grow older. This is at once both obvious and peculiar. It is obvious that this connection should have been emphasized, since religious professionals have long been heavily influenced by psychology and since the leading models of Faith Development have been borrowed whole hog from psychologists (Levinson, Kohlberg, Piaget, and others). It is peculiar, however, since aging is the one factor that cannot be halted or even greatly altered. If by some chance Faith Development proved to be entirely a product of the aging process, nothing much could be done about it, except perhaps to appreciate it as one grew older. The important feature of aging as far as the faith development project is concerned, however, is not that it has a determinate, inexorable impact on faith development, but that aging is the unique, existentially terrifying property of the individual. By linking faith to aging, faith becomes an attribute strictly of the individual. It is, therefore, incumbent on the responsible individual to do something about his or her faith—to understand it, to develop it, to nurture it along as he or she grows older. The individual becomes the potential user of the technologies that are devised to manipulate faith. It is he or she who provides the demand for these services. If the goal were merely to understand faith, social characteristics such as culture, ethnicity, and sex roles would undoubtedly be just as important as life cycle events. But if faith is to be subjected to technology, then the self-help motif so common in our culture dictates that faith be seen as the sole property of the individual.

Technological Reason to the Fore

It should be evident from the foregoing characteristics that the Faith Development schema is deeply indebted to the dominant values of American culture. The biases inherent in the Faith Development schema are not the result of unreflective or malintentioned minds. They are the product of persons who care deeply about the quality of human life and have gone to considerable trouble to identify ways of making progress toward its improvement. But these persons and the ones who have adopted their ideas are also products of the culture in which all of us must live. And that culture is dominated by what Solzhenitsyn has termed a pervasive sickness, an unreflective reliance on *technological reason.*[6]

Technological reason is itself a faith. It is the belief that human betterment is best achieved by turning life into objects which through rational reflection can be manipulated in order to give us greater happiness. It is the faith to which many in positions of authority—in education, in science, and in religion as well—are devoted. Technological reason stresses the virtues of the mind, its application to problems posed by empirical data, the exclusively humanistic quality of life, and the importance of making progress as reflective individuals. This is the milieu in which the Faith Development schema has been nurtured and, despite the disavowals and caveats put forth by its chief proponents, this will be the set of assumptions most likely to shape the discussion of Faith Development in the future as its complexity is further reduced to researchable and practical models.

If the great "masters of suspicion," as Paul Ricoeur has termed them—Marx, Nietzsche, Freud—were unable to make religion go away by subjecting it to rational criticism, the new challenge to religion posed by the masters of technological reason is both subtler and more dangerous. In the name of helping out, it promises to further subject religion to the process of secularization. Max Weber recognized that the Protestant Reformation was a significant step down the path toward what he perceived as an "iron cage" of rationality in that it made the individual alone responsible for his destiny on earth and in the hereafter. The recent rationalization of the Faith Development process now provides a model for progressing further down that path. No longer is the individual simply responsible to heed the calling of God; his obligations are now neatly set before him in a sequence of rationally ordered developmental tasks. Just as the earlier work on moral development sought to differentiate morality from the domain of religion in which it had formerly been cast and set it on a plane of thinly disguised, value-laden assumptions more consistent with the pervasive cultural assumptions of technological reason, now the

Faith Development schema promises to further erode the domain of religion by attacking and differentiating the concept of faith on much the same grounds.

Two Journeys

For some, the biases in the Faith Development schema toward technical rationality may seem neither so important nor so maladaptive as to warrant serious concern. For those who, like myself, perceive grave pitfalls in the further development of this schema, however, it may be valuable to search out alternative models for the future, models that can suggest other courses for the discussion of faith or that can be held up as images of hope and corrective insight. I would like to conclude this essay by offering briefly two such models, each a story about a journey taken under circumstances resembling those at the present juncture in the discussion of Faith Development.

The first is the journey of Robert Bellah, a sociologist at the University of California, Berkeley, and one of the leading contributors to the study of modern religion. Bellah is of special interest in the present context, since Fowler cites his work approvingly and draws on similar sources, such as Paul Tillich, H. Richard Niebuhr, and Wilfred Cantwell Smith. In the middle sixties Bellah published an article entitled "Religious Evolution" which has since became a classic in the sociology of religion.[7] In this article Bellah outlined a sequence of developmental stages much like Fowler's stages of faith. The stages traced the changes in religious belief and practice from a simple association of the divine with the everyday world, through a sequence of cognitive differentiation, culminating in a complex world view in which symbolism of many kinds, taken metaphorically, enriched the individual's sense of the transcendent. The schema, like Fowler's was rooted in cognitive psychology, although Bellah drew primarily on the work of Harvard psychologist Jerome Bruner, rather than Piaget or Erikson. One crucial difference was that Bellah was describing *cultural* evolution rather than individual development; in his schema, it had taken thousands of years for humans to progress to the highest level of religious development, unlike Fowler, who has assumed such progress can occur in a single lifetime!

The reason why Bellah poses an interesting case, however, lies in his own thinking subsequent to the development of his schema. In *Stages of Faith* Fowler recalls a conversation with a rabbi which took place in the early seventies, shortly after he, still in his early thirties, had worked out the basic structure of his theory. The rabbi, clearly skeptical of the theory, asked Fowler if he really believed personally in this theory, to which Fowler attested that he did. The rabbi responded by asking Fowler rhetorically whether or not he would still believe in it by the time he was forty. Fowler tells this story to assert that he turned forty while completing the book and that he still believes.

Most authors believe in what they write while they are still writing it, of course; so Fowler's own testimony may not be the final answer to the rabbi's question. Bellah's journey suggests another possibility. Bellah was also in his thirties when he formulated his developmental theory. But by the time he was in his early forties, he had begun to have serious doubts about the premises on which it was based. In particular, he questioned the assumption that religious styles could be ordered along a continuum connoting progress and sophistication. By the time he was fifty, further reflection and a series of deep personal tragedies had led Bellah to renounce the "Enlightenment fundamentalism" on which his earlier work had been based and to devote his energies to examining with a more appreciative eye the wisdom contained in religious symbolism of all kinds, including the totemic myths of African tribes, the earth and sky symbolism of native American religions, and the covenantal roots of his own Protestantism.

The second journey is that of Jürgen Habermas, currently the leading proponent of critical theory and one of the world's most renowned social theorists. Habermas is relevant to the present discussion because, like Fowler, his recent work has been deeply influenced by Kohlberg and Piaget. Habermas has subjected the developmental schemas of Kohlberg and Piaget to searching philosophical analysis and has arrived at several conclusions that might usefully inform the discussion of Faith Development as well.[8] While Habermas shares Fowler's enthusiasm for cognitive structures, he has shown little interest in religion as such, viewing it primarily as a stumbling block in the way of truly rational reflection. In this, of course, he differs from both Fowler and Bellah. For Habermas, however, religious symbolism can be made to facilitate sharing and the expression of deep-felt values (he points to liberation theology as an example). Religious symbolism, therefore, constitutes but one type of utterance or action which Habermas places at the center of his model of human communication. *Communication* for the purpose of arriving at shared values which go beyond self-interest is the primary concern of Habermas' work. This emphasis suggests a valuable corrective to the exclusive emphasis thus far in the Faith Development literature on purely individual concerns.

Habermas' emphasis on communication nevertheless leads him to address the issue of meaning and purpose which has been of vital interest in the faith development literature. Like Fowler, the issue of meaning consists of establishing a *relation* with some symbol or set of symbols. What Habermas adds, however, is the insight that this relation needs to be differentiated into a number of component elements. Whereas Fowler focuses almost entirely on the cognitive structures which define the relation between the individual and whatever symbol is at issue, Habermas suggests at least four other relations that need consideration:

    a. A relation of truthfulness or *sincerity* between the individual and the symbol; that is, the person's conception of the transcendent (in the present case) must be articulated in such a way as to suggest that this is what the person really believes, that there is a sense of emotional and volitional involvement as well as cognition.

    b. A relation of *comprehensibility* between the symbol articulated and the language in which it is expressed; in other words, utterances about the transcendent convey meaning only if they conform to established patterns of grammatical and syntactical usage, the implication being that conceptions of faith are conditioned by cultural content rather than cognitive structure alone.

    c. A relation of *legitimacy* between the symbol expressed and the norms and rules and values implicit in the social context in which it is expressed; that is, any conception of the transcendent acquires meaning only in the context of a community of persons who understand, modify, and articulate these conceptions on the basis of shared experience.

    d. A relation of *truth* between the symbol expressed and the objective reality it seeks to express; in other words, Habermas leaves open the possibility that some conceptions may be more meaningful than others because they square better with the facts—in this case, with the objective character of the transcendent or sacred.

Keeping these distinctions in mind would be of considerable value in further discussions of Faith Development. Establishing a meaningful, fulfilling relation with the transcendent depends not only on the development of one's cognitive ability, but also on development or growth in all of these areas—in the sincerity of one's own commitment to the transcendent, in the degree of comprehensibility of one's utterances about the transcendent, in the extent to which these utterances reflect the shared experiences of a community of individuals, and in the degree of articulation between these conceptions and the nature of transcendent reality itself.

These are but two journeys. Bellah's suggests that a denial of technical rationality may require alternatives more complex and less easily reducible than any schema of Faith Development. Habermas' suggests that even if some elements of the basic schema arc adopted, major work must still be done if a truly comprehensive model of Faith Development is to be obtained.

Notes

1. Readers may consult my book *The Consciousness Reformation* (Berkeley: University of California Press, 1976) for an example of quantitative survey research which attempts to examine questions of meaning and purpose such as those of concern in the faith development literature. The essays in Roger Johnson, ed., *The Anatomy of Faith* (Philadelphia: Fortress Press, 1982) also contain examples of survey work concerned with the measurement of alternative styles of faith and reflective essays on this work by theologians and religious educators.

2. For useful introductions to this perspective, see David Held, *Introduction to Critical Theory* (Berkeley: University of California Press, 1980) and Paul Connerton, ed., *Critical Sociology* (New York: Penguin, 1976).

3. Wilfred Cantwell Smith, *Faith and Belief* (Princeton: Princeton University Press, 1979).

4. I have discussed these developments in approaches to the study of religion more fully in "Two Traditions in the Study of Religion," *Journal for the Scientific Study of Religion* 20 (March 1981): 16-32.

5. Herbert Richardson, *Toward an American Theology* (New York: Harper & Row, 1967).

6. Aleksandr Solzhenitsyn, *A World Split Apart* (New York: Harper & Row, 1978).

7. Reprinted in Robert N. Bellah, *Beyond Belief* (New York: Harper & Row, 1970). Also see this volume for much of Bellah's subsequent thinking on religion.

8. See Jürgen Habermas, *Communication and the Evolution of Society* (Boston: Beacon Press, 1979).

Richard Shulik

is a licensed clinical psychologist in private practice near Boston. In his doctoral dissertation, his focus was on patterns in aging, with emphasis on the faith and moral developmental concepts of Fowler and Kohlberg. He brought to the SYMPOSIUM, as he brings to this paper, a sensitivity to the interrelationship between the understandings of psychology and the dynamics of faith. Coming from a Jewish background, he practices meditation and has visited India several times to visit with holy men there.

10

The Symposium as Viewed by a Clinical Psychologist

A SYMPOSIUM was held in St. Paul, Minnesota, during the second week of August 1981 bearing the intriguing title, "Faith Development in the Adult Life Cycle." The present writer has been invited to reflect upon the SYMPOSIUM proceedings as they relate to his work as a clinical psychologist. Indeed, the proceedings *can* be meaningfully related to psychotherapy, but the SYMPOSIUM also had a psychological significance which, for this writer, went beyond psychotherapy itself. In a sense, the SYMPOSIUM was an ecumenical event in the broadest meaning of the word, attracting members of many different religious traditions as well as many different professions. In attendance were members of the Protestant, Catholic, Greek Orthodox, and Jewish clergies, representing nearly the full spectrum of denominations within those faiths. Also present were theologians, religious educators of children, religious educators of adults, educators of the clergy, and several individuals who, in a good-natured and self-effacing manner, described themselves as "church bureaucrats." Also present were many secular professionals, including social workers, educational psychologists, clinical psychologists, secular educators, sociologists, lay counsellors, and social activists. Upon returning from St. Paul, I described this gathering to a friend of mine, a former clergyman who is now a clinical psychologist. He commented, "Well I'd have enjoyed being even a fly on the wall of a conference like that, just to overhear the conversations that took place during the coffee breaks!"

The SYMPOSIUM addressed itself to several goals. First, it sought to introduce to its participants some of the current concepts in the areas of Adult Education, Faith Development, and the Social Psychology of the Adult Life Cycle. Some of the participants were familiar with these concepts from the standpoint of academia and empirical research, whereas others were more sensitive to these concepts from the standpoint of religious ministries or the helping professions. A second goal of the SYMPOSIUM was the planning

of a new program of empirical research. The proposed research
Project would ostensibly bring together the areas of Adult Development, Spiritual/Religious Growth, and Faith Development.
Kenneth Stokes and his colleagues within the Religious Education Association, explained the attractiveness of such a research
endeavor in terms of some current North American cultural
trends. Among these are the following:

a. There is now an increased, popular sensitivity to the
   growth and change that can occur in the human personality throughout the *adult* years, even manifesting in late middle age and old age. (This popular awareness is reflected, for
   example, in the widespread circulation of such books as
   Sheehy's *Passages,* Bantam, 1977.)
b. Many of the established religious faiths in the United States
   and in Canada have rediscovered a ministry which has
   been long neglected, namely, the ministry of attending to
   the spiritual and educational needs of their *adult* members.
   Hence the faith development of adult members of religious
   congregations cannot be deemed finished, or completed,
   simply by virtue of the fact that they are adults.
c. Lastly, in the social sciences, and particularly in social psychology, a number of *developmental* theories have grown
   popular in recent years and have attracted attention. In
   particular, the works of Erikson, Levinson, and Kohlberg
   have evoked very strong reactions. And yet, to date, most
   developmental theorists have had relatively little to say
   about the changes experienced by adults, in the areas of religion, spirituality, world view, or faith. James Fowler, who
   has been refining a structural theory of Faith Development,
   has been attempting to remedy that deficiency.

Furthermore, perhaps half of the SYMPOSIUM'S time was devoted to the very practical task of planning a program of empirical
research. Members formulated and refined hypotheses and considered a variety of research techniques which might be used in
testing these hypotheses. No final program of empirical research
was firmly formulated by the end of the SYMPOSIUM, but at the
very least, the task of planning research had begun.

The SYMPOSIUM spent much time in mulling over the very terms
defining its concerns. We were encouraged in this task by Gabriel
Moran, an educator who has long been interested in religious and
social-psychological questions and who provided us, at one point,
with a fascinating and lengthy analysis of the word "adult." The

SYMPOSIUM participants generally agreed that "the Adult Life Cycle" is a concept which has firmly-established meanings both for the general public and for social scientists. However, we sensed that the concept of "faith development" is much more difficult to define. James Fowler has made a bold attempt to define "Faith Development," using language which is intended to appeal both to theologians and to social scientists. Indeed, Fowler's professional background has exposed him to both professional circles, enabling him to make the following two assertions with a substantial degree of confidence:

> a) The process that we call Faith Development *can*, indeed, be defined in a manner which even satisfies the social scien tist's stringent requirements for operational definition; b) moreover, the process that is called Faith Development occurs in the context of *structural* changes, or changes which can be assessed apart from the *contents* of the person's faith or belief. These structural changes may well be found to be consistent across individuals, across communities, and across all human cultures. A complete analysis of Fowler's work is beyond the scope of this paper. But suffice it to say, for present purposes, that Fowler's theory may, indeed, provide the research framework sought by the SYMPOSIUM. The impact of Fowler's work can readily be measured, at the very least, by the fervor of the critical reactions which it has drawn.[1]

At the SYMPOSIUM, his work drew some of the following reactions:

a. Whatever they are, "faith" and "faith development" cannot be defined;
b. They can be defined only by those who are spiritually or religiously competent (e.g., by professional theologians), but not by social scientists;
c. "Faith" or "faith development" may be definable by social scientists; but if social scientists make the attempt, then they are likely to use much less theological language than Fowler has used himself;
d. Fowler's definitions are adequate, but his contention that Faith Development occurs in the context of stages is unfounded.
e. Lastly, it is possible that Faith Development does occur in the context of stages, as maintained by Fowler, but Fowler himself has described those stages incorrectly—particularly, the last stage.

Now, the above list represents a *spectrum* of criticisms, arranged here in order of greater to lesser opposition to that which Fowler is trying to accomplish in his work. All of these criticisms were indeed voiced at the SYMPOSIUM; many of them have been voiced elsewhere. The present writer devoted part of a doctoral dissertation to an analysis of Fowler's work and therefore wishes to remain sympathetic both to Fowler and to his critics. It is beyond the scope of the present paper to evaluate each of these criticisms in detail. Yet a review of them here is useful in that it conveys a flavor of the kinds of discussions which occurred at the SYMPOSIUM. Indeed, in reviewing the work of the SYMPOSIUM, it is possible for us to say of "faith" what was said of "religion" by Marty in 1964: Almost all of us are interested in it, much is said about it, a great deal is written about it, but, truly speaking, we do not know exactly what it is.

Is There a Connection?

For the moment, let us turn again to the work of the psychotherapist by raising the following question: Does the concept of Faith Development relate, in any meaningful way, to the psychotherapist's work? My own answer to this question will be an emphatic "yes," and yet I think it important to observe that, in my training, and in my professional experience, I have encountered many psychotherapists who would answer this question with a vigorous "no." Some psychotherapists would correctly point out that not all of the people who seek counseling require attention to "the whole person." Faith is, indeed, an holistic phenomenon, and the perspective of Faith Development is, indeed, the perspective of the whole person. Nevertheless, psychiatric patients who seek relief from a single, well-defined phobia, or from an encapsulated, well-defined depressive reaction, do not necessarily require elaborate analysis of their world views or life histories. They can achieve significant and lasting relief much more quickly than that.

There are, however, psychologists who would resist the notion of Faith Development on grounds that are more ideological than practical. For example, certain very conservative psychoanalysts have stated that a client's intellectual, philosophical, and spiritual concerns, as voiced in the context of psychotherapy, really are not that important. Such concerns have little value to the therapeutic process *per se*. Rather, they are important inasmuch as they reflect the more basic, more meaningful, subconscious processes of psychosexual life occurring deep within the patient.

With regard to this perspective, I should like to relate my experiences with one particular colleague. My colleague held a PhD. in clinical psychology, and he deemed himself a psychoanalytical psychotherapist. Together, he and I would attend a case conference held regularly at a psychiatric clinic, and periodically each of us would present a case. In presenting my own cases, I often found it interesting to review my clients' philosophical, spiritual, or religious orientations. My colleague regularly descried this interest, on my part, and he insisted that he found much more meaning in those things which my clients did *not* say, than in those things which they *did* say. Often, he said, "Your client's world view is of no value to me, save in that it might be a roadsign leading into the unconscious; our task as psychotherapists is to seek road signs. Your client who insists upon discussing religion, spirituality, or philosophy with you in this manner is either highly defended or sexually repressed." Frequently, he quoted from the only book that Freud ever wrote on the subject of religion, a short work which bore the very revealing title, *The Future of an Illusion.* In it, Freud argued that spiritual/religious concerns are anachronisms, or superstitions which will ultimately be cast aside by an enlightened, mature, scientifically oriented society. Invariably, in every hospital, in every clinic, in every group practice with which I have been affiliated, I have found at least one person who is somewhat like my above-mentioned colleague in his or her views. Curiously, not all of them are conservative psychoanalysts, by any means. Indeed, those who call themselves "radical behaviorists," who turn to John B. Watson or B. F. Skinner and espouse similar views: that scientific psychology is inherently incompatible with spirituality/religion, that the psychotherapist's job is to change people, and that it really does not matter what the client offers as his or her world view.[2]

Nevertheless, there are probably more psychologists who take moderate or open-minded positions, regarding faith-related issues, than there are those who are "radical" or "orthodox" in their adherence to some particular school of thought. Most psychologists would probably agree that there is an important relationship between a person's sense of well-being and the way in which he constructs his personal reality. Many would agree that it would be worthwhile to examine the ways in which a personal sense of reality develops or grows throughout a human life. In fact, the relatively recent school of thought that is called humanistic/existential psychology goes even further. This approach, typified by the writings of such psychotherapists as Carl Rogers, Viktor Frankl, and William Glasser, emphatically *requires* that the psychotherapist immerse himself in the patient's world view, whatever the contents of that world view may happen to be. Some of the more emphatic members of this school of thought even assert that, truly speaking, we *are* what we believe. Be this as it may, Fowler is still attempting to do something which the humanistic/existential psychologists have not yet attempted: he is proposing that the world view (or, in his language, "faith system") can be captured in the context of a structural-developmental model. Hence, he agrees with them that the faith system is vitally important but he exceeds their endeavors by providing an embryology, so to speak, for the faith system.

Toward a Better Understanding

The present writer will be satisfied if he can succeed in demonstrating that the Faith Development theory possibly can help us come to a better understanding of the process of psychotherapy. Similarly, it may be possible to show that the Faith Development theory can help us, in some sense, to become more sensitive to the experiences of people who are not at all like ourselves.

Toward these ends, I would like to present some details taken from one of my own psychotherapy cases. I would like to begin by presenting a condensed transcript of my psychotherapy session with the client. Thereafter I would like to discuss the contents of the psychotherapy session from two psychological perspectives, these being a) a more traditional, psychodynamically-oriented perspective and b) James Fowler's faith-development perspective. Now, it should be made clear at the very outset that this young client, who saw me only twice in late 1980, cannot be numbered among my therapeutic "successes," for he declined to return after his second session, and at last sight he manifested no outward or visible signs of therapeutic change. Nonetheless, I have chosen him for presentation here, in part, because he was remarkably articulate and, in part, because I think that he demonstrates the ways in which clients can bring Faith Development issues into psychotherapy—the question of therapeutic success or failure notwithstanding. Here, then, is the first therapeutic conversation.[3]

Therapist   Why don't you tell me a little bit about yourself, so that we have some background information? Then I'll ask you more specific questions.

Client (1)   Very good. I'm thirty years old, married for just over two years. I'm a middle-level executive with [Boston-area technology firm], I should say, I am a supervisor in one of the sales divisions. My mother was a Protestant woman who didn't work outside the home. My father was a high school graduate who worked for [supermarket chain in Boston] and who managed his own supermarket for several years before he retired; he was of Irish-Catholic descent. I was the second of three children. My brother, my sister, and I are all college graduates. I took a B.S. in business administration at [East Coast university with good academic reputation]. My wife and I just had our first child six months ago; it's about a year since we bought our first house.

Therapist   That's a very helpful outline of the major details of your life. Now, let's get to the issue of why you came into the clinic. How can I help?

Client (2)   Now, there's a tall order. I don't know exactly *why* I am here. I don't *think* I am mentally ill, disturbed, whatever. But you're the expert, and you're the one who is going to decide that. [Looks nervous.].

Therapist   It would help you to know that possibly a majority of the people who came to these particular offices are not seriously disturbed; many of them are having some specific situation or difficult problem.

Client (3)   Well I'll *tell* you what it is. [Very determined facial expression.] Something just isn't right *with me, that is certain. My life just isn't right in some way, isn't the way I'd like to have it.*

Therapist   How do you know this?

Client (4)   I find myself resisting my appointments book, of all things! I have many appointments each week, and I must log them all, together with the mileage that I put on in my trouble-shooting visits, to submit at the end of each week with the head supervisor of my corporate division. Many times I just can't get myself to do it. Or only with great effort!

Therapist   Your interpretation may well be right. You are perhaps resisting the appointments? Or not entirely pleased with your career?

Client (5)   Oh, I [love] my work and my career! Or, I should say, I [thought] I did. That's the damnable part of it! I can't

231

[figure out] what is wrong or what I shouldn't like! I mean, I do quite well and supervise all the people that we have selling software related to word-processing and information-processing systems to [a certain segment of eastern Massachusetts]. I didn't start out that way, you know.

Therapist   You are a supervisor of sales people? How did you become that?

Client (6)   This is an interesting story. Out of college, I was drafted. It was the end of the Vietnam war. But I had a computer background and so did not have to go to Vietnam, thank heaven; I stayed stateside and worked with military computers. The experience was good and showed me I might like this kind of career. I spent my entire tour of duty in the United States and actually had a good time. I avoided protest.

Then after service I had several jobs, one as a "computer bum" with [research department of a New England university]. I should explain to you what a "computer bum" is. [He explains.] Then I worked for [main rival to his present firm] and switched over to [present firm] when the opportunity for advancement in salary and responsibilities came. I began designing software systems, though not trained for that, and I wasn't involved in sales at all. One day, almost on an emergency basis, one of our client companies needed to have someone come down and close a sale on a system which I knew pretty well. For some reason, illnesses and vacations or whatever, their usual sales people were not available to go to that client company. I went instead, successfully closed the deal, did even more. I explained to them some facets of the system they were buying which our *regular* salesman had not described to them. They were very impressed. To make a long story very short, they ended up buying a word-processing system which, prior to my visit, they hadn't intended to buy, but I told them about that, too. The vice-president of this client company was so impressed that he telephoned my supervisor and said that I was a better salesman than their usual salesman, because I seemed to know how to *use* the equipment myself. That was important, he said. I was offered the opportunity of going into sales after that.

With commission I found that I could make much more than I had been making helping to design the systems. I did so well, in fact, that I was made supervisor of all sales people in [given segment of eastern Massachusetts]. As a sort of hobby I still play with the equipment and keep in touch with what it is capable of doing. I have a knack for sales that I never knew I had.

Therapist   That is an unusual story.

Client (7)   Well, not as unusual as you might think. Ours is a fast-growing firm.

Therapist   And yet something is missing.

Client (8)   Yes, that is the damnedest part. I'm doing so well that I haven't the right to think something is missing.

Therapist   You feel what you feel; it isn't a question of having a "right."

Client (9)   I suppose that is correct.

Therapist   What then is missing?

Client (10)   I wish to high heaven that I knew! Everything seems to be here. Everything that I had ever imagined. . . .

Therapist   Except. . . .? You are grateful to your firm for your success?

Client (11)   Yes. . . .no. . . .I can't say. Grateful to them for what I learned about myself, that I could do this well. But grateful to them in a deeper sense, no. I contribute a great deal to their profit; they in turn are helping me. It is mutual self-interest, and there is no genuine sense of loyalty there. If I were to cease being successful, I would be replaced. I know that, am vaguely aware of that at times and find it like a minor nuisance, but really not all that troublesome. I know I'll continue to succeed.

Therapist   Then not being all that loyal to the firm, where do you place your loyalties?

Client (12)   To my wife and son, there's no question about that. I married relatively late, at twenty-eight, but I wanted to be sure she was my best choice. And my little son is everything. We bought the house when we knew he was on his way. I don't hesitate a moment to say I'm loyal to them, but I think I should be able to say also that I'm loyal to myself. I can't say that, don't know what that would involve.

Therapist That is indeed part of the problem?

Client (13) You tell me.

Therapist No, I can't yet; I don't know enough.

Client (14) Did you ever have anyone else describe to you a sort of problem like this? What was the diagnosis? What happened to them in the end?

Therapist Are you saying that you would like it if I gave you a diagnosis?

Client (15) Diagnosis, yes. I would at least then know what I've got!

Therapist I don't know that I should say. I don't know how it would help you if I gave you a diagnosis right out of the book. But this sounds in some sense like a bit of existential anxiety to me.

Client (16) Wha-a?

Therapist Well, let me try to make myself clear. When you were in university, did you take any philosophy courses?

Client (17) I took one introductory philosophy, yes, to satisfy a humanities requirement, but there was no existential philosophy in it. I have heard the expression used before, but I don't know what existential philosophy is.

Therapist A branch of philosophy which has to do with the search for meaning in life, particularly in our modern sort of society.

Client (18) Oh!! Well, I haven't read it. I didn't like philosophy all that much.

Therapist Well, no matter, really. I did not mean to confuse you. You asked me for a diagnosis, which I couldn't give you, just yet, but I was only trying to describe to you some reaction to your problem, which you can't readily seem to describe yourself.

Client (19) Well, I can't imagine many people would have a problem like it. I've never heard of any such thing. Until six months or a year ago I would not have considered it possible for me to feel this way, either. Mainly, especially, during the last two weeks.

Therapist   You always felt fairly sure of yourself, up until now?

Client (20)   Perhaps I haven't been all that sympathetic to other people who were unsure of where they were going. In college, you know, I was very unsympathetic toward hippies, toward war-protesters, you know. I had no use for them at all.

Therapist   You always seemed to know what you wanted? Where you were going? Then you were fortunate, weren't you, to get what you thought you wanted.

Client (21)   Very fortunate, you are right, and things always have come easily to me.

Therapist   True enough, when you think of how difficult it can be for some people.

Client (22)   I am beginning to see that more and more. I just never noticed it before. Still, I was thinking that this uneasiness that I have; it has a name of some sort, and I was thinking, you could tell me what it is. You seem hesitant to do that.

Therapist   Well, let me see if I can help you further by asking you some more different questions. If that's all right. Then I'll have a broader background.

Client (23)   That's quite all right, and I am expecting certain questions which, in fact, you haven't asked me yet. I suppose (laugh) that sooner or later you want to know something about my sex life as well! (Laugh.)

Therapist   (Laugh.) Well, not necessarily, that is, not unless you think that it has something to do with your problem.

Client (24)   (Laugh.) You know that the psychiatrists on television shows always ask about that, sooner or later. My sex life is quite fine, by the way. There's never been any problem with it.

Therapist   That's very good; I'm glad. I was going to ask you about something personal, but it wasn't going to have to do with sex. I did want to ask you a bit more about your religious background, all right. Now, you did say to me that your father was Irish-Catholic and that your mother was Protestant, didn't you?

Client (25) Yes, I did, and I imagine that you want to know whether I follow either of those two traditions. Well, you see, I have to tell you that *both* sets of grandparents were quite upset about it, when my parents decided to get married. That was in 1935 or 1938 or thereabouts, and there were still some strong feelings along those lines, you know, in those days. A classical case of the old New England Yankees against the invading hordes of the Irish-Catholic poor. Strange to say, my Irish grandparents were as strongly opposed to the marriage as were my Yankee grandarents. My parents married in the Episcopal church, in the end, only because my mother's parents were more headstrong and stubborn about the matter. But the entire experience really turned off both my parents, and they decided that all of religion must be a form of hypocrisy, whose major purpose is to keep different types of people apart in the name of some superstitious, ritualistic mumbo-jumbo. Out of a sense of habit, or out of some lingering wish for tradition, my father would take me to Mass or my mother would take me to the Episcopal church, but then again neither was capable of taking it seriously, and so, having their example in front of me, I couldn't take it all that seriously either.

Therapist Then you're rather sealed off from religion, and it doesn't mean much to you as an explanation of the world or as a source of comfort.

Client (26) No, not at all. [Looks a bit uncomfortable.] *Should* it comfort me or explain the world to me?

Therapist Well, no, or I should say, it's not for me to say that it should.

Client (27) I'm a computer specialist with a scientific education. I believe more in science than in the churches. As the churches say that God created man, I rather say that the forces of nature created man, and that man in turn created atomic energy.

Therapist And have you ever had any thoughts about dying?

Client (28) What? [Looks very uncomfortable.] How do you mean that? Why did you ask me that? I'm in perfect health, and I don't think that I've ever thought about dying at all. That seemed a very strange question.

Therapist   Well, then, let me explain to you why I asked it. I'm not trying to force any religious questions or concerns upon you. However, I often find that questions about death are important in that they help us to have some sense of perspective concerning life, or what we think is important in life, or what we'd like to accomplish in life.

Client (29)   Oh!. . . . Well, in that sense, I understand. But I rarely think about death at all. I've not had any contact with it. [Again looks uncomfortable.] I'm quite firmly convinced that there isn't anything beyond death for us, you know. I believe that this is it, and that what we accomplish here is all that there is. After death, eternal sleep, no awareness of anything at all.

Therapist   And in turn I apologize if my question made you at all uncomfortable.

Client (30)   Well, I can understand why you ask me certain questions. You, after all, understand why you ask, and these are things that you need to know. If you are going to give a patient a diagnosis, you have to know these things. I did think, however, that you were going to tell me that I was having a religious problem of some kind! (Nervous laughter.)

Therapist   Well, you should remember that I told you it was a sort of existential problem, but there you go again, asking me for a diagnosis.

Client (31)   Don't you *have* to give everyone a *diagnosis?* I thought I understood that it was required.

Therapist   No, I will say it again. I think that helping you is more significant and more important than the diagnosis.

Client (32)   Wow!. . . . I begin to think that you don't understand what is the matter with me, because you can't tell me what it is.

Therapist   Now, listen to me: I am trying to understand you. I want you to tell me as much as you can about what is troubling you. But *you* must understand that it doesn't necessarily help either one of us, if I try to package you neatly into some psychiatric, some diagnostic category on the basis of one *one* visit, without hearing all that I should hear. You are not a machine; my giving you a diagnosis won't necessarily help, because this isn't the sort of "troubleshooting" repair work that a computer repair specialist does.

Client (33) Well, I'm not a psychiatrist by any means, but I had thought that you could tell what was the matter with me on the basis of just a single visit. Most of the problems in my life, you know, I've been able to solve them, or to find someone who could solve them, in a fairly short time. When you say what you just said, I'm beginning to think that this is something quite serious.

Therapist No, that's not necessarily true, either. I feel that you are trying to jump to conclusions and that you want me to, also.

Client (34) What do you propose?

Therapist I would propose that we meet again, discuss these matters further, and see where it goes. Naturally I'd like to have you think about everything that we have discussed today so that, when we meet again, you can tell me whether there are any important things that you have omitted today.

Client (35) That seems fair enough, and I do want to come back.

Therapist Have you felt comfortable with today's discussion?

Client (36) Frankly, no, not really. You asked some questions that surprised me a bit, and then you didn't give me a diagnosis.

Therapist Well, there's an honest reply. You are a very honest fellow, and quite articulate, too. I appreciate that.

Client (37) Thank you. My supervisors always told me that they appreciated my ability to express myself well.

Therapist Well, then, until next time.

The rest of this case study is easily described. The client returned for a second visit, during which he seemed even more uncomfortable than he had seemed at first. He told me that he could not think of anything more, of interest, to share with me, about his current situation or his past background. Surprisingly, he expressed a great deal of envy for his nonworking wife "who gets to stay at home with the baby all day and doesn't have to go out and face the world, its pressures, or all of these rather foolish questions which the world has stirred up within me." (Would one call this male chauvinism in reverse?) He reiterated, even more firmly, his wish for a psychiatric diagnosis. He intimated that I was inadequate or ignorant as a psychotherapist if I could not diagnose him "on the basis of *two entire visits!*" Yet I remained steadfast in my refusal to affix a label to him. I sensed that his wish to have me label him reflected a curious sort of passivity, in which he expected me to solve his problem for him, entirely through my own efforts. I, in turn, impressed upon him the opinion that I did not consider him "ill" but that I considered his anxiety and his questioning to be a natural aspect of growing older. This opinion did not comfort him at all, and in fact it even seemed to make him more uncomfortable. He told me that, in the end, since I could not label his "disease" for him, he probably did not need to see me any more; my inability to label him must demonstrate that, despite his lingering sense of anxiety, he must still be quite healthy. I told him that I respectfully disagreed but that I would be willing to meet with him if I could help him come to any greater sense of self-understanding. I told him that the decision to continue or to end with only two visits was entirely his.

Two Interpretations

How, then, can we formulate this two-session course of psychotherapy? Let us first consider psychoanalytic or psychodynamic formulations. We can, indeed, say that the young man was suffering an anxiety neurosis, or a depressive neurosis, of mild proportions. We may also speculate that he is very highly defended and that he prefers the defensive mechanisms, or styles, of intellectualization and rationalization. We note, for example, that there are a great many issues in life which he has never contemplated, including death, the suffering of others, or the fact that life could be so difficult for many people despite the fact that "things came so easy" to him. We note, further, his tendency to view his own problem almost as though it were a mechanical breakdown of sorts, and his statement that he has never known a human problem which could not be solved in a relatively short time (see statements #32 and #33). Psychodynamic formulation would also impress upon us the possibility that this young man suffers a character disorder—that he is basically immature, despite his intelligence, his successful marriage, and his career advancement.

239

Indeed, his immaturity is reflected in his subtle passivity. His attitude toward the therapist is somewhat passive. The therapist is expected to make him well and to "cure" him of his anxiety, simply by performing certain procedures with him. These procedures include the important first step of making a diagnosis, a step which is avoided by the therapist, much to the bafflement of the client. Moreover, in this "repair process," the client, himself, is not necessarily expecting to have to do anything. (See statements #2, #15, and #32.) I believe that all of these formulations are loyal to the psychodynamic or psychoanalytic perspectives.

But the perspective of Faith Development may lead us to a different view. If we borrow James Fowler's progression of Faith Development stages, we need to focus, with particular intensity, upon his stages three and four to understand this young man. In stage three, the individual strives after "synthetic-conventional" faith, or a faith system which aligns him with conventional values or widely held social norms. The stage-three person wishes, more than anything else, to reflect "good" and "right" values in his faith system, mirroring those values which others around him also deem "good" and "right." Moreover, the stage-three person likes to believe that there are certain easily identified authority figures who can function as the sources of good or right values, or proper ways of thinking. Truly speaking, the young man in question has mastered the developmental tasks of stage three. His values, his beliefs, and his convictions are those which are socially acceptable to his family, his community, and his firm. He readily identifies those "experts" who are the source of right thinking; indeed, even his therapist, who is supposed to give him a psychiatric diagnosis, is such an expert. He deals with conflict, tension, or intellectual ferment by ignoring it or by backing away from it. That is why he has largely avoided issues of religion (see statement #25), which he strongly associates with the battle between his Protestant and his Catholic grandparents; that is probably why he "avoided protest" and "had a good time" during his stateside tour of duty during the Vietnam war (see statement #6).

Yet there are signs of a definite movement into Fowler's fourth stage. We can sense a strange and unfamiliar world view dawning within him—a world view which makes him very uncomfortable and which he resists. He begins to wonder whether there is any spark of individuality within himself. We note that he says that he can experience a proper sense of loyalty to his wife and his little son, but that he does not know whether he could express any sense of loyalty to himself (see statement #12). We know, too, that he is a very pleasant and likable person, and that these personal qualities have contributed to his success as a software salesman, and ultimately as a supervisor of software salespeople within his firm (see statement #6). Yet he has also come to understand that this sense of "niceness" and "pleasantness" in the business world has its limitations and that truly speaking, his relationship with his firm is a relationship of mutual self-interest (see statement #11). He is "vaguely aware" of this reality and finds it "like a minor nuisance," but then, in his rationalizing style, he quickly adds that these discoveries are "really not all that troublesome." But they are indeed troublesome to a person whose once-comfortable world view may soon be supplanted by something new. Let us consider what Fowler says of stage-four faith. He calls this type of faith system the "individuating-reflective" type. At this stage, the person begins to sense his own individuality much more saliently. He understands that, whereas he *is,* indeed, a member of the community, nonetheless there are many different individuals *within* the community, reflecting many different patterns of belief, conviction, values, and faith. He still tends to view the overarching faith system of his community or his culture as being "basically correct," but he now realizes that it is no longer sufficient for him to voice the conventional or popular convictions of the community in a conforming style. He senses that he has, within himself, a responsibility to make those convictions his own, to examine them and to understand them.

The Holistic Approach

Here, then, is the central question of this paper: Which of the psychological perspectives is more appropriate for the young man in question? Would we be serving his needs more effectively by diagnosing and treating him according to the psychodynamic model? This strategy, of course, would entail affixing the diagnoses of "anxiety neurosis" and "mild character disorder," with special attention given to his mechanisms of defense (intellectualization and rationalization). If we were comfortable in so doing, we could then prescribe a course of psychoanalytically-oriented psychotherapy in which we would address these "disease processes" according to traditional methods. But is it possible that we would be serving his needs more adequately by adopting a structural-developmental or life-cycle strategy? Indeed, a review of the psychotherapy transcript reveals that this is the strategy which I actually adopted. It is a more holistic perspective, in which the processes of development and change are not necessarily deemed pathological. It is true that this holistic perspective, at first glimpse, pays less attention to the client's unconscious processes and meets his consciously expressed concerns in a more direct manner. Yet I do *not* believe that the structural-developmental approach necessarily inhibits sensitivity to the client's unconscious.

Which strategy, then, should be used? This is a question which I shall not answer. In my refusal to answer this question, I shall remain a humanistic psychologist to the last! *The way in which one answers depends, naturally, upon one's own world view, or the structure of one's own faith system!* My faith system impresses upon me the integrity and the validity of so many different perspectives within my own profession. Accordingly, I cannot say that there is any one "right way" in which to practice psychotherapy in general. Nor can I say that there is any one "right way" in which to practice psychotherapy with any particular client. I will be satisfied, however, if I have demonstrated, in this brief paper, that the Faith Development paradigm, presented by James Fowler, *can* be used by clinical psychologists in attempting to understand their clients. I firmly believe that the Fowler paradigm has helped me achieve a better understanding of some of my own clients. And indeed, the case study which I have chosen for review in this paper may not be an obviously successful case. But, on the other hand, I am not convinced that it is a decided failure, either.

If the Faith Development paradigm *can* be used productively by psychotherapists, then let us consider this further question: *Should* it be used by psychotherapists? Indeed, do we want to urge psychotherapists to understand their clients—or even themselves—as evolving people who are in the midst of faith journeys, as people who are subject to internal, structural change? My answer to this question may seem a bit paradoxical, and yet I offer it here in fullest sincerity: If the practicing clinician can establish his own sense of faith in the faith-development paradigm, then he may indeed be able to use it productively. Perhaps it can truly be said that the established schools of thought in psychotherapy (e.g., psychoanalysis, behaviorism, and humanistic-existential psychotherapy) are truly faith systems in and of themselves. Indeed, even the Faith Development paradigm should be regarded, perhaps, as a faith system, or as a philosophical position. If this be the case, then let us say to psychotherapists the following: If you can establish faith in faith, then progress forward in good faith! And may you and your clients all be better people for the effort!

Notes

1. Perhaps there is something backward about measuring the impact of a theory or an idea by observing the degree of opposition which it attracts. Yet the present writer notes the observation of Thomas Kuhn (1970), that many of the most important new theories and ideas have been met, initially, with uproar and outrage!

2. The tension between spiritual/philosophical interests and the notion of a scientific psychology is by no means a new phenomenon, for it was described as early as 1897 by William James, and again in the 1940s by Gordon Allport. This tension seems to reflect a nineteenth-century carryover that sees the basic goals of science and religion, in the broadest sense, as antagonistic and unreconcilable.

3. It should be noted that any details which would reveal the young man's identity have been changed or deleted, and that, for purposes of clarity in presentation, much of this transcript is condensed and is not presented as a true verbatim reproduction of the session.

References

Allport, Gordon. *The Individual and His Religion.* New York: Macmillan, 1950

Fowler, James W. *Stages of Faith.* San Francisco: Harper & Row, 1981.

Frankl, Viktor. *Man's Search for Meaning.* New York: Simon & Schuster, 1959

Freud, Sigmund. *The Future of an Illusion* [W. D. Robson-Scott, Transl.]. London: The Hogarth Press, 1927 (1961).

Hall, Calvin, and Lindzey, Gardner, *Theories of Personality* [Third Edition]. New York: John Wiley and Sons, 1976.

James, William. *Varieties of Religious Experience.* New York: Random House, 1902.

Kuhn, Thomas S. *The Structure of Scientific Revolution.* Chicago: University of Chicago Press, 1970.

Marty, Martin E. "Religious development in historical, social, and cultural context." In M. Strommen [ed.], *Research on Religious Development.* New York: Hawthorn, 1971, pp. 42-77.

Rogers, Carl. *On Becoming a Person.* Boston: Houghton-Mifflin, 1961.

Skinner, B. F. *Beyond Freedom and Dignity.* New York: Appleton-Century-Crofts, 1976.

Paul Johnson

is a Dominican priest and campus minister at the University of Minnesota's Newman Center in Minneapolis. With nearly twenty years in campus pastorates in several states, he brings a unique and sensitive understanding of the particular needs of young adults to the study. In 1980, Fr. Johnson spent a portion of his sabbatical working with James Fowler at the Center for Faith Development in Atlanta. In his paper, he suggests the intriguing concept of "faith stances."

11

Faith Stances, Imagination, and Campus Ministry

"At least I knew enough to ask a good question!"

This was one college student's response when asked why he had joined a Bible-based student group.

"I grew up with religion," he continued, "but I didn't know what to say or even to ask when I ran into all the other opinions on campus. My Bible group didn't give me all that technical stuff you may think is important, but I learned enough with them each week to have a way of formulating a question."

During my twenty years in campus ministry I have noticed students who have strong religious interest but little background in religious studies or theology. They hesitate when invited to put their interest to work. A common response is: "I feel so dumb. I don't know where to start."

As students face competing views and claims on their lives, they seek to explain their own views. "Where am I? What do I hold? I know a few things, but I just can't express them."

Thus while some students seek to articulate their convictions, others seek independence and new experiences. Still others may display little interest in religion. ("I know all that. It's old stuff to me.")

The research reported in this volume holds some clues which can help campus ministers understand the underpinnings of students' different searchings. But for me, and I suspect for others, the scope and complexity of the research and issues seem overwhelming. I wonder how I can get at what may help me in a hectic and multifaceted campus ministry.

In this paper I offer a notion of "faith stances" and how campus ministers use imagination and symbol as a way of exploring the research and applying it to campus ministry. I indicate some benefits I see in studies of faith structures and the Adult Life Cycle but

I also point out that we need to be mindful of other dimensions of faith broader than faith structures. I briefly describe my notion of a faith stance as a way of reading current research and drawing out leads for campus ministry. I show that campus ministry deals with a mixture of faith stances and suggest that imagination and symbol are avenues by which campus ministers can relate to and work with different faith stances. Lastly, I suggest some possible applications in day-to-day ministry and some further resources to explore.

Benefits for Campus Ministers

Studies of faith structures and the Adult Life Cycle raise questions by which we can examine our ministry. This is one benefit. Awareness of what is at work within the feelings, expressions, thoughts, and lives of students is enormously helpful. We need not be trapped into a trial and error setup: guess and success; try this, drop this; chalk up this year to win some, lose some; let us push ahead and hope something works better. The questions raised help us examine how we identify what paralyzes or constrains movement in faith. What helps intensify, energize, and expand faith? How do I relate where I am in faith to where students and faculty are in their faith? How does my faith stance help or hinder others with whom I work on campus? How do I accept and respect where others are in faith, and engage their heads, hearts, and hands allowing or catalyzing growth? Do two aspects of faith— "faith as the knowing, composing, integrating, imaginative aspect of the self" (Fowler) or "as the act of commitment and fidelity of a centered person" (Gooden)—call for different responses in our ministry?

A second benefit is that studies of faith structures alert us to the life tasks and choices people face at different points in their lives and the processes at work (Gooden). Especially helpful here are Levinson's early adult and mid-life transitions as they relate to students and faculty: how one must conclude one form of life and create a new life structure; how one must use and know what one is and integrate the great polarities of life; how one must take time, scan possibilities, check out roads not taken, and choose a new direction or recommit oneself in a new way.

The third benefit is that faith structures studies offer us frameworks in which we can carry out campus ministry. In one sense Levinson's alerting us to life tasks can be viewed as a framework. An anthropological framework comes from Clifford

246

Geertz as he identifies the capabilities activated when agitating events lacking interpretability confuse and stress us.

> . . . three points where chaos . . . threatens . . . at the limits of his powers of endurance, and at the limits of his moral insight. Bafflement, suffering and a sense of intractable ethical paradox are all . . . challenges to the proposition that life is comprehensible . . . challenges with which any religion, however "primitive", which hopes to persist must attempt to cope.[1]

As these experiences confront us, we attempt to map out and make sense of life. The traditions and religious teaching of different groups symbolize and express how communities have discovered meaning, coped with suffering, and chosen the good, mixed as that may be at times.

Fowler's research seeks to go inside and view the ways in which we work at these issues and make meaningful a puzzling existence. He identifies seven aspects which work differently at different stages. Sharon Parks draws upon William Perry, Kenneth Keniston, et al. and expands Fowler's study, speaking of ten strands in adult development which interact and the various forms these strands take in adolescence, young adult, adult, and mature adult life. Parks examines Fowler's broad description of faith throughout all of life and concentrates particular interest in how college students can move in faith in an academic setting. Parks's summary of that movement is worth quoting here to express the framework offered.

> What we perceive is that the journey toward mature faith begins with what we may call "dependent, authoritarian, conventional, adolescent faith." Then when such faith is no longer "fitting" there is a movement through a "counter-dependent, relativistic faith" to the faith of a self-aware young adult. Young adult meaning-making is formed by a "fragile, fresh, self-dependence which seeks and clings to an explicit, ideological, ideal" system centered in an identifiable community. Young adult faith must be worthy of the promise of the self emerging from within, and it must empower the testing of the new and ideal structures of truth in probing commitments into the world it has inherited and is prepared to critique. Such young adult faith emerges at the great cost of lost certainty and the terror of responsibility.
>
> If young adult faith is confirmed and given place, it can emerge from its fragile form to a self-confident strength that

can make meaning in the world-as-it-is, while maintaining sufficient integrity with the ideal of one's vision. This new "adult" faith can sustain a significant awareness of communities other than its own; it can trust its own inner authority, though remaining dependent upon some outside community of validation; and it can tolerate, if not embrace, the felt tensions between inevitable choices. Adult faith can engage the world because it has a sense of agency—the power to transform. But adult faith is won at the cost of the loss, great or small, of the purity and clarity of fidelity to one's young adult "ideal" vision.

If the call to that quality of fidelity or the "ideal" is not utterly stifled in its encounter with the "pragmatics," and can continue to find place and expression, it may (sometimes quietly but surely) persist, eventually calling out "mature adult faith." For beyond the developmental truce between self and society in adult faith is the reorganization of meaning we call "mature faith." Compelled by the awareness that life is half spent and that all persons participate in the fateful ordering of others, mature faith knows that therefore one *is* responsible to everything; but not everything has been given into one's keeping. Mature adult faith knows—at the price, if necessary, of the loss of the props of community and ideology—that life is irrevocably interdependent. The mature adult must act congruent with the knowledge that the self is intricately woven into the tapestry of life and is essential to its quality and strength. Mature adult faith lives with the paradox that one is both "woven" and "weaving."[2]

Dimensions of Faith

Fowler's and Parks's research into faith structures emphasizes faith as a way of knowing, an inner activity, and the structures that shape meaning. They do not speak of God's call or activity within us. As we pursue the faith-knowing emphasis, it is helpful to keep in mind other dimensions of faith. Useful in this regard is Avery Dulles's description of three components of faith—conviction, commitment, and trust—and the intellectual, performative, and fiducial approaches that emphasize each of these components.[3]

Carlos Cirne-Lima describes the religious attitude and lead characteristic of faith as a reaching beyond self to the *personal* reality of another. Faith is an act of my personal center, a commitment of my whole person. Faith is an acceptance of another and letting the other influence my life. Acceptance and influence interact, and the content of faith is expressed in whoever the other is that I accept and the way of life lived because of the influence received. For Christians, the other is God, Jesus, community of faith, and the like. The strength of faith, the adherence, varies with our relationship to the other, a relationship of strangers, acquaintances, or friends. The wary acceptance of a stranger is significantly different from the unreserved acceptance of a friend. What is our image of God or of Jesus, and in that image do we accept him as stranger or friend?[4]

Cirne-Lima points to a condition for each level of faith: personal knowledge on the level of intuition or experience, personal knowledge that goes beyond concepts and works in an image aware of its own truth. An intuition is knowing another. What makes faith to be faith is the free attitude of acceptance of another whom I know by my whole person. I see others in my image of them and take them into myself, say yes to them from the core of who I am. From this acceptance of the other person we accept their assertions or teachings.[5] Any images of others and consequent awareness of them as stranger or friend indicates the importance of images as they mediate faith. Also, the way our life history and events of life shape our ability to accept others plays a major role in the intensity of faith possible for us.

In an unpublished paper, "The Three Movements in Faith," Jim Fowler explores Hebrews 11:1-3, faith as understanding, assurance, and conviction, or what I call faith-knowing, faith-loving, and faith-serving. I see this description closely connected with Dulles's components of faith as conviction, trust, and commitment and parallel to the challenges of ignorance, suffering, and evil which faith must confront. As one inquires into the structures by which we make sense out of life, we need to keep the activity of faith-loving and faith-serving in mind. I find myself asking how the work of our hands is a form of knowing; how love yields experiential knowing that goes beyond concepts; how the understanding we have enlarges our hearts and activates our hands; how the embrace and service of our hands, prompted by love, continues when no signs of success or hope are apparent. I call attention to these aspects because a faith stance includes knowing, loving, and serving—head, heart, and hands—and the multiple interrelationships and interactions between them.

249

Faith Stances

The many dimensions of faith are not easily held together. Nor is it easy to connect the many aspects of structural developmental studies, the disparate views of adult development, and the many dimensions of faith open to development. Helpful distinctions are made in various symposium papers—in Fowler's chart, for example, which contrasts psychosocial perspectives on the life cycle and constructive developmental approaches. Fowler and Levinson describe their efforts as "theories in process," unfolding and unfinished. I suggest the notion of a "faith stance" as a more inclusive notion that can draw upon the insights of faith stages and the meaning-shaping structures at work in them but can also include insights of other studies that I see as important to faith.

I use the word "stance" to mean the way I position myself, ready or unready to give or to receive. *Stance* implies that at times I hold a tenuous position, unsure of my footing, at times off balance and trying to rebalance. I can take a stance I have not yet tried, or I may stumble into a stance I never knew was possible, recognize its newness, and want to learn how it happened so I can stand that way again. Each stance I take offers possibilities and limitations for who I am or what I can do in that position. What I deal with and what I do from different stances may be similar, but the way I do it and the intensity of activity may differ widely.

The notion of stance bypasses the hierarchical connotation of stage theories, in which more differentiated and complex faith structures are the ideal. The notion of a faith stance allows me to explore Gooden's point that a twenty-year-old is not at a lower point of development but may have a faith which appropriately deals with the tasks of life at that time of life; there can be other faith stances able to deal with other experiences at other times. In circumstances of failure or of success, are there other approaches or patterns of acting for me? Is there an appropriate faith stance for me at this time and situation of my life? What makes up that stance? I suggest five components in a faith stance: meaning-making structures (e.g., Fowler and Parks); life tasks (e.g., Levinson); preferred ways of acting; intensity of love; and my spirituality. First there are the structures by which I receive and shape meaning in my life. Different constellations of structures carry strengths and limitations. The structures—aspects or strands of Fowler and Parks—most helpful to examine for strengths and limitations of a faith stance are the following: dependence–independence–interdependence or the appropriate attachments for nurture, affection, and belonging; where we base authority—in others, in self, or between self and others who are in groups different than our own; world coherence, or how we put to-gether our sense of what life is all about and the terms in which we express that ordering of life; our ability to take the viewpoint of others and the different ways we do that; and lastly, how we seek to be separate from, yet connected with, others and various groups.

A faith stance with such structures faces life tasks, the second of my components. The life task of developing a dream or vision of who I can be in the world and what difference I make in the world usually occurs in young adults. The review and revision of that dream or vision in mid-life is what faculty or today's returning students often face. What will open up the possibilities for life and support the search and struggle for that dream, new or revised? Levinson proposes the role of mentor and others in significant re-lationship to us as we look at what we face with faith and who stands with us as we face it.[6]

A third component in a faith stance is my preferred ways of act-ing. As structures identify patterns of similarity in how we shape meaning, we note differences in our preferences which affect how we act. Some prefer to draw energy from contact with people (75%), and others energize themselves in solitude (25%). (The per-centages and preferences are taken from Keirsey and Bates's *Please Understand Me*, applying the Myers-Briggs temperament styles to marital, learning, and work relationships.)[7] Some people prefer living with facts, experiencing the present (75%), while others prefer innovating, imagining new possibilities and new fu-tures (25%). People split equally on making choices based on a clear line of argument or choosing on the personal impact of the decision. People also split equally on those wanting life and events settled and nailed down or those keeping their options open and fluid. These preferences and the various mixes possible explain why people take this or that faith stance at a particular time or event in their lives.

A fourth component of a faith stance is what I call energy and largeness of heart, the intensity of love present. My affective ca-pacity is grasped by another person or object. I feel a fit, a conge-niality, a common sharing as though I have always known the other, even though it may be our first meeting. This felt affinity energizes. I open myself and reach out to understand and let the other person influence me. My love enables me to "know" in deep and profound ways because we feel together. Each faith stance is capable of various levels of energy, depending on my affective connections at that moment.

This experience of being in love with God, or with the reality in which I believe, is a basis for an experience of a-conceptual knowledge. My adherence of faith is animated by love. God's gift of love in me and my being in love with God opens me to the Spirit's activity and understanding, which go beyond conceptual knowledge. Being in love with others opens me to their gifts as they mediate God to me. I think further exploration of experiential knowing in love relationships, as well as experiential knowing through suffering, is a needed area of study today.[8]

A fifth component of a faith stance is my spirituality, how I live at the center of who I am. I live at a center with an image of who I am, how I am embodied and in touch with the concrete, and with work, a career, and a calling. I have my individual family history, and I can draw upon my religious heritage. I stand in a particular social class from which I look at the world, and I do not see as others see from other social classes. I do not stand alone, but interact with others and am a part of several different communities. I feel strange toward, or unfamiliar with, or a companion with, frailty and death. My spirituality is the way I live at my center and connect within myself these factors in my life. There are times when I need to shift my center, or realign it, allow the connections to loosen or to break and be redrawn. I may passively wait to be changed, but often find I need to be open to, seek out, or recognize the emergence of a new center and accept it, which in turn may allow me a new faith stance.

Faith stance is a broader, looser, and more inclusive term than the specific notion of faith stage in structural developmental studies. I am greatly helped by Fowler's and Parks's descriptions of faith stages. In naming faith stances with descriptive language from the faith structures, I want to include all five components identified above. Four faith stances are:

1. Interpersonal and unexplicated faith;
2. Personally appropriated, reflective but vulnerable faith;
3. Explicit, confident, world-engaging faith;
4. Interdependent and paradoxical faith.

The rich dimensions of faith, the many components of a faith stance and the varieties of faith stances possible in a campus setting impel campus ministers to see and decide how we can relate to them, how we help or hinder movements of energy and activity within a particular stance, how we help or hinder movement from one stance to another. We need also to recognize our own faith stance in relationship to others' faith stances.

Imagination and Symbol

I suggest that campus ministers can catalyze movement in faith by an imaginative use of symbol, which engages affectivity and explores meaning, calls forth new dreams and possibilities, respects and allows people to use their preferred action styles.

There are two kinds of movement we can consider: movement within a stance and movement to a different stance. The imaginative use of symbol enhances and/or digs into the interpersonal, reflective, world-engaging, and paradoxical strengths of particular faith stances and can also call forth movement to a different stance. Symbols do this by engaging our affections, evoking response, and opening up new directions and possibilities.

I use the word "symbol" to mean a tangible reality which makes present another deeper reality, engaging us and involving us with that reality and evoking in us a new way of being or acting. Religious symbols, faith symbols or symbols used in a religious or faith context, mediate realities beyond everyday life—the transcendent—and convey a sense of utter actuality; we touch it, and it touches us.[9]

Sapir lifts up two constant characteristics of symbolism: a symbol refers to and substitutes for some more closely or directly experienced reality; a symbol condenses energy whose significance is beyond the apparently insignificant form of the symbol. Both referential and condensation symbolism are usually blended in daily human activity.[10]

An example of this blend from my own experience is the following. In the summer corn dance at Cochiti pueblo in New Mexico in 1962, the dancers were growing weary. They had danced from early morning. It was now mid-afternoon. The sun was hot, and the sand upon which they danced was hotter than the 96° air temperature. An old Indian lady came out of the crowd, dancing vigorously and wildly, a marked contrast with the disciplined step of the Cochiti dancers. She had two swirls of cotton candy in each hand. She swung between the dancers, shaking the cotton candy at their mouths. forcing them to take a bite. She smiled and laughed. The dancers kept their ritual step and nipped at the swirls, restraining their laughter which danced in their eyes and bodies. The fatigue of the dancers dissipated; the tempo and energy of the dance rose.

I asked the Indian with whom I had gone to the dance whether the old woman was a clown figure and a part of the ritual. This action was not called for in the ritual. It was an improvised, quiet mocking of the tourists who surround the plaza watching the dance. The symbol of cotton candy not only refers to the tourists and their culture but also condenses many attitudes, feelings, experiences into this shorthand symbol which evoked new energy in the dancers. The symbol in action was an *experience* of the tourist *as* cotton candy, fluff. The ideas of tourist and fluff are brought together. A new perspective was provided to the dancers. This symbolic action of eating the cotton candy and mimicry evokes the entire relationship of the pueblo people and tourists with all the overtones of feelings, attitudes, pains, and understandings. As the action is interpreted, this terse but layered symbol can develop into a more conscious, intellectual elaboration and eventually simply refer to the relationships. The relationships in a symbol can aim at knowledge, action, or emotional attitudes and sentiments and refer to this singly or all at once.

Symbols, then, can serve many purposes and touch on many dimensions of life: they can maintain and deepen traditions through recall and remembering; provide directives for action; stimulate the mind to new connections; select and embody values as normative for human activities; and serve as a means of communicating and developing cooperation with a society. A symbol, such as communion or eucharist, may remain relatively unchanged throughout years, but the experience of it and the symbolic interpretations may vary widely depending on the attitudes of the people.

It is helpful to be alert to two ways we use symbols, as referring to another reality and appealing to our understanding or as engaging us head, heart, and hands with the reality. Communal symbols—in Christianity, for example, of baptism, eucharist, the cross, the tomb—may be employed both ways; there is a beneficial interplay that unveils the richness of a religious tradition.

Individuals also have their individual symbols which develop from the life lived and their awareness of it. For example, Jesus may be experienced or referred to as brother, Lord, Savior, teacher, compassionate healer, teller of parables, and in any of these be accepted as stranger, acquaintance, or friend. Individuals vary widely in which symbols and images are active for them. Primary images of water, mountains, or light may be more active than any religious symbol. I refer you to Robert Wuthnow's paper in this volume in which he discusses the conditions which allow any symbol to be meaningful for us.

The diversity of a campus setting, where the mix of students and faculty in their differing faith stances, poses a problem. Do I as a campus minister address one faith stance, or do I try to relate to more than one stance? If the latter, how do I do that? The many components of a faith stance are all at work: structures shaping meaning; life tasks; temperamental preferences for action; felt affinities, inclinations, affective energy, and resultant understandings and commitments reason can recognize but not explain; and how we live at the center of who we are. The clues from faith structures and the use of imagination and symbol can touch this diversity and richness. I turn now to some applications and resources that may be helpful to you.

Applications

The university setting is a mixture. There is a mix of faculty: some researchers, others mainly teachers, others faculty who teach or research but have a gift of counseling students about their studies and direction in study. Students are a mix in many ways, one of which is their various faith stances. Campus ministers need to use a mix of faith stances that relates to the emphasis on our own campus. A heavily interpersonal faith stance on our part may touch the lives of undergraduates but bypass faculty. Similarly, a highly reflective, world-engaging faith stance in liturgy, or in our programs, may leave undergraduates searching for someone to understand and work with them on more immediate issues of coping with who they are and where they want to go.

Our ministry needs to foster two movements: 1) deepening and enhancing the strengths of interpersonal faith into a reflective and world-engaging faith and 2) calling reflective faith into the paradox of strong commitment which embraces and appreciates other religious and faith understandings and ways of life.

I want to illustrate briefly applications in three areas: social justice, liturgical celebration, and programs of prayer and informal learning.

I hear people in their thirties and older say that students today do not have a sense of social justice as students did in the late 1960s. A recent newspaper account might reinforce this viewpoint. In April 1981, students at the University of Massachusetts in Amherst were not bothered by U.S. advisors in El Salvador or budget cuts, but they were troubled by the proposed change of coed bathrooms in the dorms to single-sex status. Harvey Ashman, 18, a leader to retain coed bathrooms, said this was his first political action. "On something like El Salvador, I don't see where we could make much of an impact. But this is different. This is an issue that directly affects us right where we live"(*San Francisco Sunday Examiner and Chronicle, Sund Punch, April 19, 1981, p.5*). If and when the budget cuts affect students remaining in college, that may become a political action. Harvey's action may be resistance to what he sees as destructive of his family atmosphere in the dorm. It may be a beginning step of self-awareness that he can take a stand and challenge decision-makers. Rather than say, "Harvey, deal with what is really important, with global issues!" and reject his first political action, we need to see the beginning of Harvey's developing sense of justice. The immediacy of the draft and the Vietnam war was the issue that affected college students right where they lived in the late 1960s.

Movement to broader issues can happen in many ways. Calling on the research and reflective abilities of students, J. Edward Anderson, at the University of Minnesota had students study the MX missile system in a course on Technology Assessment; the system was studied further in a Peace and Issues Forum of faculty. This reflection critiqued reasons for the MX system and found them wanting. This type of reflection calls students to engage the world as it is and can build on their major interest and studies and lead forward to the global issues. College students tend to emphasize this reflective, critical ability. Mary Wilcox, in her symposium paper, highlights some of the questions of higher education and faith development. The students who can critique the MX may not be similarly reflective in scriptural studies, where they may function with a strong interpersonal faith stance. Social justice issues can be one way of moving students along, and Robert Marstin's *Beyond Our Tribal Gods* explores that approach.[11]

If students function reflectively and critically in classroom pursuits, they may still function uncritically in religious questions. The movement to reflective and paradoxical faith in Fowler is paralleled in the work of Paul Ricoeur and Richard Palmer in their views of hermeneutics, the ways of interpreting texts. Liturgical celebrations are open to this kind of movement. The movement is from living in the symbol, to drawing out its coherence by critique, to retrieving the fullness of the symbol by critique and emotional intensity held in tension.[12] Speaking the experience moves to explaining the context and situation of the scriptural event and then translating or bringing together the world of first century Palestine with, for example, the computer world of today.[13]

256

In liturgy one can engage people in the proclamation or saying of the scriptures and help them move by dramatizing or enacting them. This living in the symbol can bring about experiences not had before. I recall enacting the temptations of Jesus on the first Sunday of Lent a year ago. This was dramatized very simply with a narrator, Christ, and the devil. The devil was portrayed by a drama major who prowled the balcony, cleverly presenting the enticements. A student mentioned afterwards that he felt for the first time the real appeal, the real threat of greed, honor, and power. He stood with Jesus for a first time and felt threatened.

Two years previously we rewrote the scriptures and enacted with humor the temptations, not aimed at Jesus but at a contemporary Christian student with local symbols of wealth, power, and honor. This needs to be done well, and the advantage of a campus is the theatre department and people in the congregation who have these skills. The symbols can evoke the affective side.

The homily can be a movement from that new experience gained from liturgy to a reflection, a critiquing and eventually bringing the two worlds together, the world of Christ and our world today. G. B. Caird's commentary on *Saint Luke* in the Pelican commentaries reflects briefly but well on the temptations of Jesus as sorting out our claims of who he is to be. This reflection could relate easily to the time in students' lives when they sort out their future, their dreams, their visions. One can at least hint at connecting the world of Jesus and the students' world together. My point is not that people quickly move to different faith stances. People are at different faith moments; we need to recognize and touch the diversity so people can say, "I never thought of that before!" or "I never saw that before!" and can move if and when they see new images.

Lastly, with liturgy, I can see a movement of the school and liturgical year that offers possibilities for campus ministry. Students begin, especially freshmen, in an unfamiliar and perplexing world. Welcome, face-to-face understanding of the confusion and support are all needed. As the fall term moves on, many diverse voices call. The end of the liturgical year readings lift up questions of what is life all about, where is it headed. These worlds of scripture and college can be connected. Advent is a time of visioning the future. Perhaps we can reflect and call forth visions in the students of their own personal calling in the broad sense of that word. The whole Lenten season of reflection and renewal can leave the heavy interpersonal emphasis and focus on reflection. The Death–Resurrection–Ascension–Pentecost season is rife with paradox. Perhaps that is why so many prefer Christmas time, with its interpersonal emphasis on "God with us," to the bewildering paradox of life out of death. The faith stance in paradox can be highlighted, however, and the movement toward the paradox through the reflection on parables and Christian growth in the rest of the liturgicasl year reflects the variety of faith stances with which our people are working.

Programs of prayer and informal learning offer other possibilities. There are many ways of using imagination in prayer and methods of reflection. The simple hand gestures of different types used with the Our Father create images and experiences that enhance faith. Others use reflection sessions and personal imagery to explore how we ask and intercede in prayer, how we ask for forgiveness, and how we cope with temptation. Primarily, we need to use a variety of prayer foci and employ imagination for ourselves and for others.

In informal learning, I offer one example and a reflection. Two law faculty professors told a group of law students about: how they became interested in law and chose it as their career; how they met their spouses and chose to marry; how they would deal with and whether they could fairly defend a person whom they knew from other knowledge had actually committed a murder. This personal account and a conflict of approach between the two professors on the fair defense questions allowed the students to see a different side of the professors. The analysis and critique of the classroom gave way to personal approaches and paradoxes in life unseen in the other setting. It opened up the possibility for the professors to assume Levinson's mentoring role. In any informal program, we can foster different voices speaking and interchanging from different stances. My point again is respect for the mix and recognition of different ways of presentation and interpretation. John Dominic Crossan, in *Cliffs of Fall,* explores two ways of presenting and two ways of interpreting and commenting on the parable of the sower.[14]

A rhetorical presentation starts with the needs of the hearer, uses what is known and familiar to them, and holds that up for approval. A dialectical presentation scrutinizes, disturbs, does not answer, and leads one to discover. What is our preferred way of presenting our programs? There is a time for each.

Crossan speaks of interpreting under the guidance of rabbi and of poet. The rabbi seeks to decipher origins, to draw out meanings and connections. The poet turns to play and moves us to a destiny to be enjoyed. We need to do both. Current work with humor and play and how humor can open us to new possibilities is important in our ministry. The works by Cormier and Trueblood on the humor of Jesus, the efforts of Doug Adams at Pacific School of Religion on humor and faith, including mime and dramatizations of scriptural episodes, and the performances of such groups as the Fountain Square Fools release our numbness and remove blinders from our eyes. Music and the arts free us, surprise us, and challenge us in many ways.

Resources

The examples given above in the applications can be enhanced by seven resources that I have found helpful in my attempts to understand how campus ministers can foster movement in faith. These seven are: Walter Brueggemann's *The Prophetic Imagination*; William F. Lynch's *Images of Faith*; Robert T. Gribbon's *The Problem of Faith Development in Young Adults*; Evelyn and James Whitehead's *Christian Life Patterns* and *Method in Ministry*; Robert Jay Lifton's *The Life of the Self*; James Loder's *The Transforming Moment*; and James Bacik's *Apologetics and the Eclipse of Mystery*.

Brueggemann's *Prophetic Imagination* talks of the prophet's role in helping us remember, see the present anew, and evoke a new consciousness of what we have been called to be, which has been numbed by present consciousness.[15] Imagination engages the numbness with symbols adequate to the horror of what is wasting us; imagination helps us explore concretely the death that gnaws at us. The commitment to a new consciousness is critical. This commitment moves by grieving rather than by anger and by energizing with the language of amazement, which reclaims the newness forgotten. Holding together grief and awe is essential. This twofold process of dismantling and energizing is important, because there is a tendency to grieve over and dismantle current oppression without energizing; or there are attempts to energize without the necessary preceding grieving, which breaks the barriers to newness.

William Lynch's description of faith and human time shows how faith makes the imagination take an active role in different moments of life from birth to death.

> Birth and death have faith carved into them. But in between is the need of the development, in forms both subtle

and simple, of what I am calling irony. Not any irony but the irony of faith. The irony of Christ.[16]

Robert T. Gribbon summarizes the basic transitions and development in young adulthood, intellectual and ethical development, Christian belief and faith development, and concludes with seven guidelines for young adult ministry. This brief overview is most useful for those with limited reading time.[17]

Evelyn and James Whitehead, in *Christian Life Patterns*, describe the tasks of intimacy and mutuality for young adults and how religion can relate to and support that quest. They illustrate their reflection well with examples related to marriage, divorce, the gay Christian, self-understanding, and self-acceptance.

In *Method and Ministry,* the Whiteheads offer an image of Christian tradition, personal experience, and cultural information as sources that contribute to and shape ministry. The method is the movement of reflection by which ministers understand more clearly and act more effectively. I see this work as helpful as we formulate and articulate our faith stance as campus ministers.[18]

Another perspective on the inner workings of the campus minister and of students and faculty is Robert Jay Lifton's description of the basic, psychological process forming the self.[19] This process is dependent upon the interrelated capacities for *centering* and *grounding*. Centering is the ordering of our experiences of our self with three dimensions of the moment: bringing older images to bear on the present and anticipate the future; unifying the immediate concrete and bodily involvement with the abstract and more distant, ultimate meaning; and discriminating between the passionate, core images of self and the less passionate, marginal images of self. Centering, ordering one's self and one's experiences, requires decentering, moving to a distant place to see the familiar better. Victor Turner describes a pilgrimage as going to a far place to understand a familiar place better. Decentering is the inner process of detachment that allows us to see anew and apply ourselves to new challenges.

This centering–decentering calls upon the capacity for a grounded imagination which is in touch with one's individual and social history and one's body and temperament. When the grounded imagination is blocked and one cannot symbolize and recreate certain experiences, there results an impaired capacity to feel and to order our experiences.

Another rich source to explore faith stances and movements of faith is Jim Loder's *The Transforming Moment*. He describes the pattern of convictional experience and knowing as a transforming event engaging and articulating the human dimensions of "world," "self," "void," and the "holy" in the five-step process of conflict, interlude for scanning and searching, imagination yielding insight or new vision, release of energy, and interpretation.[20]

Lastly, James Bacik looks for a concrete way of achieving an increased self-awareness and a more accurate description of the depth dimension of common human experience. He proposes a religious interpretation of human experience in terms of mystery through two models of mystery, human questioning and human freedom.

> Our discussions of questioning and freedom should be viewed as complementary: only taken together do they give us a balanced understanding of human transcendentality. The cognitive and volitional aspects must both be included: we are knowers and lovers, we question and are free, we seek the absolute truth and the absolute good, we are self-present and self-giving. These aspects are not simply set side by side in us but mutually condition one another and flow from a primordial unified source. Our deepest responses issue from our unique personal subjectivity and include cognitive and affective elements joined in an inseparable unity. Love is the "light of knowledge" and knowledge is "the luminous radiance of love."[21]

Conclusion

As campus ministers recognize their own faith stance, its strengths and limitations and the faith stances of students and faculty, I suggest we employ imagination and symbols to provoke reflections and carry reflection forward into paradox and depths we seek but cannot fully understand. This gift and service we can offer in our ministry is described by C.S. Lewis in speaking of symbols and the fantastic or mythical mode:

> ... if well used ... it has the same power: to generalize while remaining concrete, to present in palpable form not concepts or even experiences but whole classes of experience and to throw off irrelevancies. But at its best it can do more; it can give us experiences we have never had and thus instead of 'commenting on life' can add to it.[22]

261

Notes

1. Geertz, Clifford. "Religion as a Cultural System." *Anthropological Approaches to the Study of Religion*. Ed. Michael Banton. London: Tavistock, 1966, p. 14.
2. Parks, Sharon. *Faith Development and Imagination in the Context of Higher Education*. Thesis. Cambridge MA: Harvard University, 1980, pp. 197–199.
3. Dulles, Avery. *The Survival of Dogma*. Garden City NY: Image Books, Doubleday, 1973, pp. 15–16; "The Meaning of Faith Considered in Relationship to Justice." *The Faith That Does Justice*. Ed. John E. Haughey. New York: Paulist, 1977, pp. 13–16.
4. Cirne-Lima, Carlos. *Personal Faith*. New York: Herder & Herder, 1965, pp. 21–44.
5. Ibid., pp. 45–52.
6. Levinson, Daniel J. *The Seasons of a Man's Life*. New York: Ballantine, 1978, pp. 91-97, 245–256.
7. Keirsey, David, and Bates, Marilyn. *Please Understand Me*. Del Mar CA: Prometheus Nemesis. Distributed through Center for Applications of Psychological Type, Inc., 414 SW 7th Terrace, Gainesville FL 32601.
8. Maritain, Jacques. *The Degrees of Knowledge*. New York: Scribner's, 1959, pp. 292–293, 313, 322–323; O'Brien, T.C. Appendix 3, "Faith and Truth About God." St. Thomas Aquinas. *Summa Theologiae*, Vol. 31. "Faith." New York: McGraw-Hill, 1974, 195–204.
9. Schneiders, Sandra. "Symbolism and the Sacramental Principle in the Fourth Gospel." *Segni e sacramenti nel evangelo di Giovanni*. (Studia Anselmiana 66.) Rome: Anselmiana, 1977, pp. 223–226; Geertz, Clifford, op. cit., pp. 26–28.
10. Sapir, Edward. "Symbolism." *Encyclopedia of the Social Sciences*. Ed. R. A. Seligman. 14:492–494.
11. Marstin, Robert. *Beyond Our Tribal Gods*. Maryknoll NY: Orbis, 1979.
12. Ricoeur, Paul. "The Hermeneutics of Symbols and Philosophical Reflection." *The Philosophy of Paul Ricoeur*. Ed. Charles Reagan and David Stewart. Boston: Beacon, 1978, pp. 44–46.
13. Palmer, Richard E. *Hermeneutics*. Evanston IL: Northwestern University, 1969, pp. 13–32.
14. Crossan, John Dominic. *Cliffs of Fall*. New York: Seabury, 1980.

15. Brueggemann, Walter. *The Prophetic Imagination*. Philadelphia: Fortress, 1978.
16. Lynch, William F. *Images of Faith*. Notre Dame IN: University of Notre Dame, 1973, p. 175.
17. Gribbon, Robert T. *The Problem of Faith Development in Young Adults*. Washington: The Alban Institute, 1977.
18. Whitehead, Evelyn Eaton and James D. *Christian Life Patterns*. Garden City NY: Doubleday, 1979; *Method in Ministry*. New York: Seabury, 1980.
19. Lifton, Robert Jay. *The Life of the Self*. New York: Simon & Schuster, 1976.
20. Loder, James. *The Transforming Moment*. New York: Harper & Row, 1981.
21. Bacik, James. *Apologetics and the Eclipse of Mystery*. Notre Dame IN: University of Notre Dame, 1980, p. 103.
22. Lewis, C.S., "Sometimes Fairy Stories May Say Best What's To Be Said," in *Of Other Worlds, Essays and Stories*, edited by Walter Hooper. New York: Harcourt, Brace & World, 1967, p. 38.

Barbara Gould Pelowski

combines two professional careers—teaching at Findlay College and coordinating the Parish Education Division of the Episcopal Diocese of Ohio— with her family responsibilities. A specialist in higher education for persons in mid-life, Dr. Pelowski's reflections provide particular insights on the faith development of those in the middle years.

12

Higher Education as a Resource for Faith Development in the Adult Life Cycle

Propinquity is fifty percent of the impetus to form a relationship. Having internalized the aphorism recited for years by my mother, I approach new experiences with considerable curiosity. Besides the anticipation of making new relationships with the people who happen to be in a given place, there also exists the expectation that there will be an opportunity to explore new connections with ideas and feelings. It was with such a mind set that I joined with the three hundred participants gathered for the SYMPOSIUM, "Faith Development in the Adult Life Cycle." A number of new relationships and explorations were to be had with people, ideas, and feelings. From the perspective of a professional in higher education, the new connections were a vital part of the SYMPOSIUM as a formal and informal educational experience. As with many experiences, the SYMPOSIUM served as a life-enhancing transition from the past to the future.

For most of my early adult life, I had worked with traditional college students. Three-and-a-half years ago, I returned to graduate school to complete a doctorate in higher education. Returning to graduate study seemed timely in exploring new relationships with people and ideas and in discovering new aspects about myself.

It was with both a personal and professional motive, therefore, that the choice was made to conduct doctoral research in the social-psychology of adulthood. Adult life cycle literature and decision-making theory formed the conceptual base of the doctoral study. The questions focused on the differential process by which mid-life women and men chose an educational resource as a means of effecting a change in their lives.

The findings in my research revealed a highly differentiated process of decision-making between the mid-life women and men. Women made the decision to enter graduate school through a complex network of human relationships. Men arrived at the same decision in an independent manner. For both women and men, however, the decision-making process involved some similar faith issues.

For example, most of the mid-life graduate students were dealing with feelings of ambiguity in their perception of self-in-world. The felt need to change, to take risks, to take a broader view of their lives had contributed significantly to an evolving sense of identity. As my research project progressed, it became apparent that education was being perceived by the adult students as a resource for integrating both old and new dimensions of the self in relation to their "ultimate environment."

My dissertation on "Decision-Making at Mid-Life" generated new opportunities to meet people and to apply the research findings. One such opportunity was a national conference, "In Celebration of Life Transitions," held in Kansas City in November 1980. I met several women and men there whose presence was significant. One of those people was Kenneth Stokes, who talked about the budding research Project on Faith Development in the Adult Life Cycle.

The subject was of personal interest for two reasons, each of which has become a focal point for reflection in this particular essay. First, it was possible to visualize the potential for building through a study of faith development new relationships between higher education and other institutions committed to the growth and development of human beings. For example, resource people in colleges and universities might find new connections with health care professionals, clergy, personnel in community service agencies, and other educators. In such a vision, the lifelong education of women and men might be viewed holistically as the broad concern of all human service institutions, not just the narrow purview of higher education.

Secondly, Faith Development in the Adult Life Cycle also interested me as a possible source of insight into the developmental paradoxes of adulthood. For example, the critical self-awareness which often evolves in middle adulthood emerges at a point in the life continuum when familiar ways of being and doing are becoming uncomfortable. Perhaps it is at that point of uneasiness when women and men at mid-life are most ready to grow in their view of themselves and others and to develop in their need to be attached and to be separate. A study of possible relationships of Faith Development in the Adult Life Cycle may reveal new perspectives of a person's level of faith development and a commensurate capacity to manage such paradoxical issues as separateness vs. attachment.

Few assemblies of which I have been a part of have had such diversity in its make-up, as did the SYMPOSIUM at the College of St. Thomas. Ranging in age from approximately 25 to 75, and representing a myriad of occupational backgrounds and religious traditions, the participants met initially as an aggregation of strangers. Five days later, the group dispersed as a community of caring companions and colleagues.

In less than one week, the participants had faced many of the major dialectical issues related to Faith Development in the Adult Life Cycle. In a schedule which at times resembled a marathon, individuals were involved in lectures, reflection groups, meal gatherings, and personal conversations. Each afforded an opportunity to examine the implications for faith development in such adult life issues as work and love, changing identities and commitments, and the growth toward deeper self-knowledge.

Both the process and the content suggested implications for higher education. As a process, the SYMPOSIUM served the purpose of providing the adult participants with an opportunity to examine their own shifting identities and commitments. The content itself stimulated ideas about the developmental needs of students and the educational environments which are most likely to support that development.

For example, young adult students may use higher education to help build their evolving identities as independent persons making initial choices about occupation and personal relationships. Toward that end, the educational environment offers activities through which students might learn to express and integrate new images of themselves and others, and thereby enhance their own need for self-certainty. Those activities might be formulated with an understanding of a theory of Faith Development.

Observing as well as participating in the SYMPOSIUM, I witnessed and joined the struggle to relinquish old images and to affirm new views. Participants may have been presented with "a paper in progress," but the gathering was of a people in process.

All that was experienced pointed out the challenges in the appointed task of seeking to bridge the gap between Adult Life Cycle concepts and Faith Development theory. As an *ad hoc* community, the women and men worked to differentiate between such polarities as structure and content, perception and behavior, nature and grace, abstract and concrete reasoning.

(How many times have faculty members been heard battling over course structure and content? How often do advocates of student development struggle with issues of perception and behavior? Perhaps the familiar scenes would change in tone if more were understood about the evolution of reasoning and the structure of meaning.)

Other dialectical forces which shaped our encounters suggest a developmental-type journey. First, creating ideas by brainstorming, then by rejecting the parts which seemed superfluous, a balance was finally struck at a point called "building." There was a rhythmical flow in our daily routine: in one moment meditating in the solitude of the early morning gatherings; in another moment holding hands at dinner in thanksgiving for new friends. There was a search for meetings of the mind to take home. With the familiar having been made strange, it was possible to imagine how these new ideas and relationships would be integrated into accustomed processes.

It was in the struggle for balance, in the exchange of conflicting ideas that new relationships were conceived. For the sake of growth, various religious traditions were shared and different views heard. With the hope of discovering a kindred spirit, individuals chose to be vulnerable in the company of strangers. Each person was confronted with an opportunity to nurture the self and others into new ways of being.

Such opportunities for growth lie at the heart of all educational enterprises. For those who focus on higher education and the growing population of adult students, the chance to connect with the shifting identities of women and men is an exciting personal challenge and responsibility. It is imperative, therefore, that attention be focused on the natural life processes of people, including Faith Development, that systems be created to implement them, and that human-service professionals collectively learn how to help people get the most out of their involvement in life processes.

Because of the new relationships fostered within a professional as well as a personal context during the SYMPOSIUM, it is possible to envision the effects the current research project might have on the formal educative process as well as on student development. For example, if in the course of research the educational components of Faith Development were identified, what might be learned about the process of faith development as an educational activity? The writing and research available on the developmental processes of moral and cognitive reasoning opens up two avenues of insight into learning behavior. Understanding the observable consequences of faith, as Malcolm Knowles suggested, or accepting faith as an "imaginative recomposition of experience," as Winston Gooden called it, might offer new ways of thinking about how adults learn.

While several implications for higher education have been discussed above, other questions were raised in the *Hypotheses Paper* distributed to participants regarding possible relationships between Faith Development and education. For example, if more were known about faith as an activity with moments of "peak learning readiness," how might that affect the design of educational experiences? If faith development were generally understood as a natural life process with evolving stages in the lifecycle, how would that affect the perceptions and behavior of adult learners and educators?

Certainly, faculty and staff within colleges and universities might better understand the developmental paths of students if more were known about the relationship of faith development to such factors as socio-economic status, ethnic background, gender role, and life stage. Perhaps, faculty advisors might be used more effectively as guides if more were understood about the relationship between faith development and mentoring.

However, there may be more to the relationship between faith development and education than is suggested by a quantitative study or its implementation by even a wise mentor. The chief value in the current project may lie in its potential to reveal to adults new ways of seeing and being. Propinquity presents the opportunity to discover new relationships. Self-knowledge, through the exploration of new relationships, shapes perception and choice.

As more is known about how and when individuals ascribe certain meaning to their lives, more may be understood about the choices perceived by women and men at different life stages. In Jim Fowler's discussion of the ways in which a person perceives life, two elements were cited: centers of value and images of power. Defined as those centers in which both self and others invest trust and loyalty, these are the dynamic points of "resting one's heart."

Applying such a concept to the educational environment, learning experiences might be developed to facilitate the knowing, valuing, and interpreting processes of students. Furthermore, greater understanding might evolve regarding students' continuing use of education as a resource in their lives. What remains to be determined is how a theoretical framework of faith development will be viewed and implemented in the field of higher education. Or, for that matter, how a theory of Faith Development from the experience will be applied to any understanding of Adult Life Cycle concepts.

The likelihood of discovering concrete, quantifiable relationships in faith development in the adult life cycle is sufficiently uncertain at this point. Perhaps, asking the questions, the ability to wonder, is always more important than having the answers. The growing theory of Faith Development may serve its highest purpose if it affirms the existence of mystery in the lifelong development of human beings.

Such a position may seem too inconclusive to some, and indeed the human desire for solutions and the recognition of growth in conflict and failure is the greatest paradox of all. A paradox, by definition, has no clear answers and carries with it a spirit of alternating and conflicting perceptions of the truth. Using an earlier example, it is not possible for a person to be wholly and simultaneously separate and attached to the self, to another person, or to God. The natural paradoxical process of living demands a flexible response to relationships. The ability to integrate such experience changes as a person evolves from one life stage to another, and therein lies the importance of searching for the relationships which may exist between faith development and education.

To highlight the major points presented in these reflections, two stories follow which describe the human process experienced at the SYMPOSIUM. One illustration involves an observable shift in one person's perception of meaning. The other story is a poignant example of propinquity.

In one of the reflection groups, a transformation occurred within a fundamentalist Protestant minister who was living out his Christian vocation as an academic administrator. In the five-day period, he moved from an expressed need for absolute truth to an expanding receptivity to the sometimes conflicting views of others. As he reorganized his experience—often supported by the rest of the group, who listened empathically and disclosed concerns of their own—one man struggled to retain the old while assimilating the new. Perhaps, there is no other way to face the paradoxical issues in adulthood other than to be vulnerable to change and wise enough to be able to identify and use both internal and external resources.

Knowing that internal resources are available, such as faith, self-confidence, courage, and love is important. Equally important is the awareness of external resources such as a home, family, friends, and education. As relationships with people, ideas, and feelings meet with conflict in the natural process of living, it is essential that human beings know how to recognize a resource, particularly the internal, when they see one. It is just as important for people to be able to acknowledge the gift of its presence by taking the resource to heart. The second story illustrates the point.

Propinquity is fifty percent of the impetus to form a relationship. On the bus, making the transition from the SYMPOSIUM to a return flight home, I located a seat for two and asked another participant to join me. We began talking about our respective reentries into our families.

By the time we reached the airport, we had shared a number of stories of family history with each other and had agreed to continue our coversation in the cafeteria over lunch. By that time, I had recognized in a new relationship, the gift of propinquity or the happenstance of being close in time and space. My companion was a seminary student, returning home to her husband and children, enthusiastic about the SYMPOSIUM experience and anxious to share it in her work and relationships. We appreciated what we had shared in our experience as SYMPOSIUM participants and that we would be taking home new aspects of ourselves because of the experience. Paradoxically, we would never be fully able to share the experience with our families and friends, yet the experience had to be integrated into family life and used in our work as educators and human beings.

With the transitions back to the familiar and occupations on our minds, we welcomed another participant to the cafeteria booth. She was returning to a religious community where she lived, but going by way of her parents' home. She expressed her reluctance about the visit to her family home. She explained that it stemmed from the fact that her mother had died a few months ago and she had not been back since to visit her father and the house.

One circumstance after another which she reported reminded me of my own life experience with my family. As I listened to the person across the table from me, I empathized not only with memories of family history but also with an understanding of the process which allows human beings to let go ultimately of a relationship. I felt her conflict in approaching her parents' home in the absence of her mother and appreciated the ambivalence she expressed in articulating her feelings of loss. In that moment of propinquity, three people shared a bit of time and their lives in a paradoxical confrontation in which they were finding even more to keep by letting go.

The three of us were expressing the painful reality of transition, namely, while one experience is ending, another has already begun. Our mutual empathy and acceptance might not have ever been found and shared, but they were. In such reality lies the wonder, the contingency, that while we might never have met, we did. With eyes to see the possibilities of learning and loving, we were blessed with the capacity to know and trust. In such wonder and mystery may we all be educated.

Reflecting on higher education as a resource in the faith development of adults, I am reminded of a paradoxical theme suggested in my experience in higher education. It is the expressed hope that as growing persons we might always seek a place:

> between pride and abasement at a point called acceptance;
> between selfishness and display at a point called sharing;
> between rebellion and acquiescence at a point called responsibility;
> between dogmatism and mindlessness at a point called commitment;
> between arrogance and ignorance at a point called wisdom;
> between hate and self-indulgence at a point called love;
> between cruelty and submission at a point called tenderness.

Ultimately, if we are able to accept ourselves, share our lives in a spirit of responsibility and commitment, then, with the gifts of wisdom and love and a dash of tenderness, we will be open to moments of propinquity.

Linda Jane Vogel

is Assistant Professor and Director of Continuing Education at Westmar College in Iowa, married and mother of two children. With a degree in religious education, she is a Certified Director of Christian Education in the United Methodist Church with specialization in adult education and gerontology. Dr. Vogel stresses the importance of including the elderly in this or any study of faith development, bringing the perspective of *total* life cycle which is too often overlooked in an emphasis on young and middle adulthood.

13

A Symposium: Creative Tension at Play

Introduction

"Tension," according to one definition, is "a balance maintained in an artistic work between opposing forces or elements" (*Webster's New Collegiate Dictionary*, 1980). Given that definition, "creative tension at play" seems to me to be the most apt description of what I experienced at the SYMPOSIUM on Faith Development in the Adult Life Cycle. I want to share the experiences and the observations that led me to describe the SYMPOSIUM in this way.

Envisioning the Task

The SYMPOSIUM grew out of a dream. That dream was that the time had come to explore the insights that come out of developmental psychology, social psychology, and adult education regarding the adult life cycle and insights gleaned from recent literature in moral development, theology, and religious education regarding faith development. Perhaps, the dreamers dreamed, a serious examination of these areas of study would lead to the discovery of "a potentially significant relationship between the psychosocial dynamics of the Adult Life Cycle and the psycho-theological Development of a person's Faith" (*Overview of the Project*).

Responding to the Task

It soon became apparent that many persons were eager to buy into the dream. In spite of the uncertainty of flight schedules due to the air controllers' strike, three hundred persons invested a week of their summer and several hundred dollars to be a part of the SYMPOSIUM.

So it was that Phase I of this three-phase dream culminated in the bringing together of a highly diverse group of scholars and practitioners for an intense week of listening and questioning, of reacting and suggesting.

Just who were these dreamers? I was one who teaches college classes in Christian education and gerontology. My interest in faith development, then, is obvious. Here was an opportunity to learn and perhaps to advocate for the need to expand our study of the life cycle to be more age-inclusive. Many studies seem to end at age 60 or to lump all persons over 60 in one large group. I had caught a vision and determined to find a way to attend the SYMPOSIUM. My roommate was a nun who directs an adult education program in religious education for nontraditional college students.

I met and dialogued with pastors and priests, denominational representatives, and lay persons who were serving on Mennonite and Baptist and Roman Catholic and Presbyterian and United Methodist commissions or agencies or who were working in local churches. There were representatives from Jewish, Unitarian, and Ethical Culture communities. There were persons whose interest was not in religion at all. There were social workers and professors and psychologists and theologians and adult educators and religious educators. The stage was set for an intense and exciting week of exploration and dialogue.

Dialoguing about the Dream

It is not surprising, with the diverse backgrounds and interests of the SYMPOSIUM participants, that there were differing ideas about where to begin, what language and methodology to use, and even what the desired ends should be.

I have diagramed the tensions I saw in the following way.

Symposium Tensions

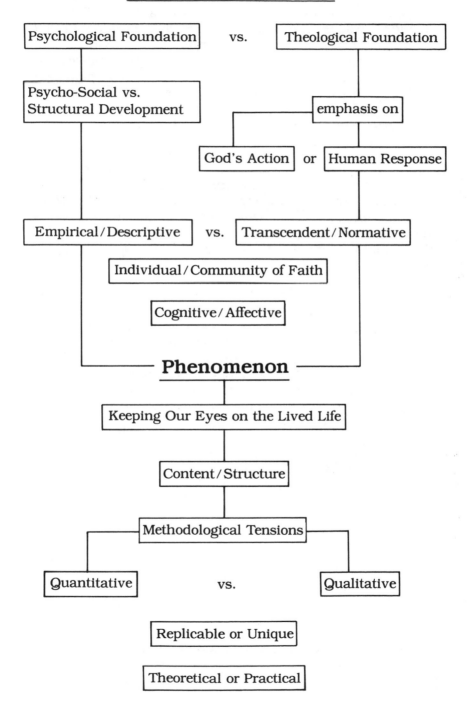

Psychological/Theological

There was an almost continual cry for "operational definitions." And, indeed, valiant efforts were made in that direction. But it is not easy to come up with even an operational definition for a concept like "faith." Some persons insisted that psychological language must be used, since that is all we can study empirically, and they did not want to "muddy the waters with God-talk." On the other hand, there were those who were disturbed because the transcendent seemed to be almost totally absent.

As the week progressed, this creative tension between a theological and a psychological beginning point seemed to begin to be resolved. From my perspective, there was an increasing recognition that it could never be either/or; in fact, it had to be both/and, even if that sometimes muddied our waters. The dialogue was on, and most persons recognized that we had to find ways to communicate meaningfully while holding on to the insights from both psychology and theology.

The task was complicated further, however, because there were not monolithic psychological and theological positions. There were those who took a psychosocial perspective to examine and understand the life cycle (following persons like Freud, Buehler, Jung, Havighurst, Erikson, Levinson, Sheehy, Neugarten, Vaillant, and Gould). There were others who were more interested in a constructive developmental approach which focuses on epistemological questions (following persons like Kant, Hegel, Baldwin, Dewey, Piaget, and Kohlberg).

The theological perspectives were probably even more diverse than the psychological perspectives. There were those who understood faith as a gift from God; there were others who saw it as a human response. There were, and I think continue to be, questions about whether faith is "a generic or universal feature of the human struggle for identity, community, and meaning" (Fowler's paper), or whether it should be understood as religious belief and action. For some persons at the SYMPOSIUM, faith by its very nature must involve the transcendent. Once these persons agreed that, for them, faith involved the transcendent, they were still left to ponder how beliefs and actions relate to faith.

Growing out of these varied perspectives, additional tensions arose. Was this study of Faith Development in the Adult Life Cycle to be viewed as descriptive or normative? How does one do an empirical study that takes cognizance of the transcendent?

Fowler suggested in his presentation that the key to this study would be to focus on the "lived life"—to keep our eyes on the phenomenon being studied. The suggestion is a good one. Nevertheless, the lenses through which persons look have a great deal to do with what they see. It seems to me that one of the great strengths of the SYMPOSIUM—indeed, of the project—was that there were people with so many different lenses who were focusing on the same issue. A holistic approach to this study, in which all perspectives would be taken into account, could generate some exciting new insights regarding our understandings about faith development and the adult life cycle.

Content/Structure

"Keeping out eyes on the lived life" seemed a viable approach. But then the questions surfaced. Fowler is concerned primarily with structure rather than content. Can such a distinction be made? Is it possible and/or productive to study "faithing" as a process apart from the content of faith? In addition, can we describe styles of interpretation without being judgmental? Is it possible to be descriptive without becoming prescriptive?

For me, a major question which remains has to do with the interrelatedness between content and structure. If one of the desired outcomes of the study is discovering if and/or how persons may be enabled to develop faith, then this interrelatedness is a crucial concern.

Methodological Tensions

Much of the week's discussion revolved around what would and would not be appropriate and fruitful research methodologies. There emerged a dichotomy between those favoring quantitative research methods and those committed to a qualitative approach. While it is no doubt true that both approaches offer certain strengths and have some limitations, the primary direction which the research design would take was a very real concern for many participants.

There were obvious constraints affecting research design—money and time, to mention two. The Gallup organization had already been contracted to develop an initial instrument and to do a pilot study. This made some who favored a more qualitative (e.g., in-depth interview) approach somewhat anxious.

Those favoring a quantitative approach emphasized the need for a replicable study that was both reliable and valid. They saw a need for a research tool that could be used by many persons in different settings.

On the other side of the issue, Knowles and others spoke out in defense of a more qualitative research design. They asked: "How does one elicit meaningful data about faith development from a phone interview or with a paper and pencil questionnaire?" Words like "faith" and "religious" have extremely diverse connotations for persons. An approach that is not interactive, many believed, could not provide helpful results.

"Are we at a stage where we have a theoretical base and a viable methodology that will make a reseach project of this magnitude viable?" some wondered. Others pointed out that you have to start sometime and daring to dream dreams and attack the perhaps-impossible will move us forward.

It is my sense that the methodological issues are far from solved. Can operational definitions be formed in ways that capture the intent and purpose of those interested in the study? Can the hypotheses be reworked so that they are testable? Can a variety of methods be used which will maximize the strengths and avoid the pitfalls of both quantitative and qualitative research? Can we limit our study in light of our financial resources and the state of existing knowledge in a way that does not sell our dream short?

These are not easy questions. The answers will be worked out over time. But I left the SYMPOSIUM believing that while compromises will have to be made, there was excitement in the air and that most of us believed that the tensions between a holistic/realistic/visionary/practical approach would, in fact, be maintained in a viable way.

Theoretical/Practical

Underlying persons' methodological concerns was the question, "To what end?" In other words, what, after all, is the purpose of all of this?

There were those who were excited about the theoretical implications of this study. Knowledge will be advanced. The way we understand how persons make sense of their world and the constructions they use will be fascinating discoveries.

There were others who were concerned primarily about the practical applications which this study would have. For them, the whole purpose is to enable churches or synagogues or psychologists or teachers or social workers to help persons develop, in order to live more whole and fulfilled lives. Some of these persons exhibited little interest in the research design.

Other tensions are inherent in the theoretical/practical issue as well. Is faith development strictly a personal, individual phenomenon, or is it integrally tied up with a faith community? What is the relationship of faith development to cognitive and affective development? What is the relationship between faith and Levinson's seasons, which interpret development as the evolution of the life structure, or Erikson's more maturational understanding of stages?

All of these questions are seen to have either or both theoretical and practical ramifications. The success of the study will require a clear understanding of just what the theoretical/practical focus or balance is to be. There are some key concerns which have important implications for both the theoretical and the practical value of this project. These, too, can be viewed as tensions which emerged during the week of the SYMPOSIUM.

Conceptual Framework

No decision about the precise nature of the conceptual framework had evolved by week's end. There were some who favored developing a model which relied on Levinson's seasons and Fowler's stages of faith development. There were others (e.g., Wilcox) who were convinced that Perry's work must be incorporated into the framework. There seemed to me to be a consensus that it was not possible to be totally eclectic. Some clear schema is required. On the other hand, it seemed that the dream would be seriously and negatively altered for some if the study were to be based on the research of only two persons.

The project staff and design team seemed to be given the unenviable task of coming up with clear operational definitions as well as with a conceptual framework that is broad and includes as much relevant data as possible while being coherent and tight! That is not all. There were additional pitfalls which they were called upon to avoid.

Sex Bias

Many women (and some men) were extremely concerned that the data on which the conceptual framework would be based contains a male bias. It is obvious that Levinson's study involved forty male subjects. To suggest, then, that his eras (much less his periods) provide the basis for the foundational structure of this study created much concern.

The need to remain cognizant of this limitation from existing research was mentioned in the original *Hypotheses Paper* and was expanded on by Gooden. Nevertheless, the fear of many is that a conceptual framework which relies on studies with a male bias will, in fact, begin to be seen as normative.

The plea was made that women who were sensitized to this issue and who are competent scholars in theology and psychology be integrally involved in designing, conducting, and interpreting the research. In addition, it was suggested that special attention be given to collecting data on women to see if another stages or seasons framework might emerge.

The challenge is to build on past research while attempting to correct for the sex bias which clearly exists. This illustrates, once again, the dangerous consequences which can result from taking descriptive data and viewing it as normative, prescriptive data.

Age Bias

A concern of mine, and one that was evidenced in several small groups I was in, had to do with the age-bias of much of the existing life cycle literature. For example, Gould, Vaillant, Levinson, and Sheehy all end their discussion of the life span around age sixty. Erikson provides some help here, but his primary focus was on children and adolescents. Peck expanded Erikson's work on the last half of the life span, and his work needs to be given serious consideration.

For too long we have used the phrase "the adult life cycle" to mean young and middle-aged adults. To pick an arbitrary chronological age (e.g., 65 years) and lump everyone from 65 to 100 years old in a category called "old" is neither descriptive nor helpful. Gerontologists often speak of the young-old (55-64), the old (65-74), and the old-old (75+). There is an urgent need for research which focuses on the upper end of the adult life cycle in order to balance the overemphasis in the past on the middle-aged.

There are some exciting suggestions in Peck's work which might be fruitfully pursued. He suggests that issues of central concern to older adults include 1) ego differentiation versus work-role preoccupation, 2) body transcendence versus body preoccupation, and 3) ego transcendence versus ego preoccupation (Peck, pp. 90 91).

A possible reason why the structural-developmental literature does not give much attention to the old is that age-related stages seem to be less apparent. Another reason for less attention being given to the upper end of the life span may relate to the negative feelings which pervade much of society regarding old age. James Feibleman illustrates this negative perspective when he writes that in old age "the individual's powers fail, and his ill-humor and even bitterness is a logical consequence of the fact" (Feibleman, p. 228). Moran also illustrated this reality when he pointed out in his presentation that Norton writes about moving *up* from childhood to adolescence and from adolescence to maturation and then experiencing a sharp decline from maturation to old age!

These reasons seem to demand empirical studies which can help us grasp the developmental tasks and the periods or seasons which characterize those who are at the upper end of the adult life cycle.

Cultural Bias

Several persons raised crucial questions about the mostly white, middle class, American bias of much of the existing research on the adult life cycle. Once more, the dangers of using descriptive data about a certain group of persons as if it were prescriptive for all persons emerged. The SYMPOSIUM participants were agreed that we must avoid as much as possible an egocentric approach which has a cultural bias. At the same time, we must be clear and up-front about the extent of the cultural bias, which cannot be avoided in this project. There was a vital interest in attempting to collect cross-cultural data as an outgrowth of this study.

One manifestation of cultural bias is the tendency to equate faith development with cognitive/logical/rational/verbal skills. If, in fact, hypotheses like "the amount and nature of one's formal education is a positive factor in one's Faith Development" (original Hypothesis #3) and "there is a positive correlation between higher socioeconomic status and more advanced Faith Development (original Hypothesis #11) are found to be true, one might profitably ponder once again the extent of cultural bias in the research instrument or design.

Crisis Bias

A review of life cycle literature suggests that crises or traumatic events may not be as important a change-factor as some have supposed (Glass, p. 11). There remain real questions about the role of crisis in stage or developmental changes. Just how crisis is related to transitions in human development is not clear.

If this research focuses on life crisis, we might miss the role that something like relationships with significant others may play in adult development. There are many intervening variables which complicate a research project of this magnitude and complexity. Crises in life are an example of an important variable that should not be too readily assumed to be the sole cause of developmental change. In addition, we must remain aware that both the causes and the consequences of traumatic events are not easily ascertained.

Faith Development and the Adult Life Cycle: Potential Application

"What use is all of this for your work with the elderly?" I was asked as I rode the bus to the Chanhaussen Dinner Theater to see *On Golden Pond* with other participants. That is a question I have been asked to address in this paper. A corollary question might be, "What use is all of this for those who work as Christian educators in the church?"

Both questions imply that there is a practical application which is expected to result from this research project. That is indeed the case. The expectation is that Phase III will involve disseminating the findings from Phases I and II in the form of "books and other resources designed for professional educators and counselors, both religious and secular, for teachers of adults in religious settings, and for individual readers interested in their own faith development" (*Overview of the Project*).

It may be premature to speculate on the applications of information that is yet to be collected and analyzed. Nevertheless, I believe I can point toward some areas of potentially valuable application which are included in my dream (grounded in the reality of the SYMPOSIUM experience) for this massive research project which is being designed to study "the relationship between the dynamics of the Adult Life Cycle and an individual's Faith Development" (*Overview of the Project*).

Applications in Gerontology

There are many exciting possibilities and as many frustrations when one begins to ponder what happens when you try to interrelate insights from three quite young fields of study—the adult life cycle, faith development, and gerontology. There are many problems with the data which exist in all three areas.

For example, Levinson's work contains both age and sex bias, though it is longitudinal, which is a positive factor. Fowler's work, while impressive, is also somewhat age-biased, and there has not been time to generate cross-cultural data. Much of the past gerontological research has been cross-sectional. Institutionalized persons tend to be overrepresented (they provide an easily accessible group) in the research. The need to consider period and cohort effect in gerontological and life cycle research is crucial.

This means that it is important *not* to assume that we have normative data which tell us what older persons' faith should be or how it should develop. There is a need for many more descriptive studies involving older adults—studies that are longitudinal and cross-cultural. Nevertheless, while acknowledging the limitations of existing data and being cautious about how we use it, these fields of study can be helpful to older persons and to those who work with older persons. Some examples follow.

Facilitating Transitions

The existing literature does suggest that transitions are a part of experiencing adulthood. Transitions involve a reworking of our past, a letting-go of some things, and a building of other things. In a youth-oriented culture like ours where advertising illustrates our passion for looking young and thinking young, the research on the adult life cycle can be of immeasurable benefit.

Understanding the need to move from stage to stage or from period to period should free us from the destructive tendency to hand on to our youth or to hang on to our middle-age values. It should provide a rationale for facilitating persons in transition. An important beginning point is communicating the normalcy reflected in moving from young adulthood into middle age and from middle age into old age. Persons need to be helped to see that the tasks and concerns which face a middle-aged person should be different from the tasks and concerns which we confront in old age.

Practically speaking, then, we can help adults understand what is happening and what likely will be happening in their lives. Workshops and discussion and sharing groups are possible settings for concretely accomplishing this task.

Levinson suggests that late adulthood begins in the early sixties and that it should be seen as a distinctive and rewarding season in one's life. His middle adult era and late adult era seem to parallel Erikson's developmental tasks of generativity vs. stagnation and integrity vs. despair (Fowler's paper, p. 194). Peck points out that the fact that death is inevitable really impacts a person's life in old age. Fowler maintains that there may well be significant parallels between Levinson's eras, Erikson's psychosocial stages, and his own faith stages (Fowler's paper, p. 195).

These insights and issues all suggest that older persons might benefit greatly from an opportunity to explore in some depth their questions and hopes and fears regarding the meaning of death and life. Knowing this, I was somewhat startled by my own reaction several years ago when I was asked to teach a death and dying course in a nursing home. Why did I hestitate? Would you have hesitated, too?

Once I accepted the opportunity, I was amazed at the eagerness with which my sixteen students (half nursing home residents, half staff members) responded. The depth of the older students' experiences and the wisdom they shared were a valuable learning experience for me. One eighty-seven-year-old woman said, "I've got a lot of questions, and I've never ever been able to talk about dying before."

If we pay attention to the tasks which Havighurst includes in later adulthood (see Knowles's paper), we will begin to experiment with ways to facilitate older adults' preparation for and/or experience of living on a reduced income, the death of their spouse, reexamining their values, finding a new self-identity, and preparing for death.

Providing resources in the form of books, tapes, television, and radio presentations of these issues is one practical application. Developing adult education classes which provide a dialogical setting for exploring issues like these is another good approach.

Here again, the information we have on adult development can help us in designing both programs and resources. For example, we know that older persons often are constrained by having less financial resources and by physical limitations. This knowledge must inform our planning. An important key is the recognition that since many elderly persons are adjusting to retirement and may be seeking new ways to be useful, they are well equipped to be integrally involved in program and resource planning.

Attention must be paid to the insights Knowles offers regarding andragogy when planning educational experiences for older adults. The temptation to ignore the need that older adults have to be self-directed is one that must be avoided. In addition, we must remember that readiness to learn grows out of the needs persons experience in order to cope with life.

The experiences older learners bring are a vital resource for meaningful learning and must be utilized. Finally, the time, place, and pace which are appropriate for particular older learners must be given consideration.

Enabling Mentoring

Much literature is currently being written on mentoring. Levinson points out that mentors for persons in his study were generally half a generation older than their proteges (Levinson, p. 99). I wonder whether persons who have successfully made the transition into old age, with all that that entails, might not be helped to understand how the mentoring process works, so that they might be enabled to serve as mentors for those who are approaching retirement and/or entering upon widowhood.

This seems to me to be a topic worth exploring. The practical benefits to both protege (easing the transitional period into old age) and mentor (feeling useful by being of help to others) seem obvious.

Applications in Religious Education

What is said in the preceding section on applications in gerontology is relevant here. Church and synagogue have been shown to provide the setting for about half of all adult education for older adults (Vogel). In addition, many older adults who are not involved in any adult education classes depend on church and synagogue for worship and fellowship. Church and synagogue, then, are vitally important institutions for older persons in our society.

Furthermore, a primary concern of religious institutions is or should be faith development. The practical applications which could result from this study, which seeks to discover the relationships between faith development and the adult life cycle, are immense.

For example, pastors, rabbis, and religious educators could be much more effective preachers, counselors, and teachers if they would pay serious attention to the developmental tasks which each season or period of life brings. Understanding the various faith stages or styles in which adults find themselves should enable religious leaders to communicate with persons at all stages more effectively. It is neither necessary nor desirable to categorize individuals as "Stage 3" or "Stage 5." Rather, religious leaders need to attempt to convey their messages and raise their questions in a variety of ways, so that they will be both relevant and challenging to persons at differing stages.

Perhaps the most challenging and exciting potential application for me has to do with the possibility of learning how to enable persons to grow in faith toward a more whole and fulfilled life. That possibility, of course, carries with it a host of problems and dangers.

What makes lives whole? Is Fowler right when he talks about Stage 6 approximating the Kingdom of God? Does developing in faith really require increasing complexity? How does this contention relate to Jesus' saying, "Truly, I say to you, whoever does not receive the kingdom of God like a child shall not enter it" (Luke 18:17)?

Nevertheless, as this Project tackles a myriad of difficult issues, I am convinced that it will yield some new insights and define clearly many questions relating to how adults move through the life cycle and how they respond in faith. The scope of the task and the attempt to include scholars and practitioners from many disciplines and persuasions suggests to me that the answers may be useful precisely because they will not be simplistic.

If, as I understand and share the dream, we can learn anything at all about enabling wholeness in the lives of persons, this project will have been of great value. My prayer is that it will be so!

Bibliography

Clements, William M. *Ministry with the Aging.* San Francisco: Harper & Row, 1981.

Clinger, Donald. *Aging Persons in the Community of Faith.* Indianapolis: Indiana Commission on the Aging and Aged, 1975.

Erikson, Erik H. *Childhood and Society.* 2nd ed. New York: W.W. Norton, 1963.

Feibleman, James K. *The Stages of Human Life.* The Hague: Martinus Nijkoff, 1975.

Fowler, James W. *Stages of Faith: The Psychology of Human Development and the Quest for Meaning.* San Francisco: Harper and Row, 1981.

Glass, J. Conrad, Jr. *Growing Through Adulthood: Can the Church Help?.* Nashville: Discipleship Resources, 1979.

Gould, Roger L. *Transformations Growth and Change in Adult Life.* New York: Simon & Schuster, 1978.

Kimmel, Douglas D. *Adulthood and Aging.* New York: John Wiley and Sons, 1974.

Levinson, Daniel J. *The Seasons of a Man's Life.* New York: Alfred A. Knopf, 1978.

Neugarten, Bernice L. *Personality in Middle and Late Life.* New York: Atherton Press, 1964.

Peck, Robert C. "Psychological Developments in the Second Half of Life." *Middle Age and Aging,* Bernice L. Neugarten (ed.) Chicago: University of Chicago Press, 1968, pp. 83-92.

Sheehy, Gail. *Passages: Predictable Crises of Adult Life.* New York: E. P. Dutton, 1974.

Vaillant, George D. *Adaptation to Life: How the Best and Brightest Came of Age.* Boston: Little, Brown, and Co., 1977.

Vogel, Linda Jane. *How Older Adults Perceive and Legitimize their Adult Education Participation in Schools and Churches.* Ph.D. Thesis. The University of Iowa, 1981.

Wilcox, Mary M. *Developmental Journey.* Nashville: Abingdon, 1979.

Joan Cronin

is Coordinator of Religious Education and Family
Life Education for the Carleton Roman Catholic
School Board in Ottawa. As both teacher and administrator, Sister Cronin has served in a variety
of positions in which religion and family development are of central concern. She brings this focus
to the issues of the SYMPOSIUM and the Project,
reflecting the important tradition of Canadian Ca-
tholicism in her comments.

14

Implications for Adult Religious Education

After attending this exhilarating SYMPOSIUM on Faith Development in the Adult Life Cycle, I am attempting to suggest implications for the adult learning situation, particularly in the area of adult religious education.

I have realized a growing awareness for the importance of adult religious education. In fact, *General Catechetical Directory*[1] places this orientation of adult catechesis as the major focus:

> . . .catechesis for adults, since it deals with persons who are capable of an adherence that is fully responsible, must be considered the chief form of catechesis. (20)

To Teach as Jesus Did,[2] the American Catholic bishops' pastoral message on Catholic Education, states:

> Consequently the continuing education of adults is situated not at the periphery of the Church's educational mission but at its center. (43)
>
> The full content of revelation can be communicated best to those able by reason of maturity and prior preparation to hear and respond to it. Religious education for adults is the culmination of the entire catechetical effort because it affords an opportunity to teach the whole Christian message. (47)

Adult religious education is an exciting process wherein people revise former religious attitudes as well as become aware of new ideas of ministry. This shift in consciousness is very important, because we are speaking of a kind of faith which is significantly different from that of a younger person. The recent research in the adult life cycle enlightens this shift in emphasis and carries very practical pastoral and educational implications. A sensitivity to the principles of adult learning which has emerged from this research and from the professional experiences of professionals is of enormous value to persons initiating adult religious education.

To begin, Malcolm Knowles suggests that we might use the term "andragogy" (coming from two Greek words: "Aner," meaning "man," in the sense of a grown-up person; and "Agogus," meaning "the leader of"). He believes we should deal with adults andragogically because of certain qualities that are characteristic of most adults. He sees the adult as independent instead of dependent, possessing a self-concept of self-directedness and the authority of his/her own experiences, which may be great and enriched. Adults are attracted to problem-centered learning; they want help with the tasks they are facing now. In the process of self-directed learning, Knowles addresses such elements as the learning climate, goal-setting, planning, diagnosing needs, designing a learning plan, learning activities, and evaluation.

Directors of Religious Education and other pastoral ministers need to be very sensitive to the principles of adult learning which have emerged from research and experience within the past decade.

The interesting Faith Development theory of James Fowler also has implications for adult religious education. Adult religious learning is concerned with the maturing of faith within the context of total human development. Faith, in this perspective, is more a way of knowing or understanding than what is known or understood. Fowler describes faith as that knowing or construing by which persons or communities recognize themselves as related to the ultimate conditions of their existence. Therefore, faith is an active potential for growth within persons by which they come to know their centers for values, their images of power, as well as their master stories. In Fowler's perspective, faith involves the total person's growth, vision, and response to life.

There is always the temptation in developmental theories to perceive the stages of development as levels of achievement. Stages can become stereotypes in the post–Vatican II church. However, Fowler warns against so interpreting his theory and cautions that each stage has its own special grace or merit.

Fortunately, stage theories require us to look closely at the person, and they identify milestones in development. It is not the milestones themselves which are significant, but the movement they represent. Developmental stage theories emphasize growth and help us to discover the processes of growth. It is the process of growth that are the proper starting point for adult religious education.

292

We have learned that the processes of human development are influenced by the person's own experience and by his/her own efforts to accommodate to and assimilate the events of one's life. The growth is the whole process of a new experience displacing the old without repudiating it.

It is difficult to ascribe to Fowler's theory without believing that higher stages of faith development are more adequate and that it would be better if more people were at a higher stage. The adult religious educator, then, has the task of creating the learning experiences to assist this movement to a higher stage. I believe that this happens most creatively with adults in discussion groups focusing on appropriate issues. However, the purpose of the groups would not be to come up with solutions, but rather to explore the reasoning leading to a given solution. Hopefully, over a given period of time, adults who are exposed to this process with peers may move to higher stages of faith development.

This is quite a different approach, but one which is being faithful to the principles of adult learning suggested by Malcolm Knowles. For too long, adults have been indoctrinated by the authority figure telling them what and how to believe. Adults must also learn to trust their own experiences and learn from those in their peer groups.

For faith education for adults, Fowler's approach would suggest a personal challenge for growth, a focusing on faith itself rather than on just a list of things to believe, on an environment wherein adults can honestly speak about what they believe, and on a change in attitude between the roles of teacher and learner as well as on small group size.

If adult programs are going to be constant with Fowler's theory, adults are going to have to be critical, question former beliefs, trust the facilitator, be connected with a religious community that would help synthesize meanings for life.

It seems very encouraging that post–Vatican II Roman Catholic documents have placed adult education at the center of the Church's ministry. Fowler's theory supports this position, because he is speaking of a faith which is quite different from that of a child. It is seen as something brand-new that can happen with adult's faith development, and certainly this is the stuff of adult religious education.

In my own experience with adult religious education programs for teachers, I have always found a real tension between content and process. Out of the past creeps the belief that learners need new knowledge in the areas of theology, scripture, morality, liturgy, and so forth. I have come to believe that learning has to do with more areas of the person's life than the cognitive domain. If one listens to Fowler, one would focus more on the process, or the quality of responses and interactions among the participants. The hoped-for growth does not result from acquiring more knowledge as much as from the increased dissonance created from the dynamic at work.

Adult religious education, in its fullest sense, uses religious knowledge as a means to develop the potentials within persons for knowing and understanding religiously. Other SYMPOSIUM professionals encouraged exploring our human experience in our adult programing. This type of sharing of life experiences could develop common understanding and mutual support.

Coordinators of religious education and all other pastoral persons must be conscious of andragogical principles in the designing and implementing of continuing education programs.

From the adult education research, I suggest the following key guidelines for people dealing with adult religious education:

—The climate of the center of learning needs to be respectful of self-concepts, positive and supportive to self-directed learners. Signs of affirmation are important for effective adult learning.
—It is of great importance to be aware of religious culture, socioeconomic status, ethnic background, parish situation, and past educational experiences of the adult learners.
—Adults need to participate in the planning of their own learning and set their own goals.
—The programs should recognize a response to a wide variety of needs, as well as a variety of learning experiences.
—The adult needs to learn to trust his/her experiences, which lie within reach, waiting to be enlightened and directed.
—Adults learn well when they are with peers, freely learning in groups. Therefore, a variety of models of learning need to be employed in adult learning.
—Adults need to see immediate results and progress. With the many demands of living, adults need some rewards for the time they put into learning. Programs need to be realistic and flexible in terms of the involvements of peoples' lives.
—Adults sometimes resist change and are often slow to accept new ideas.

—Adults live in the midst of great cultural change and are often looking for a new faith experience.

—Adults need to have the opportunity to experience the movement of God in their everyday experiences. In adult programs, elements of prayer, liturgy, meditation, and shared reflection all contribute to this development.

—Adults need to evaluate themselves according to the goals set.

These guidelines for adult religious education are not all-inclusive statements, but are intended rather as important principles for the whole process of adult programming.

There has been a significant number of changes in the Church since Vatican II. During the 1980s, as the new orientations begin to consolidate, as believers continue to search for truth and justice, the adult religious educators must continue to be attentive to the best known research of the social sciences.

Notes

1. *General Catechetical Directory.* Washington: United States Catholic Conference, 1971, page 21.
2. National Conference of Catholic Bishops. *To Teach as Jesus Did—A Pastoral Message on Catholic Education.* Washington: United States Catholic Conference, 1973, pages 12, 13.

William "Bud" Phillips

is the Director of Advanced Studies in Ministry, Vancouver School of Theology, with particular responsibility for the continuing education of clergy. Dr. Phillips is ordained and experienced both in the local pastorate and in the academic setting and brings an important focus on theological education in his reflections. As a Canadian, his participation underscores the international diversity of the research.

15

Faith Development and Theological Education

The emergence of exploration and research into the relationship between the Adult Life Cycle and the Development of Faith meets the world of theological education at a most opportune time. It is a time of rethinking and reevaluating a confusing curriculum situation and a time in which there is a prospect of radical reshaping of the elements within theological education activities. Theological educators are convinced that contemporary forms of and approaches to theological education are not serving to prepare people for the kind of ministry that the schools know to be needed and that the churches and communities are calling for. There are now clear signs that there is motivation both from within and beyond the institutions of theological education which could have the effect of creating vital and new teaching and learning patterns. Faith development theory can, and will, play a part in the critiquing and reforming of those patterns. Just what part will depend to some degree on where and in what direction faith development theory moves. A symposium on the subject suggests where the theorizing may take us, but the message of the symposium is, so far, an uncertain one.

The uncertainty is partly due to the present evolutionary state of the Project, as outlined and reported in this volume, and to the fact that not all of the principal issues in the matter of Faith Development have been articulated. The uncertainty is also the result of the fact that both the Faith Development movement and the enterprise of theological education are themselves in some ill-defined state of maturing and growth. It is suspected that the movement is in fact as much a product of the world of theological education, both in the latter's immediate past and its convulsive present, as it is a separate entity, and if so, each will be critiqued by the other.

There are problems related to the SYMPOSIUM that are explained by the mere recognition that in any movement in search of an integrating process some parts move more rapidly than others, some move in directions that cause them to appear isolated and inconsistent, and some seem to come from somewhere else altogether.

We shall need some perspective!

The project is occurring in a context. Participants at the SYMPO-SIUM were dealing with the end of the first stage of a three-stage Project. The Project is itself a part of the larger Faith Development movement, and the movement is, as I have suggested, an expression of, and at least a stepchild of, the enterprise of religious education, a subsystem of theological education.

As an example of the differing rates of development within a movement, there is the fact that while we were supposedly working with a common document, the *Hypotheses Paper*, some had in their heads, if not in their hands, a more comprehensive and integrating study of the field which had been published a few months earlier. Jim Fowler's book *Stages of Faith* had been impatiently anticipated by early participants of the movement, and both the perception of the field and the methodologies of exploration integral to Fowler's work provided something of a constant but largely unexamined counterproposal throughout the SYMPOSIUM.

The fact that many people attending the SYMPOSIUM were unfamiliar with some of the basic theories and assumptions so far established in the movement gave the meeting the flavor of a continuing education event as much as a symposium. While it was an excellent continuing education event, it appeared at times that the purpose of the Project would take a secondary place to the excitement of adult learning in the personal timetables of the participants. More importantly, as a continuing education event, it pointed to the fact that many who will need to be involved in the ongoing dialogue were conspicuously absent. For a full SYMPOSI-UM on the subject at hand, biblical scholars, theologians, liturgists, and specialists in pastoral psychology and comparative religion will need to be present in sufficient strength to have impact on the direction and shape of discussion.

In order to bring the research project along, it was believed by project organizers that the choice of a research methodology and an agreement with the team of researchers had to be made before the SYMPOSIUM. This led to some discomfort when many, if not most, of the participants came to believe that a methodology of *qualitative* research would more appropriately serve the subject matter and help us to get at the kind of information we need at this time in the theory-building stage. Since we were working with one of the world's outstanding *quantitative* research organizations, there was and remains some tension over methodology. While the distinction between quantitative and qualitative research should not be held as absolute, nor should the research organization be perceived as only able to work in a quantitative milieu, input from the researchers present did not ease the tension much. "Methodology" is one of the linkages which must be examined in the relationship between Faith Development and our concern for theological education.

A Question of Readiness

There is much to be done to bring the faith development movement to the place where it has articulated its theory clusters, defined its issues and relationship, and recognized its prophets, leaders, and historians. The research project may be a catalyst for some of this, but it may also be true that some of the work needs to be done before the project can proceed fruitfully. Much of the interplay within the SYMPOSIUM was about the matter of timing and the maturing of ideas. It was about the uneasy feeling that the Project is not ready to test its hypotheses, because the Project hypotheses do not ask the deeper 'movement' questions. Have we questioned our assumptions sufficiently to have come to agreement as to what we are studying when we examine "faith," "development," and "adult" as concepts interdependently linked?

For some the question is one of epistemology, a matter of our need to understand in what way we know when we are concerned with the subject of faith. As shall be demonstrated later, there are serious concerns to be raised both about how we know and the nature of our knowledge when the subject is faith. This epistemological question is shared by theological educators, and the issues involved strike at the heart of a research project determined to use *faith* as one of the variables. Questions concerning faith are answered by responsive activity as well as words. Since responses are expressed in habitual behavior, in posture, in attitudes toward institutions and persons, and in the ownership of symbols, as well as with a "sense" of belonging to one community rather than another, the inquirers' and researchers' tools, methods, and sophistication within the sphere of faith and faiths are of critical concern.

For others the question of readiness has to do with whether all the major disciplines and fields of knowledge have been consulted in projecting a research focus of such magnitude. The value of explorations of the faith of individuals will surely depend upon the ability of the researchers to understand the peculiar nature and use of religious symbolic communication and the interplay between symbols that describe and symbols that lead to attitudes and behavior. Since the scriptural tradition of religious people becomes both normative and suggestive in the symbolic expression of the faith of that people, and the expression of faith—either lived faith or faith hoped for—are rooted in the communities and traditions which have affirmed the validity of those symbols, it seems presumptuous to proceed toward a study of faith without defining which symbols are to be examined and in what way those symbols will be understood.

Of course, there will be those who will argue that we must not lay on some definition, but rather let people define the terms the way they wish, in order not to preclude or precondition responses. The problem here, however, is that a research project must, if it is to serve its purpose, define its terms. It will, of course, then limit its findings and discover inadequacies in the chosen definitions; but without defining terms in such a way as to make them measurable, we have no subject to research.

Gabriel Moran is right in calling for the definition of meanings in the use of the term "adult" in both the *Hypotheses Paper* and in the work of researchers and students of the adult life cycle. Equally, if not more important, is the need to define "faith" for the project purposes so that those who are using it as a research variable and listening for it in the research project will know it when they hear it. To state the problem bluntly, the long and complex definition of faith development offered in the *Hypotheses Paper* is clearly unmanageable for quantitative research, and the shorter phraseology offered by Fowler in his book, namely "centers of value and images of power," has not been discussed nor agreed upon, nor have alternatives been compared and contrasted. Could we not as easily and perhaps more fittingly, use what people see, experience, and express as "substance of things hoped for and evidence of things unseen" (Hebrews 11:1) as a working definition of faith? Such a definition would set us looking in slightly different directions but may be more likely to keep us on a path that is in touch with a religious tradition and has some authority—at least, within that tradition.

The *Hypotheses Paper* does not help us much by simply laying out a variety of quotes and offering as summary Fowler's comprehensive and complex wording, since Fowler's definition presupposes a different methodology of inquiry. That we could have a usable definition for quantitative research purposes is not being argued, only that such a definition needs to be debated and generally agreed upon for the sake of the Project, since a research project that uses words uncritically stands in jeopardy of having most of the people it seeks to serve reject the findings, whatever those findings may be, on the basis of inadequate and "unowned" definitions of the terms being used.

Faith Development Movement and Theological Education

In order to address the question of the impact of the Faith Development movement on theological education, it is necessary to outline some of the features of the ongoing dialogue concerning theological education in North America. Theological educators, at least on this continent, have been described as being in "an historical cul-de-sac,"[1] and reform within the movement is believed to be possible only with the application of a theological solution to the problem of unity within the branches of theological study. The attempt at unity within those branches has generally taken the form of attempts at bringing various fields of study, isolated over time from one another, to various contexts simultaneously, in the hope that integration would take place. Even that process has been resisted because of the assumptions of some that each of the various pieces of the theological education mosaic has its own method which does not easily allow for imposed agendas and irrelevant contexts. The historical, critical, and systematic methods all reflect the "discipline" approach to learning that is so common in universities and theological schools. The emerging emphasis upon praxis theology shifts the center and method of theological education but is as yet not widely translated into curricular or methodological concepts. Praxis theology would attempt to bring together the critical and rational approach to, and the existential and experiential motivation toward, understanding a single point of context. What is important in the praxis model of theological education is that it begins with the identification of contexts in which theology is being done and works with both rational and experiential tools to understand, interpret, redefine, and inform the theology in context. Such an approach has yielded some hopeful suggestions for curricular reform in theological education. The reform would see teams of students and faculty cluster around problems dealing with major global issues facing the church and the world today. Obviously, it is hoped that such activity would break down the traditional divisions of theological studies by focusing on the point of praxis.

Faith Development theory and theological education share this concern, since reflection in the Faith Development movement calls for the same type of clustering of disciplines. It will be necessary to bring together biblical, historical, dogmatic, ethical, and educational disciplines to reflect on Faith Development experiences. Anything short of that will be open to criticism as ill-informed reflection. The shared dilemma created by the need for such an interdisciplinary approach raises nearly insurmountable curricular and methodological problems.

Another shared concern is that of the definition of terms. If faith needs to be examined as to definition before it can be measured or manipulated as a variable in a research project, so theology and the theological task need to be revisited with a view to assuring that those involved are not using the term ambiguously or in an uneven manner. A recent issue of a theological education periodical takes the task seriously and points to the need for historical, biblical, and traditional reflection on the terms "theology" and "theological education." This presents, incidentally, a reminder to the Faith Development movement that such historical studies should not be excluded in the development of theory, since history can help a movement evaluate, at any given moment, how it got that way.

In the theological education periodical cited, Ed Farley and Bob Lynn both address the historical problem of the use of the terms "theological" and "theological education," and Farley distinguishes four different meanings of theology as a genre. He suggests that theological education is in the aforementioned cul-de-sac as a result of the loss of two of the four meanings that inform the field. Farley contends that in its original Christian use, "theology" simply meant the knowledge of God, "a scientia, an act or cognitive disposition in which the self-disclosing God is grasped and disclosed." Here we see the linkage between the present state of the evolution of faith development theory and theological education. As Farley puts it:

> Theological education like all education has a matrix in which it exists and from which it receives its mandate. . . . The normative reality of that matrix to which theological education is subject and by which it measures its task is Christian faith itself.[2]

In pointing to this linkage, however, Farley makes us aware that there are at least three issues involved for Faith Development theory. First, there is the recognition that to speak of theology in this sense and faith in this context is to limit the discussion to the Judeo-Christian tradition. Secondly, faith understood as an expression of "a disposition in which the self-disclosing God is grasped and disclosed" is to recognize and place the initiative for theology and faith outside the individual person. The third problem raised for us, if we work with this definition of theology and its implications for faith, is that we must, of necessity, enter into the mystery of revelation which engages humans in a way that relates to their *habitus*, or disposition, and to acts of the soul itself. Some writers argue that this disposition, or *habitus*, is "an existential, personal act and revelation of the human self-naming wisdom." A difficult subject to examine as it develops!

The most important issues inherent in this struggle with meanings and problems attached to the meanings, both for the Faith Development movement and for theological education, are the issues of method and all that entails of data gathering, symbolic communication, and, most specifically, epistemology. In this case the epistemological question is: How do we come to *know* the things hoped for and unseen, since our lives express substance that we do hope and evidence that we trust the unseen?

The second meaning of theology which seems lost in antiquity is that understanding which recognizes theology as a discipline of inquiry and study, not in the sense of theology as compared with biblical studies or ethics, but on a par with philosophy and astronomy with its own object and proper method. Here theology embraces and is expressed through ethics and the tradition of believing communities and their writings, as long as the living communities respond with appropriate method to theology's object. The point here is that biblical studies, church history, ethics, and other studies are all informed by and responsible to theology where theology is a single science.

What in fact has happened is that each of the subdisciplines developed its own object and its own method, and theological education therefore became a study of the disciplines rather than a single discipline. Now, again, we engage the matter of the interface between the Faith Development movement and theological education. There was an excellent metaphor for the relationship within the SYMPOSIUM. Representing as it does a part of a movement, the research project proposes to study faith in the context of other disciplines—adult education, human development, developmental psychology, moral education, and the like. Within the SYMPOSIUM, many felt a deep uneasiness which, while not articulated in this way, is believed to be related to the basic question of genre. Indeed, we do not need to deny the existence of relationship between faith and the many disciplines, but rather ask whether faith can be studied merely as it relates to subdisciplines.

An even deeper issue is that of the nature of the "given." Fowler's work undertakes examination of faith as a "given" but uses a generalized and, some would think, secular definition in order to avoid critique from those who would label as bias a more obviously religious definition. The SYMPOSIUM paper and much of the discussion at the meetings assumed that the "given" is the life cycle or developmental stages. What needs to be challenged, as Winston Gooden points out in his observations, is our ready acceptance of the assumptions about the naturalness of development where faith is concerned. It may be that the nature of one's faith is essentially decided as an issue at what Erikson calls "stage one"—the stage at which trust or mistrust is set. All else is a response to, and a struggle with that given. Evangelicals would say that the nature of one's faith as it relates to trust/mistrust can be altered, but only by going through the trauma of a return to stage one of Erikson, a rebirth of the notion of trust and a rejoining with the source and object of that trust.

Some of us in theological education are becoming used to saying, "People will do theology, but the question is whether that theology will be well informed." A similar question could be asked of Faith Development, namely, that while we will have faith, the question is whether our faith will be informed, effected, and interpreted by a well-articulated theory of growth.

When, with the development of the institutionalizing of the modern university, theology was influenced into a definition which was related to the critical principle and became a subject of study parallel with other subjects (biblical, ethical, psychological, and the like), theology as a *habitus,* or way of being, and theology as a structure of interpretation gave way to theology as a science, among others, to be compared and contrasted with other types of theology as sub-categories of a subdiscipline. What is at issue here for theological educators is a question of whether persons can learn to be theological persons and think theologically about their various contexts and conditions by bringing a number of well-developed individual disciplines together and overlaying them, much as acetate sheets are overlaid on a projection machine, to search for a pattern. The parallel between Faith Development theory and the mistaken development of theological education is in the method that emerges as a result of the assumptions made. Theological educators have come to realize that one does not develop a theology by carefully mastering a series of separate sciences or fields of knowledge and then applying them to various contexts. Rather, we recognize that persons have a theology with which they engage their various contexts, and the question is whether that theology is well informed. At this point, exponents of Faith Development theory, if they are aware of the potential for their input, can nourish the ongoing discussion within theological education by encouraging those of us within it to think differently about our tasks. Indeed, at Iliff Theological School, where Mary Wilcox and Ed Everding and others are working, and at other places as well, there is serious resistance to the compartmentalized approach to preparing people for ministry. Theological educators are feeling pressure from many sides to work with a methodology which, as Jim Fowler recommends in another context, "keeps its eye on the phenomena."

In theological education circles this means giving attention to focus not on the many disciplines which compartmentalize the educational process, but rather on the lived theology that is evident in the stories of individual persons, both students and faculty alike, and the faith communities, both historical and present. The result, it seems, is a way of thinking about ministry that takes seriously the context in which theology is done and examines it against historical and other related knowledge. The tools for ministry then become a self-conscious theology and an understanding of those "principalities and powers" that undermine, distort, and attack, as well as those gifts which bring to birth and nurture, one's posture in relation to the object of theology. If faith is the substance of that which we hope for and the evidence of that which we do not see but nevertheless trust, what we are measuring when we measure faith is that which expresses itself at any given time and in any given context. Snapshots of such an expression, even millions of snapshots, can have meaning only if understood within the historical and symbolic dimension.

If we assume faith and theology to be static throughout our encounter with various contexts, then it is possible to observe what happens at one point or anywhere along the life journey and to describe what we see. One simply freezes the experience at a given time and in a specific context and describes the faith or the theology that is expressed. But if faith and theology are the responses of persons who are changing and expressing themselves in similarly changing contexts—in short, if both elements being studied in the relationship are moving—then research must take the movement into consideration when determining the method. In the case of both theological education and faith development, the method must be longitudinal, narrative, and particular. For theological education this may mean severely reduced periods of "schooling" and extended periods, indeed a lifetime, of theological reflection with required observation, supervision, and peer support to assure historical, traditional, and technical critique of the theological journey.

In the case of Faith Development theory, care to the point of near-paranoia will be needed to assure that something dynamic is not defined by a method that examines it in frozen forms.

The intent to study the phenomena of faith in persons against a backdrop of various contexts—in this case, stages in the development of adulthood—has its problems. But at least it suggests a method which, while only in its infancy and not at all accepted by the colleagues of theological education, holds promise. Such a method would use data drawn from the actions of persons responding in faith to investigate the meaning of faith. Thus, different questions are asked, and the disciplines engaged to examine the lived faith are used in a creative new way where the "given" is not the "method" of the discipline. This is the crucial point of praxis and where, so often, we could misstep. The revealed living faith of people may not necessarily be good or well-informed faith. It is important, therefore, that persons who are going to assist in the faith development process come to those contexts well prepared to offer their resources in the way that will critique and enrich the context in the direction of growth, insight, and change.

The work of Gustavo Gutierrez and others who articulate the liberation theology movement provides a case in point. Gutierrez depends on basic Christian communities—small groups of persons with varying levels of awareness, involvement, and skills, struggling with the interface between their faith and the context in which that faith is to be expressed—to raise and respond to theological questions. The liberation theologians resist the North American tendency to want to impose structures and categories on the contexts they engage, preferring to let the problems identified in the contexts determine the focus for resources and perspectives. Each situation begs new questions and draws on new and different fields of knowledge or on the old fields in a different way.

As examples of resources and fields of knowledge that will need to be consulted both by theological educators and Faith Development practitioners, we will mention two specific areas. There are more.

The first has been given a thought-provoking analysis by Peter Slater in a book entitled *The Dynamics of Religion.*[3] It is the study of the interplay between symbols and the meanings and purposes they express. In any attempt to "hear" the expressions of living faith people offer, it becomes significant for enquirers to possess a sensitive understanding of symbolism in human communication generally and religious expression in particular. Slater, without being a part of the SYMPOSIUM, the faith development movement, or the adult life cycle field, nevertheless addresses what may be at the heart of our concern. Speaking from his background in the field of comparative religion, he states:

> Whether they are primary or secondary, central or auxiliary, symbols are not meaningful in a void. We cannot simply take terms from one tradition, look for their nearest equivalent in another tradition, and then suppose that by comparing them we have studied religion.[4]

It requires little imagination to recognize that if this is true of persons who represent different religious contexts and traditions, it is also true of the general population of North America whose lives have been influenced by a wide variety of traditions which, while having some commonality, are subtly and significantly differentiated.

Slater indirectly challenges and questions the value of quantitative research in areas of understanding where faith is concerned. He says:

> The whole cycle of stories and symbols which develop in the history of a tradition is what provides the context for religious meanings. It is the network of relationships among stories and symbols that gives content to the particular faith.[5]

Since he believes that truth is most often realized *between* the stories and that the ability to pass over from one viewpoint to the next becomes an essential element in making sound judgments in religion, Slater holds that it is important that we understand the full nature of the symbols used in our faith stories. "Through them,' he says, "our future takes shape."[6]

Slater, as well as others, would have us distinguish between *in-*

dicative symbols (those wherein the focus is on expectation) and *transfiguring* symbols (those which suggest harmony, glory, rest, and fulfillment). Before we go far in listening for and assessing the faith development level of persons, we will need to be clear that we know if the symbols being used are indicative or transfiguring. Otherwise we will not know whether we are measuring present faith or the faith of expected futures.

In his study of religious symbolic expression, Slater notes:

> The faithfulness of a given stance or attitude or a given story waits for confirmation from a faith community which understands the tradition and embraces the significant symbols.[7]

This suggests that we will be wise to question the assumption of objectivity, not only as to whether objectivity is possible but also whether it is advisable in religious and faith research.

Again indirectly Slater asks a question which our project and indeed the faith development movement must engage. It will also be a challenge to the theological communities, if taken seriously by them. He wonders "what identifies a movement as religious?" He goes on to express his understanding that the very least that can be said on the matter is that a religious story is one which moves from past to present experience and shapes our convictions concerning personal fulfillment in both present and future.

According to Slater's theory, there are central symbols that have the effect of concentrating both actions and thoughts on their distinctive way toward the realization of some transcendent end. Following Christ, for example, is that central symbol that concentrates the way into the kingdom. Keeping the Torah is the central expression of the way to become truly Israel. To understand the meaning for individuals of any given symbol, however, central or otherwise, it is necessary to know both what the individuals are rejecting as well as what they believe they are accepting in the use of such central stories. To understand those dynamics the observer will need to use a methodology that pays attention to the life narrative of the one whose master story conveys the ways he/she chooses to express faith in a given tradition, as well as the spirit in which that tradition is lived.

Slater asks a question that will need to be raised in faith development research: "To be a faith story, does there need to be a plot which brings central figures to salvation, or healing, or wholeness?" He then goes on to assert that a faith story "must communicate some affirmation of identity with integrity, some hope of personal fulfillment, or self-realization, which enables its characters to transcend the negativities of existence."[8]

Slater's discussion of symbols should serve to remind us of an issue which has concerned this writer through the evolution of Faith Development theory. It has to do with the motivation for and object of Faith Development. It has to do as well with the role of intentionality and of models of completeness, wholeness, or fulfillment which play into an individual's development. In the specific case of Christian faith, the meaning and definition of the term is so intrinsically associated with the person of Jesus as to render irrelevant any description of the development of personal faith which is unrelated to one's affinity with him. Without a Christology, discussion of the highest stage of Faith Development for the Christian is irrational, and any non-Christological models and motives which would call persons toward development of faith are partial and incomplete.

Other resources that need to be consulted as we move toward faith development theory are illuminated by William Bridges, in a little-known book entitled *Seasons of Our Lives.*[9] Bridges, in a fresh and most stimulating series of essays, refers to classical literature, nature, and primitive societies to raise contrasting, contradicting, and suggestive images and models of the life span. These will bear consideration before we accept as a given, "adult development" as it is known in North America.

Bridges believes that our view of the life span, when compared with views of other cultures and traditions, is quite unusual and that our language about life span reflects the basic metaphors of our culture. He also believes, therefore, that our views and language need to be culturally critiqued before we use them as norms. Since *expectations* of the life span play a major part in *experiences* of the life span, it becomes important to be aware of the easy trap of self-fulfilling prophecy. His image of the "braid" of life, rather than the chain, or stages, or steps, suggests that what we are working with in our changing and growing, in areas of identity, intimacy, and generativity (to use Erikson's terms), must be examined in a holistic and inclusive way. He suggests that what may be happening, in mid-life for instance, is explicable, in part at least, by the fact that during that period there is a cross over; masculine giving way to femine characteristics and vice versa, and *yin* (the holistic and inclusive outlook) developing in contrast to *yang* (the categorical and analytical outlook). Bridges suggests that part of what is happening to us in mid-life is an attempt to fill "voids and empty places" in our development.

In a most revealing and penetrating way, Bridges also lifts up alternative ways of seeing the "predictable crisis" of one period of life. By identifying the image of the "neutral zone" he again, quite unintentionally, challenges the developmental assumptions. By using excerpts from literature—biographical sketches from Tolstoy, the revelatory work of John McLeish in *The Ulyssean Adult* (McGraw-Hill, 1978), to mention only two—Bridges challenges the "declining years" image and suggests there is much work to be done before we accept the cultural assumption of adult development. He ends in a way that recalls the implications of religious symbols on our task. He reminds us of the deeply personal and human basis of the great festivals of rebirth and describes Easter, for some, as a time of turning, "a reminder that rebirth begins with dying and that new forms begin in chaos. . .," if Easter is a significant symbol for some, it may be because it speaks of what is ending and what is being begun in our lives today."[10]

Another issue that is raised by early reactions and responses to the faith development movement in general and the research project in particular is that which could be described as the spectre of a new rationale for ministry which could threaten to divert the present, creative dialogue within the field of theological education. While this emerging role for ministers and others helping in the process of faith development is welcomed in some ways, it must not be allowed to be blown into the basis for a rationale of ministry. This sort of thing has happened before, and theological educators and the churches we serve are still recovering.

When Anton Boison, Carl Rogers, and others brought together the many inviting "loose ends" of knowledge and skills from a variety of fields of study to the clinical contexts of human relationships identified as hospitals and institutions, what emerged was a way of thinking of ministry that was, as much as anything, defined by those disciplines and contexts. What was frequently missing in the early development of that concept of ministry was the careful examination of the essential biblical, theological, and historical elements. What was also treated with less emphasis than appropriate was the liturgical and church community contexts of the theological enterprise.

The parallel with the pastoral counseling movement is a reminder that we will be wise to avoid, in the early stages of the faith development movement, omission of some traditional theological questions. Only laterally for instance, did the pastoral counseling movement engage questions of "revelation," of "eschatology," and of the "sin/salvation dynamic." It took too long for the movement to get over the need to use the established, authorized language of the other disciplines and only with some difficulty come to speak of "grace," "redemption," "conversion," and the like. The field of pastoral counseling has had to labor aggressively in the recent past to prove its theological and biblical responsibility. Only recently has the church and the parish been discovered as an appropriate alternative to the hospital and the institution as a setting worthy of being considered a clinic for supervising students who are preparing to be pastoral theologians. The irony is laughable but points to the acute danger of defining ministry by gathering tools, theories, and methodologies from a number of sources and integrating them into a methodology of ministry.

Having stated this warning, however, I think it is important to examine what may be learned from pastoral theology in general and the pastoral counseling field in particular that will assist in the process of Faith Development theory-building. Pastoral theology has encouraged the assumption that persons can be helped to understand themselves, to reinterpret and reengage the brokenness in life, if they can be helped to "bring to word" and name, in ways that allow for critical analysis, the hurts, emptinesses, and longings of the human spirit. In helping persons identify their experience, name it, and lift it beyond the subconscious, much can be accomplished in both faith development and faith therapy.

The perceptive pastoral theologians will ask of faith development exponents difficult and important questions. They will raise the question of sin as a function of development. Is it, for instance, a "sin" to choose to remain at a lower stage of development because a glimpse of a higher stage brings the awareness of unwanted responsibility?

An outstanding pastoral theologian, Wayne Oates, after undertaking a theological and scientific analysis of the development of personality, reflects upon several important religious implications. One of these is what he considers the "inseparability of redemption from development."[11] Here he points out that the scientific conception of maturity today is, in a sense, a secularization of the religious conception of perfection and eschatology.

A second implication for Oates is the developmental character of a dynamic ethic. Here he refers us to the work of John Bunyan and others who have recognized that spiritual life and growth is neither a smooth nor an easy path and that "the very darkest and foreboding developmental task may not only be threatening as a task but also promising as a teachable moment."[12]

A third implication of the relationship between pastoral theology and personality development has to do with theories of development and dramas of redemption. Because of those emerging theories the field of pastoral theology will be able to contribute to faith development theory by assisting in the identification of the spiritual awareness patterns of individuals based on data gethered from decades of observing and participating in the unfolding of those human dramas.

We have previously alluded to the fourth implication of the relationship between pastoral theology and faith development in suggesting that in recent years pastoral counselors have taken care to consider the implications of Christian eschatology no the meanings wo which people apply their lives. Wayne Oates puts it this way:

> Our eschatology shapes the goals of our personal strivings, whether we know it or not. These goals, in turn, specifically determine our interpretation of the developmental pilgrimage of the individual personality.[13]

Just as the early integration of psychological insights and the concerns of pastoral theologians in counseling offered a new or more holistic way of examining, measuring, and responding to the psychosocial symptoms of persons needing care, so there is the promise of such integration and insight from educational psychology, developmental psychology, moral development, and spirituality toward an improved skill and theory base for responding in "faith care." There is bound to be an adoption of this new cluster of skills and knowledge as a new specialty, especially when there has been, for some time, a kind of inferiority complex among those whose focus in ministry has been in Christian education and formation. It is also true that the emerging concern for spirituality and spiritual development, particularly in Protestantism, has been awaiting an understanding of the skills, dynamics, and theories that would shape a professional role image. This potential cul-de-sac of specialty formation could provide the space for a diversion from the important journey on which theological educators are set: a journey that seeks to avoid defining ministry in terms of competencies and skills but rather in terms of the *purpose* of the enterprise. If faith development is a purpose for ministry, along with other purposes, it will be facilitated not only, nor even primarily, by specialists in adult life stages, developmental psychology, moral development, and research techniques, but also by persons who, while conversant with these, bring compassion, acceptance, and understanding along with an historical and transcendent perspective to relationships with persons seeking to be faithful and with groups who are in process of becoming communities of faith.

Notes

1. Edward Farley "The Reformation of Theological Education as a Theological Task," *Theological Education,* (Spring 1981) 93.
2. *Ibid.,* pp. 111-112.
3. Peter Slater, *The Dynamics of Religion,* (San Francisco: Harper & Row, 1978).
4. *Ibid.,* p. 27.
5. *Ibid.,* p. 21.
6. *Ibid.,* p. 49.
7. *Ibid.,* p. 59.
8. *Ibid.,* p. 58.
9. William Bridges, *The Seasons of Our Lives,* (Rolling Hills Ca: The Wayfarer Press, 1977).
10. *Ibid.,* p. 72.
11. Wayne Oates, *The Religious Dimensions of Personality,* (New York: Association Press, 1957) p. 162.
12. *Ibid.,* p. 163.
13. *Ibid.,* pp. 167-8.

16

The Future

As this volume is being readied for publication, the work of Phase II is just beginning. Hypotheses are being revised, Project leadership and representatives of the Gallup Organization are working closely together in the development of interview questions, and the counsel and suggestions of SYMPOSIUM participants have been translated into the kinds of "mid-course corrections" that strengthen the study. Already, plans for regional conferences, Phase III resource materials, and the Project's culminating International Conference are beginning to take shape.

One would like to develop these future plans in more detail here, now, on these pages . . . . but that will just have to wait for another book.

Appendix

The Project

The Faith Development in the Adult Life Cycle Project is a three-year research study sponsored by the Religious Education Association of the United States and Canada and 18 other denominations and organizations.

Early in 1979, the Adult Education Committee of the Religious Education Association proposed research designed to study the relationship between Faith Development and the Adult Life Cycle. In May, 1979, the Project was approved by the Board of Directors of the R.E.A. and preliminary work begun. By fall, 1979, over a dozen denominations and organizations had joined the R.E.A. as "sponsors" by the contribution of $200-$500 each for "seed money" to develop the project design, and a Steering Committee was chosen from those sponsor groups to guide this development.

By spring, 1980, a Proposal was being written, with counsel from Lutheran Resources Commission in Washington, D.C. A small planning grant from the Raskob Foundation of Wilmington, Delaware made possible the completion of a Proposal for Research which was approved by the Steering Committee in September, 1980.

The Proposal was submitted to several foundations with, for the most part, discouraging results. It appears that *religious-oriented* foundations are hesitant to underwrite research and that *research-oriented* foundations are chary of projects related to faith issues. However, a grant from a small family foundation and several gifts from individuals in the fall of 1980 made it possible to begin the Project on January 1, 1981.

Many of the original sponsor groups, and others, reaffirmed their commitments in 1981 by becoming Partners with the R.E.A. in the Project through three-year commitments of $1500 and active participation in decisions related to the Research.[1]

The Center for Religious Education at the College of St. Thomas, St. Paul, Minnesota, serves as the academic research base for the Project, and was the host organization for the 1981 SYMPOSIUM.

Purpose of the Study

Although important research related to the Adult Life Cycle has appeared during the past 20 years, little of its is addressed to the dimension of faith in an individual's life. Similarly, the Faith Development literature, although cognizant of and sensitive to the Adult Life Cycle, has dealt directly with the relationships only minimally. The purpose of this Project is to explore such relationships in some depth.

The ultimate concern of the study will be to shed light on such questions as:

1. What is a "mature" faith vis-a-vis an "immature" faith? Are there stages of faith development that can be measured? If so, but what criteria?
2. How does the faith of adult persons develop? How is this development affected by classes? Reading? Prayer? The "TV Church"? Interpersonal relationships? Conversion experience(s)? The Charismatic Movement? Significant events and crises in life (marriage, death of a loved one, etc.)?
3. How does the development of an individual's personal faith relate to the dynamics of the life cycles in contemporary culture, such as the beginning of a family, the changing role of women, vocational uncertainty, physical aging, the "empty nest," divorce, retirement, alternative lifestyles, preparation for one's own death, etc.? How does the faith of one's spouse impact on his or her faith development?
4. What educational implications may be identified from such information? How can churches, parishes, synagogues, and other agencies concerned with the development of the individual's personal faith provide appropriate learning experiences which better serve the changing needs of their people through the life cycle?
5. How can an increased understanding of the changes that occur throughout the adult life cycle help persons to take responsibility for the nurture of *their own* faith development during their adult years?

Possible Utilization of the Study

A primary concern of the Project leadership is that, although the research itself be scholarly and based on good research methodology, the end result be of value to the practitioner and to the individual. For this reason, Phase III of the proposed research will be directed toward the development of practical resources based on the data collected. These could be utilized in many ways, among them:

1. They will help individuals understand the development of their own faith throughout the adult years.
2. They will enable those persons—ministers, priests, rabbis, parish workers, educational directors, and others—who are directly responsible for the educational leadership of adults in the *local* religious community to understand better the dynamics of faith development within the context of the adult life cycle, and to apply them to their work.
3. They will provide a foundation for the development of educational curriculum and programmatic resources in faith development by national and regional denominations and other organizations representing a broad spectrum of religious traditions.
4. They will comprise a significant and useful contribution to the literature of the fields of human development, adult education, and religious education.

The Research Design

The Project is being carried out in three phases, one in each of its three calendar years. Three broad goals, one for each phase, have been established.

Phase I Goal (1981)

To establish hypotheses, based on current literature and research, about the dynamic relationship, actual and potential, between the patterns and causes of change throughout the adult life cycle and the development, in terms of both growth and regression of an individual's faith.

An extensive study of the literature was made by a Research Team of six persons under the direction of Research Consultant Charles Bruning between January and May, 1981. Its findings were reported in the *Hypotheses Paper*

317

which was the basic document on which the papers and discussions of the SYMPOSIUM were based.

Phase II Goal (1982)

To test the hypotheses, by means of questionnaire and / or interview methodology with a statistically valid sample of the American and Canadian population.

The Princeton Religion Research Center, affiliated with and utilizing the extensive research capabilities of the Gallup Organization, is responsible for developing and guiding the Phase II research, in cooperation with the Project leadership. As this is written, this phase is just beginning and should be completed in 1982.

It should be noted that, in addition to the broad interview sample obtained through the Gallup resources, provision also has been made for additional data to be gathered by means of in-depth interviews with a more limited population.

Phase III Goal (1983)

To suggest and develop the implications of the findings of the research design identified in Goals I and II for individuals and those in the helping professions related to ministry, counseling, and education.

Six to eight regional conferences will be held throughout the United States and Canada early in 1983 to focus on the transition from the data gathering phases to the resource development phase of the Project. The Project leadership will pursue the development of publications which seek to translate the findings of Phase I and Phase II into resources of value to a relatively wide audience of professionals and interested individuals. This volume is the first of these resource publications.

It is anticipated that Phase III will culminate with an international conference in 1984.

Project Leadership

Overall direction of the Project is vested in the Steering Committee, representatives of eight of the Partner organizations. The Steering Committee meets twice a year.

The Project Committee, a group of Twin Cities scholars, meets regularly with the staff to review and evaluate the progress of the study from a research perspective.

The Phase I Research Team functioned early in 1981 to review literature related to the topic and to help in the preliminary development of the *Hypotheses Paper*.

Dr. Charles Bruning, Associate Professor of Education, University of Minnesota, as Research Consultant played a major role in the oversight of the Phase I research and the development of the *Hypotheses Paper*.

Dr. Mitchell Cohen, Senior Researcher, the Gallup Organization, has been the primary representative of that organization in working with the Project staff in the development and oversight of the Phase II research design. Mr. George Gallup, President, has been closely related to the Project since its early beginnings. Dr. Robert Wuthnow (cf. Chapter 9) serves as a Consultant in the Phase II research development.

Dr. Connie Leean directs the in-depth interview aspect of the Phase II research design.

Ms. Connie Davis, Administrative Assistant and Registrar for the SYMPOSIUM, provides secretarial and administrative assistance for the Project.

Dr. Kenneth Stokes, Director, is Assistant Professor of Education, College of St. Thomas and an independent consultant on Adult Education and Adult Life Cycle issues.

In addition, nearly 100 Field Consultants throughout the United States and Canada, and abroad, review and comment on periodic updates related to the study.

The Project has stimulated considerable interest among members of the theological, psychological, and education communities. Countless persons have participated in the Project through suggestions and ideas, many of which have been incorporated into the research design.

Notes

1. As of August 1, 1982, the following have joined the R.E.A. in this Partnership:

Adult Christian Education Foundation
American Baptist Churches in the USA
American Ethical Union
American Lutheran Church
Anglican Church of Canada
Canadian Catholic Conference
The Episcopal Church
Fuller Theological Seminary
General Conference Mennonite Church
Institute of Pastoral Studies at Loyola University of Chicago
Lutheran Church in America
Mennonite Church
National Association of Congregational Christian Churches
Presbytery of New Covenant
Sisters of St. Martha
Unitarian Universalist Association
United Church of Canada
United Church of Christ
United Methodist Church
United States Catholic Conference
University of the South